THE
BIBLE AND
MODERN DOUBT

THE
BIBLE AND
MODERN DOUBT

Mack B. Stokes

Fleming H. Revell Company

Old Tappan, New Jersey

TO
Rose and Elsie Pauline

Scripture quotations are from the *Revised Standard Version of the Bible,* copyrighted 1946 and 1952.

SBN 8007-0410-X

Contents

3

Preface

In each generation questions have been asked about the Bible. But in this era when men are looking toward the twenty-first century the questions are more insistent and radical than ever. Can the Bible speak to modern man? Does the idea of revelation have authentic meaning? Are the basic teachings of the Bible true? These and similar questions keep returning. The aim here is to interpret the teachings of the Bible for the general reader in such a way that their truth and relevance in the modern world will become increasingly clear.

I shall proceed on four assumptions. First, I shall assume the major teachings of the Bible are true but that this cannot be taken for granted in the modern world. Therefore, all Christians share a common responsibility for interpreting the Bible afresh for man today.

Second, I shall assume the Bible is relevant, but that its relevance has to be shown through persuasive interpretation. The basic teachings of the Bible, though emerging in and through historical persons and situations, can be identified and related to the universal needs of men. For this reason they speak to men in all ages, including and especially to men in the modern era.

Third, I shall assume that the major teachings of the Bible, in their intellectual content, are indispensable to the Christian religion. The major ideas or beliefs of the Bible are particularly important in this time of competition for the *minds* of men. Revelation goes beyond propositions to disclose the presence and action of God; but it includes ideas or teachings that can be discussed. There are other ways of approaching the Bible

5

than through its teachings. The Bible is a religious book and it deals with man's encounters with God through faith. It might be urged that to deal with the teachings is to miss the reality of the faith to which the Bible calls men. This has point, but I shall assume that if the basic teachings of the Bible are not true and relevant, all talk of religious encounter is little more than a grand hoax. Christians know only two ways of encountering men in the interest of vital religion, namely, by reporting what God has done and by discussing ideas that are congenial to faith. Both are important.

Fourth, I shall assume that the major teachings of the Bible move in the opposite direction from some prevailing modern ideas. These teachings and any nontheistic world-view, whether consciously developed into a philosophical system or unconsciously assumed as a current fashion, are at war with each other. Christians have much to learn from the secular world, but they cannot find their identity there. They are in the world but not of it. Therefore, from the standpoint of the Biblical revelation there can be no easygoing accommodation to "the secular city" nor to the various secularisms of the day. On the contrary, the major teachings of the Bible are a sustained challenge to the questionable assumptions of the modern mind in its tendency to ignore God.

Though these assumptions lie at the background of my thought, the book is primarily an effort to enter into dialogue with the modern mind by reflecting on contemporary doubts about the major themes of the Biblical revelation. To this end, the first chapter presents in brief compass something of the range and seriousness of the doubts about the Bible in the modern world. These will figure as a recurring theme in all the chapters thereafter. The second chapter states some of the basic principles of interpreting the Bible that might appeal to the modern mind. Then, as we deal with specific teachings of the Bible, these will be considered, chapter by chapter, within the setting of *alternative views and modern doubts*. These latter in particular will be taken seriously. In the last four chapters an effort will be made to show the relevance of the Biblical teaching to some of the major personal and social problems of the day. In these also I have sought to encounter the doubts arising from contemporary experience. No attempt is made in them to cover every area of concern. Nevertheless, by discussing the Biblical teachings with respect to selected personal and social problems an effort is made to show some of the principles and guidelines that are required for responsible Christian action in the complex and rapidly changing modern world.

This pattern of presenting the Biblical teachings in the setting of alternative views on the one hand, and of modern doubts on the other seems to be as good a way as I know to join in the dialogue with the modern mind. This is why, after Part I, the various options are presented at the first of each chapter and then are followed by a summary of what the Bible teaches. All this leads up to the encounters with modern doubts and the responses to them.

The word "response" is used as a heading to signify the way I propose to reflect on the modern doubts. It is an important word here. For it stands in contrast to "answer" or "solution" and suggests that I want to *persuade,* to lead, to call for *honest reflection* on the part of the reader. It presupposes that we are living in a time when persuasion, plausibility, and "making sense" are indicated in the individual Christian as well as in the community of faith. At the same time the responses are not intended to be weak or halfhearted, suggesting compromise where it is impossible or harmony when there is a clash of ideas.

I am assuming that the path before Christians is not a simple one. For in many respects we are living in a new age and we must encounter the issues of a relatively new mentality. This book is an effort to face the issues in ways that are intellectually informed and practically sensible. Of course, I realize that much remains to be said.

I am indebted to my colleagues on the faculty of the Candler School of Theology of Emory University for invaluable suggestions, often received without any full awareness on the part of those who shared them. I am indebted also to William R.

Cannon, formerly Dean of the Candler School of Theology and now a bishop in the United Methodist Church, for many insights through conversations across years of service together as a friend and as a colleague on the faculty.

I am particularly indebted to my secretary, Mrs. Sybil Oviatt, for her tireless efforts and extraordinary competence in preparing the manuscript for publication.

MACK B. STOKES

Part I

Introduction

1

THE BIBLE AND THE MODERN MIND

As we move toward the twenty-first century, the prevailing intellectual perspectives are marked by secularism. That is, they assume that if God is, He does not matter. Neither the physical universe nor human history is seen in relation to God. According to some modern assumptions the universe is heading nowhere. Man, the product of the impersonal processes of nature, is moving inevitably toward annihilation. Doom is sure. The grave gets the last word. Sin is reduced to psychological jargon, to social maladjustment or, at best, to wrongdoing without reference to God. There is no Redeemer. "Salvation" comes through culture, education, and psychological and social adjustment instead of through faith in God. Consequently, in the thinking of many, there is no real salvation at all.

The medieval mind, as was that of the apostles, was dominated by the sense of cosmic purpose. God created the world for moral and spiritual ends, and man was chosen to be a part of that goal. Similarly, the Elizabethan Age, so rich in faith and literary production, was given meaning largely through the teachings of the Bible. As William Hazlitt wrote, "It gave a *mind* to the people, by giving them common subjects of thought and feeling."

But the modern mind, dominated as it is by the idea of natural and evolutionary processes, has gradually lost this sense of purpose and promise at the heart of things. The vague notion of impersonal processes in a universe of law makes itself known in much of the art, literature, music, dance, and drama of the present century. Man has been left to shift for himself in a world without absolutes. So he broods over his plight in a pitiless universe. He is reduced to an unknown entity in an unknowing universe.

Many factors have contributed to this revolutionary change in geography and climate. The most important is the vast achievement in the natural sciences and technology. This has created a new intellectual as well as physical environment. It has gradually suggested elements of a world-view in which God is conspicuous by His absence.

Other important developments include advances in the behavioral sciences, namely, psychological and sociological studies. These also have done much to reshape the way men think. Still other factors include the rise and spread of various ideologies, such as communism with its materialistic assumptions.

One more factor bears mention here, namely, the failure of the church to present an adequate understanding of God and of His ways with men. It was much easier for men to abandon a firm belief in God when they were nurtured on caricatures of Him. Christians themselves have often contributed to these caricatures by their failure to think deeply about God.

The situation in historical perspective is this. During the past several hundred years radical doubts have been raised about Biblical teachings that required more than 3,000 years to be woven into the fabric of Western civilization. These doubts no longer concern minute difficulties in the text of the Bible or in translation. They do not address themselves to small contradictions, trivial discrepancies, and the like. They have to do with the total world-view and message of the Bible as a whole. This is why, for many thoughtful persons, the language of the Bible fails to say anything. It does not speak to them. So it cannot be God's Word in any special sense.

To be more specific, at least seven major teachings of the Bible (in relation to which all of its other important teachings are to be understood) are subject to doubt and denial by many people. These are: (1) the belief in an ultimate purpose back of the universe, (2) the belief in a personal God, (3) the belief in a moral order, (4) the belief that man needs God and is lost without Him, (5) the belief in a divine redemptive process, (6) the belief in the Kingdom of God, and (7) the belief in the life everlasting.

The result of all this is that the church can no longer take the Bible for granted. For it is not self-evident to modern men that it is God's Word. In comparison with this basic change in the intellectual and cultural environment nearly all other issues pertaining to Christianity in the modern world are either secondary or trivial.

It is no simple thing to deal with this problem. It requires many approaches by different people. Nevertheless, let me suggest three ways of confronting the challenge posed by this modern mood of radical doubt. I shall merely state them here with the understanding that the interest in the present study will be confined almost entirely to the third. The first two are mentioned because they are needed in any adequate intellectual encounter with the modern mind. They are of utmost importance, but they require a detailed presentation that is not within the scope of this effort to interpret the major teachings of the Bible. With this in mind we are prepared to take a brief look at the three ways of meeting the problem of modern doubt.

First, we must point out the inadequacies and limitations of the sciences. This does not mean they are unimportant. Science is one of the finest achievements of the human mind. But it must be made clear to everyone that no science or group of sciences is able to establish or destroy any total world-view, least of all a world-view with God as the ultimate reality. Science does not favor one world-view over another. It is neutral. It may contribute data for a world-view, but it has no resources for saying, for example, that natural process, and not God, is ultimate. (The terms "nature," "naturalism," and "natural process" have many meanings. The main thrust here is to convey the idea of *being* and *energy* as devoid of any ultimate

11

mind and purpose.) It is an illusion of the modern mind that science is the only road to truth.

If a scientist believes that natural process is ultimate, this is not because his scientific studies require it. It is rather that scientific advances have tended to make it fashionable to think in this way. Nothing can be more unscientific than to believe on the basis of fashions rather than on the basis of deep reflection on all kinds of evidence. It is no accident, therefore, that A. N. Whitehead wrote his *Science and the Modern World* (1926) partly to show that science should free itself from its naïve enslavement to materialistic assumptions.

Moreover, a little thought will show that there are other approaches to reality than those through the various sciences. Let me state five of them.

1. Men learn about the world and life by common sense. The extensive experiences of daily life teach them much about reality. In fact, science itself would be helpless without the presuppositions of common sense. Everyone assumes that there is an external world, that sense experience reports such a world, that there is a natural order, that there are other people, that memory is reliable (or essentially so), that causes precede effects, that things are interrelated, that what honest men report can be trusted, and so on.

2. Men learn of reality through esthetic experience. Beauty tells something about the nature of reality. This goes far beyond the range of the sciences.

3. Moral experience also communicates something about reality. This too is outside the sphere of science because it has to do not merely with what is but with what ought to be.

4. Religious experiences convey dimensions of reality inaccessible to the various sciences because they concern man's encounters with God.

5. Philosophy and theology also are avenues through which the mind of man orients itself toward reality. These go far beyond the reach of the sciences in seeking to understand the nature of ultimate reality. The sciences deal with aspects of

reality. Philosophy and theology seek to understand what is back of all reality and process.

What needs to be urged, then, is that it is only by dogmatic assertion and not by sound reasoning that anyone supposes that the sciences are the only roads to truth. All sound beliefs are at last confirmed in human thought and experience. But these include far more than can be subjected to exact scientific scrutiny. Life and thought are deeper than science. And no realms of reality must be excluded by arbitrary decree.

In the second approach to modern doubts, Christian thinkers must put their minds seriously to the task of developing a credible theism. That is, they must show that there are solid reasons for believing in God. These reasons should be addressed not only to Christians for the purpose of giving them more confidence in their belief; they should be addressed to all men who have sincere doubts. This aspect of the Christian thinker's work is called natural theology, or philosophical theology. Here the theologian employs those grounds of belief outside the Bible that are available to all men who are willing to think as honestly as they can.

We have already observed that it is impossible to recover the sense of the truth and relevance of Biblical teachings in an atmosphere of radical doubt. The primary consequence of natural theology would be to create the atmosphere of belief. Obviously, if we cannot honestly believe in God, or in the God of love and goodness, there is no point in talking about the God who made Himself known in Jesus Christ. Natural theology enables the honest seeker after truth to see that the belief in God is a reasonable option. More than this, it helps him to believe that God is the ultimate basis of all that is real and good.

On this level the Christian thinker strives to do two things, first, to show the inadequacies of the major alternative perspectives and, second, to reveal the strengths of a basic theism. In showing the inadequacies of world-views that have no place for God, the Christian thinker might pursue lines of reasoning suggested by crucial questions. How does it happen that the physical universe is intelligible? Common sense and science assume that man knows the world around him. This curious fact has to be explained. How can we explain it without God?

Again, everyone (including and especially the scientist) assumes that there is an ordered universe. Why should there be this ordered universe when there are infinite possibilities for chaos? Can order be explained without God? Further, why should there be creativity in nature? Whitehead wrote that atheism was unreasonable because it did not permit an explanation of creativity.

Again, why should there be esthetic experience that is so richly nurtured by physical things and processes? Can this be explained without God? What about the curious fact of moral experience? Could this be the product of blind impersonal process?

Once more, what about religious experience? Psychologists can study it, sociologists can view it in its effects upon men in community. But they cannot answer the question concerning the reality of the encounter with God. The saints know of the presence of God.

In summary, the Christian thinker might pursue these suggestions in detail to call modern men to an openness to the belief in God. There are sound reasons for this belief. We cannot develop them here, but broadly speaking there are three widely accepted grounds for believing in God.

First, it is intuitively plausible. Just as a leaf requires the tree, a whitecap the ocean, so the finite requires the Infinite. I do not accept the notion that modern men find God-talk or the God-idea meaningless. Men have an intuitive idea of the Infinite; and they have an essential grasp of what is meant by the Ultimate. Second, it is broadly reasonable to believe in God. That is, in the light of all ranges of evidence it makes more sense to believe that God is the ultimate causal Ground of things than to believe that the universe and man came from blind impersonal process. Third, it is experientially confirmable. Millions of men have sensed the presence of God. This is a continuing experience of men. This fact cannot be pushed aside except by arbitrary and hence irrational decree.

The work of the Christian thinker in all this is to prepare the way for a new appreciation of the Biblical teachings with their emphasis on God's good news for men. For it is far more important to walk with God by faith than merely to think about Him. Nevertheless, if we do not believe that He is, we cannot walk by faith in Him. If we believe absurdities about God, we shall reflect those absurdities in our lives.

This brings us to the third way of approaching modern man's doubts, namely, by developing sound approaches to the Bible itself. Christians must strive for a credible interpretation of the Bible as God's living Word. More is needed than an intellectually acceptable world-view. Men need to recover the sense of meaning and purpose. They need to become aware that God is dealing with them and calling them. Here is where we move from philosophy and theology to faith.

There are philosophical systems that move in the right direction. But they cannot be made available to the general public. Very few men have either the interest or ability to philosophize in any authentic way. Besides, even among philosophers only a limited number will be convinced by any particular system of thought. Again, philosophical systems, while serving their own important ends, appeal chiefly to the intellect. This restricts their usefulness still further. More important still, philosophy is one thing, religion is another. Men need both a responsible world-view and a vital faith. This combination alone furnishes an intellectual atmosphere in which the soul of a man can thrive. It alone opens the way to a living encounter with God that nurtures love and hope.

The genius of the Biblical revelation, in part at least, is that it affirms a world-view that is both intellectually plausible and experientially confirmable. It appeals to the best thinking of men and at the same time calls them to commitment and faith. But unless this can be made credible to modern man, with his inevitable doubts, the message of the Bible cannot get through.

The aim of the chapters that follow will be to take up the

theme of this third approach, namely, to obtain a hearing for the Bible in these times. This has to be done in some kind of meaningful dialogue with the modern mood of doubt and denial explicitly defined earlier in this chapter in the statement on historical perspective. Those seven beliefs, about which modern man raises so many questions, will be at the background of thought in the elaboration of each chapter that follows. The modern doubts about them will often emerge into explicit utterance and confrontation. They will also function behind the scenes in this attempt to interpret the major teachings of the Bible. The one clear purpose here is to strive for an account of those teachings that is both true to the Bible and plausible to the mind. Only in this way can modern men read the Bible as God's living Word.

The next chapter will indicate some important ways of approaching the Bible as a whole. That is, it will deal with certain basic principles of interpreting the Bible. After that, we shall turn to those specific teachings selected for special study.

2

BASIC PRINCIPLES FOR
INTERPRETING THE BIBLE

Christianity stands or falls upon the credibility of the Bible and its essential heritage. The basic question in the present situation, then, is this: Can modern men understand the Bible as a primary medium of divine communication? This question cannot be answered by mere talk. Nor can it be handled by referring to the church's historic stance. Men want to understand the reasons why certain claims are made. They want to consider for themselves whether or not the claims for the Biblical heritage make sense.

Before going further, some clarification of the term "Biblical heritage" is indicated. By it I have in mind the divine revelation that comes to men through the Biblical characters, events and teachings, together with those developments in historic Christianity that have grown on the Biblical soil. These two, namely, the Bible and what has developed from it in historic Christianity, are the Biblical heritage as here understood. These two are organically connected. They belong in the same life process. There are other aspects of the Biblical heritage, as in Judaism and in Islam, with which we are not primarily concerned here.

There is no possibility of recovering the sense of the authority of the Bible and its heritage as divine revelation without the aid of certain principles of interpretation that can come to grips with honest doubts. These doubts necessarily arise in this age of science, technology, and rapid change. The main purpose of this chapter, therefore, is to suggest certain principles that enable men to go beyond their doubts and to enter into a credible account of the Biblical revelation as authentic divine communication. If these principles are kept in mind while reading the Bible and reflecting on its historical significance, modern men may recover the sense of its authority without being obscurantists. An obscurantist is one who shuts his eyes to what is going on. He refuses to look at it. He is like the ostrich that pushes its head into the sand to avoid facing the problem.

The method already suggested here is to recognize the new world in which we find ourselves and to face all real doubts as honestly as we can. At the same time, the approach is one of affirmation. We want to see what the Bible can say for itself to modern men when interpreted reasonably.

There are at least four principles for interpreting the Bible that need to be made clear to those who are willing to consider seriously its truth and relevance. These four principles will be presented in succession but they really belong together in one total approach to the Bible and to its historical developments. They express a spirit or general attitude as well as particular ways of reading and hearing.

Some Christians have said that all that we know about God comes through the Biblical heritage. There and only there has God spoken. Others take an opposing view, urging that God speaks everywhere. The Bible is just one among many sources of insight about God and so has no special claims. In addition, there are the non-Christians who deny the idea of divine revelation altogether. God, if He is, does not communicate with men. Because this last idea has to do with the belief in a personal God, we shall postpone a consideration of it until the next chapter.

The idea that all we know about God comes to us through the Biblical heritage does not appeal to men today. It seems incredible to suppose that the God of the universe would restrict His disclosures concerning Himself within the narrow confines of a book or a particular historical community. So, when we stop and think, we realize that even if we knew nothing about the Bible and Christianity we could still see many signs of God's activity. In fact, people in various parts of the world who know little or nothing about the Biblical revelation believe in God and speak about Him. Modern man, who knows so much more about the universe and about human life than his predecessors, simply cannot accept the idea of a God whose revelation of Himself is wholly confined to the Bible and the Christian community. One reason for this is that the Bible itself belongs to human culture and civilization. No one can read it and understand it without assuming many things he learned outside the Bible.

Modern man can see also the inadequacy of saying that God speaks everywhere, as if there were no levels, nor spheres, nor degrees of revelation. Just as there are levels of human insight, there may well be levels of divine disclosure. Men today may see that it is a mistake to bypass the Bible as if it had nothing unique to say about God and His ways with men. The Bible must be given its chance to speak for itself. The work of reason is not to lump all religious books together as if there were no differences among them. The office of reason is to identify the differences, to reflect on the unique, to consider the levels of truth and relevance. The long history and distinctive levels of the Hebrew-Christian stream of thought and life may lead men to consider the possibility that God has spoken on a higher level and with special relevance through the Bible and its heritage.

According to the principle here enunciated, there are two realms of divine revelation, namely, one outside the Biblical heritage, the other in and through the Bible and its heritage. Many levels or spheres of revelation could be delineated. But to keep the discussion clear while holding to the central theme, the many possible levels of revelation are reduced to two.

First, God has spoken and still speaks outside the Biblical stream. Specifically, God seems to communicate His presence and activity in at least five realms that lie outside the Bible and its heritage.

1. God manifests Himself throughout the physical universe. He speaks in galaxies, planetary systems, snowflakes and flowers. He expresses His energy in cells, microscopic organisms, and in ultramicroscopic objects and processes.

2. God reveals Himself outside the Bible through the civilizations of mankind. He communicates something of His presence with us through the tools, languages, ideas, and ways of men across many centuries. Even the failures of men in history say something about the ways of God. The mills of the gods grind slowly but they grind exceeding small.

3. God communicates also through the mystery, joys, and sorrows of interpersonal relations. Friendship, universally valued, reflects the presence of God. Romantic love and marriage may be interpreted as expressing something of the divine-human involvement. The same can be said of the relationships of parents and children.

4. God makes Himself known in man's persistent concern for ideal values, namely, goodness, beauty, truth and reverence. God speaks in the pursuit of excellence in all fields. No scientist goes into his laboratory in the search for truth without God

going with him. God is present in the engineer who seeks the best use of steel and aluminum. For God, when rightly understood, is the Lord of truth and of the fitness of things. No moralist seeks justice without God being at work in him. No poet, or dramatist, or painter, or dancer sets out in the quest for beauty or artistic excellence without God. And no saint senses the presence of the holy, the sacred, apart from God.

5. God communicates through the religions of the world that are not based on the Bible. Even in the dim gropings for the sacred among superstitious peoples, God seems to be communicating something of His presence. In the world religions, in which holy men and women have appeared from time to time and in which the masses seek some ultimate attachment, God speaks. Even here, where darkness and light are mingled, God appears to be saying something to men.

These, then, are among the means outside the Biblical heritage that God uses to communicate His vast and pervasive activity. There is no direct revelation of God to men. He speaks through these different things, processes, persons, and events to express the various aspects of His being.

The question next to be asked is: Are these five media of divine revelation enough to meet the deepest moral and religious needs of men? The divine revelation in this first dimension does not speak adequately to the issues of life and death and destiny. Man is not left without help, but he needs far more than he can receive within this first dimension of revelation. Therefore, the Biblical heritage takes on special significance precisely against the background of the inadequacies of these evidences of God's activity outside the Bible. For this to make sense, man's needs, in their range and depth, will have to be identified.

Before doing that, however, a basic thought about these two dimensions of revelation must be stated. It is no part of the view here expressed that the two realms are unrelated to each other. The Bible belongs in the vast stream of universal history. The men of the Bible shared in the common humanity of all peoples. They lived on earth and knew the universal struggles for food, health and safety. Their lives, like those of all others, were affected by the same external and internal pressures all men have felt. Moreover, the same God who has spoken in the physical universe, in culture and civilization, human relationships, and in other world religions, has spoken through the men and events of the Bible. We may not always know how to pinpoint the interrelations of these two spheres of divine revelation. But there are decisive reasons for believing that, like the hemispheres of the earth, despite vast oceans, they are joined together at a common base.

The point is that there are two dimensions of revelation that supplement each other. Both are needed for man to make proper progress in his relationships with God and his fellow men.

This brings us to the second dimension of divine revelation, namely, that which comes through the men and events of the Bible and develops in keeping with its own nature. Where is the uniqueness? What does this offer that is not available outside the Bible and its heritage?

In answering these questions, I suggest that there is no revelation of God in the Bible that is not at least hinted at elsewhere. In some instances there are remarkable corroborations of the Biblical teaching. But mere hints or suggestions from nature, history, and other world religions are not enough. Isolated insights cannot communicate what is most needed. Again, flashes of illumination within a world-view that regards God as an impersonal process or being leave much to be desired. The uniqueness of the Biblical revelation is seen in the disclosure of three things about God and His aims that are not found elsewhere on the same level. These are of utmost importance because they meet corresponding needs of men pertaining to the issues of life and death and destiny.

First, God has revealed the main *purpose* for which He created man. That purpose is, with God's help, to realize moral and spiritual values in community under the leadership of Jesus Christ, the revealer of love. This primal theme will be developed in the pages that follow. But some notice of the uniqueness of this revelation is in order.

We have seen that a major change in the thinking of modern man, as contrasted with medieval man, is the loss of the belief in an ultimate purpose back of and in the universe. With this loss has come the sense of the absence of direction and meaning in human existence, which reflects itself in much of the art, literature, music, and intellectual endeavors of the modern world. This has left many sophisticated people with a mysterious experience of emptiness and futility. For them there is no sense of direction outside of man. Many of the efforts in recent theology to recover this religious experience of meaning and purpose without the belief in the God who acts purposively are symptomatic of the difficulty in which modern man as a whole finds himself.

The various sciences say almost nothing on the purpose of human life. One could study the stars and galaxies with the best telescopes for a thousand years and still not have a clear and relevant idea of why we are here. He could spend a lifetime in a first-rate scientific laboratory and not discover any deep lying aim of life. So is it in every field of humanistic study and discovery. Some philosophers have pointed their fingers in the right direction (toward ideal values) but even the best thinkers have given only inadequate hints. The other world religions also offer some light. But, in the main, they lack clarity and ethical authenticity on this all-important point. Where can we find in all literature a disclosure of the *purpose* of human life as noble as that in the Bible? At the same time, where can we find a statement of that aim expressed within a total perspective that can give meaning to man's life?

Second, God has revealed in the Bible the divine resources for realizing this purpose. These resources are spoken of in the New Testament as the grace of God. The writers of the books of the Bible assume that man needs God's help. There is a unique understanding here of the dramatic interplay of the divine and human. God is not some far-off deity who pulls the strings of the puppets. He does not force His way upon men.

He is not whimsical. He will not do for men what they must do for themselves.

God offers to go with them into the struggles and adventures of life. The God of the Bible is radically involved with men in history, in the thick of interpersonal relations where the action is. God re-enforces the efforts of all who are open and responsive to Him while seeking to realize moral and spiritual values under Jesus Christ, who made known God's boundless love. Through it all God offers His mysterious accompanying presence. According to the Biblical teaching the divine presence and resources are made available primarily within the community of faith. Here there is a remarkable balance between the community and the solitary soul seeking God's presence and help. This interplay of God, community, and the individual is itself a part of the uniqueness of the Biblical teaching on God's grace or help.

The first two disclosures would be utterly inadequate without the third. This is God's revelation concerning the rewards and destiny of those who seek to realize the primary purpose of life on this planet. What is the destiny of man beyond this life? Here man's best efforts in science and technology fail. Here too his finest imaginative creations in poetry, drama and art are helpless. But God, in His infinite love and wisdom, has revealed His administrative policy regarding the conquest of death. He has done this primarily through the long line of men and events leading up to the life, death, and resurrection of Jesus. He has done it also through the intimations in the experiences of those who have walked by faith.

In this way the primal aim of realizing moral and spiritual values in community is not lost at death. These values exist, and can exist, only in persons. But if the persons or souls perish, the main point of the whole enterprise is lost. This would turn it all into a meaningless succession of events. Here again there are hints by some philosophers who suggest that endurance and value must go together, or that happiness and virtue belong together. And in other religions too there are helpful suggestions. But in the Biblical teaching there is freedom from the crudities of a sensual paradise on the one hand, and of reincarnation on the other. There is freedom also from the mystical notion that the individual and his desires are absorbed in the divine Being. Besides being difficult to know what this could mean, it misses the Biblical stress on the reality and value of the soul.

We may summarize this principle by saying that God reveals Himself everywhere. But what man can neither decide nor discover through his own unaided imagination, God has revealed in a more distinctive way through the Bible and its continuing heritage. The Bible communicates a unique dimension of truth and reality about God, man, and the meeting of God and man.

SECOND PRINCIPLE: THE ORGANIC UNITY OF TYPE

One of the marks of an authentic religious belief is that it grows from simple beginnings into a comprehensive tool for interpreting reality. As does a seed planted in good soil, it develops. So is it with the major teachings of the Bible. They are dynamic rather than static. Just as a grain of wheat is not understood merely by what it is but by what it becomes, so the teachings of the Bible are to be understood in their developing nature. This is why we say that the Old Testament prepares the way for the New.

There are many things about God we shall never know, for He is the Infinite Being, and we are finite. But in so far as God has revealed Himself to men, He has done so by stages suitable to the experiences of men at given times. This suggests the patience of God, who deals with men where they are. At the same time He moves on toward the more perfect.

For example, many centuries separate the covenant God made with Abraham or with Moses and the new covenant in behalf of all men through Jesus Christ. Nevertheless, these are organically united. The seed, in the proper soil, led to the development of the covenant idea through a long line of persons and events. From Abraham, Moses, and David, through the prophets, God revealed His concern for His children and communicated the reality of His covenant. Then He clarified the true meaning of all this in the more perfect revelation in Jesus Christ.

From this example we can see how irresponsible it is to view any teaching of the Bible in isolation from its function in the developing revelation. The Word of God is a living, dynamic, creative force moving toward the larger and more perfect utterance through men. There are ideas and events in the Bible that seem to fall dead. They are there but they do not develop. These belong in the Bible, but their value is more negative than positive. For they were sloughed off in the process of God's further disclosures. This principle of the dynamic developing nature of Biblical teachings was suggested by Paul when he wrote, "But when the perfect comes, the imperfect will pass away" (I Corinthians 13:10).

One of the chief values of this principle of the organic unity of type is that it frees the Christian from a stifling literalism and helps him to identify the vast movement of God's living Word toward fulfillment in Jesus Christ. In this way, the Christian comes to see that the Bible as a whole is best understood and interpreted in the light of this tendency to find authentic utterance in Jesus Christ. By this means many honest questions raised by modern men can be faced and given plausible responses. For on this basis Christians are not committed to a literal acceptance of everything in the Bible. Indeed, there are events and teachings that are sloughed off in the ongoing movement of God's living Word. If we give the right interpretation on the words that follow, we may say: Not everything in the Bible is Biblical.

THIRD PRINCIPLE: REVELATION FOR RESPONSE

The third principle of interpreting the Bible is that God reveals Himself in order to awaken man's appropriate response to Him. This principle too will help us to appreciate the Biblical heritage without lapsing into obscurantism. For here we realize that the language used is aimed toward response and not merely information. The Bible is not a textbook in science or history. As it has been understood in Christian history it is

God's living Word, spoken through men and events, for awakening men. It is God's call to His children in succeeding generations through which he seeks a response. Let me illustrate this.

The signs on an expressway are not merely to give information. They have a direct bearing on the driver's aims and action. They affect what he does. On a human level we may say that these signs are items of revelation for man's response. Again, in honest advertising there is the combination of a statement of fact with an appeal. The aim is not merely to convey the facts, but to do so in a way that would bring men to spend their hard-earned money on a product. On a mundane level this is revelation for a response.

Once more, suppose there are two boys who want to get a favorable response from a girl. One of them goes up to her and says, "I don't know you and you don't know me but let me inform you about myself." Then he gives a detailed report of his accomplishments in high school and college. The girl would tend to show no interest. The other boy goes up to her and says, "I don't know you and you don't know me, but I think you're the loveliest girl I've ever seen." The girl would probably feel like saying, "This is getting interesting." Assuming the honesty of this second boy, he is sincerely revealing himself for the purpose of getting a response.

Now these are somewhat crude illustrations of what God does through the Bible. He speaks for a response. He convicts, probes, judges, appeals, persuades, calls, challenges, inspires, and promises, all for the sole purpose of getting the appropriate personal responses from His children.

This means that the language used must be appropriate to that end. This is why it is ridiculous to judge the Bible on the basis of a cold factual analysis. It deals in fact, but only or primarily to draw men to God. The Bible is divine communication for response. This is why a sermon is not a lecture. For it is an extension of God's living Word. That is, it is uttered to bring men into the presence of God. This helps us to see why the Bible is called God's living Word.

The question to be asked about the Bible, then, is not, How

does it stand up as astronomy, or as biology, or as philosophy, or as history, or as literature? The question is: Does God speak to men through the Bible and its heritage and draw them to Himself?

FOURTH PRINCIPLE: CONFIRMATION IN EXPERIENCE

The truth and relevance of the major teachings of the Bible can be confirmed only in experience. This is the situation with the great truths in all spheres. They are confirmed at last in experience. Whether or not the Biblical teachings orient the mind rightly toward God's ways can be known only in the ongoing of life.

This is why the most convincing basis for the truth and relevance of the Bible is not in a set of arguments but in a succession of lives, namely, the saints of all ages. I would state this principle in the simple formula: *We can neither establish nor destroy in the armchair what has been verified in the laboratory of the human soul.*

In summary, we may say that if these four principles are consciously used in interpreting the Bible, two results will probably follow. First, many apparent conflicts between the Bible and man's general knowledge will be resolved. In any case, much of the tension will be released. Second, God's Word will take on a more living and comprehensive form. For it will be understood in terms of the vast movement of the living God rather than of piecemeal snippets of revelation tacked onto each other.

Part II

On God

3

THE BELIEF IN A PERSONAL GOD

We perceive the plausibility of our beliefs mainly by following two procedures. The first is by asking the question, What are the major alternative views? The second is by weighing the evidence for and against those alternatives.

All sound thinking involves some effort to clarify the main theories or differing beliefs on a subject. If a man is unwilling to look at any view other than the one he now entertains, he has not put himself in a position to judge. He would be like a judge who stopped his ears to one side and opened them only to hear the other. Similarly, one who is unwilling to search for evidence, weigh it, doubt, and reconsider, is not in a position to judge. He would be like a man on a jury who slept through the evidence. As these processes go on in life they involve innumerable activities men perform without stopping to think about what they are doing.

Broadly speaking, the whole process of sound thinking is not a neat trim little process of taking one simple step after another. Rather, it is a process in which we strive to clarify the options, marshall the evidence pro and con, experience doubts, consider and reconsider, discuss with others, and judge as best we can. When there seems to be a convergence of the cumulative evidence in support of a particular view, the mind begins to see that it is on the right track. It is important to stress the *cumulative* evidences and experiences that tend to confirm a belief.

For it takes far more than a drop of blood to confirm a murder. It requires far more than isolated snippets of evidence to confirm any belief about God.

The procedure in this chapter and in the ones that follow will be to start with a brief statement of the major alternative views. Then we shall present the Biblical teaching as the option that is to be taken most seriously. This will be followed by a consideration of modern doubts about the Biblical teaching and an effort to make reasonable responses to those doubts.

THE MAIN ALTERNATIVE VIEWS

In the long history of religion four kinds of ideas about God may be distinguished. In primitive religions the gods were *crudely personal.* Though the gods of Greece and Rome were on a higher plane than those of primitive religions, they too were crudely conceived. In the religions of the Far East the deity is *vaguely impersonal.* Among some recent thinkers God has been thought of primarily as *process.* In Judaism, Islam, and Christianity, God has been understood as the *infinite personal Being.* Unless we deny God altogether, these four would seem to be the major alternative views. And because modern men cannot take seriously the crude notions of deity in the primitive religions and in the religions of Greece and Rome, only three live options remain, namely, that of God as an impersonal being, or as process, or as the infinite person.

THE BIBLICAL TEACHING

In relation to these three alternative perspectives the Bible as a whole is a monumental affirmation of personalism and an implicit repudiation of all forms of impersonalism whether ancient or modern. For the God of the Bible is a personal Spirit. The Bible assumes this with such remarkable consistency that we cannot help noticing it. The Biblical writers do not lapse into the vague impersonal ideas of the Far East, or of the Neoplatonists, or of the pantheistic mystics. They had a keen sense of the holy and of the greatness of God. They struggled to express the glory and holiness of God. So we might

29

have expected some of them, at least, to push off from the mountaintops into rarified remarks on the Unknowable, or on Being, or on the One. But they did not do it.

This curious circumstance calls for an explanation. How does it happen that in a collection of sixty-six religious books, written over a period of many centuries, there are no lapses into mystical impersonal thoughts about God? No detailed effort will be made to answer this question, but enough can be said to show how basic in the Bible is the belief in a personal God.

Abraham felt himself to be in a covenant relationship with God. This included the promise, through Isaac and Jacob and their descendants, to bless all mankind. Moses counteracted the gods of others by lifting up the one true God who had delivered the people of Israel from their bondage in Egypt. No vague pantheistic deity could have done that. This required the God who acts in history. God made a covenant with Moses and the people of Israel, and the whole community was required to show its good faith by obeying the Ten Commandments. Only then would God protect and support them. The prophets kept this theme alive and reminded the people of their failure to obey the Commandments and consequently of the disasters they were bringing on themselves.

These brief remarks will serve as the clue to understanding the personalism of the Bible. For from the start, God is thought of as radically involved with men in person-to-person encounters. The ancient Hebrews did not speculate about God as the One, or as Being, or as the Unknowable. They experienced Him in their struggles and hopes. They felt His help as they fought to free themselves. They knew Him as the Lord who communicated with them through inspired leaders. He was their Judge, their Resource, their Shepherd, and their gracious Redeemer.

Consequently, any thought of God as some vague impersonal remote being was out of the question. No such deity could enter into the issues of history. Equally pointless would have been the notion of God as an impersonal cosmic process. For at the heart of the Biblical teaching is the idea that God *com-*

municates with man, He *acts purposively* with them, and He *deals with them* in person-to-person encounters in both judgment and redemption. He judges, knows, calls, forgives, quickens, and commands. God is the chief actor in the Old Testament.

The New Testament, too, emphasizes the belief in a personal God and shows the special relevance of this belief in the individual's relationship with God through faith. Jesus taught that God is our Father. All the virtues of a good earthly father were elevated to infinity and applied to God. He said, "If you then, who are evil, know how to give good gifts to your children, how much more will your Father who is in heaven give good things to those who ask him" (Matthew 7:11)! The clue here is in the "how much more." Jesus taught that in our experience of family relationships there is an authentic basis for knowing what God is like. There is none of the suggestion, found among some philosophers and theologians, that we cannot think or say anything definite about God—not even that He exists; to do so would reduce God to some form of finite being. On the contrary, Jesus deliberately taught His followers to think of God as the Father and to pray to Him as such.

Among the apostles and others, too, there is this confidence that we know what God is like. He has revealed Himself in Jesus Christ. This would not be possible unless God were personal. For how can love embodied in the person of Jesus truly reveal an impersonal ultimate being? So the personality or personhood of God is implied in the revelation of God through Jesus Christ.

This personalistic way of thinking about God is perhaps somewhat obscured in certain passages in the New Testament on the Holy Spirit. For the Holy Spirit is referred to as a kind of pervasive presence who breaks through the bounds of our individuality and dwells within us. But even so there is no disposition on the part of any writer in the New Testament to think of the Holy Spirit as an impersonal energy. We may not know how to think our way through this problem to full coherence, but we do not doubt the personal nature of the Holy Spirit as described in the New Testament.

The Biblical writers were religious men, not philosophers. But there are clear implications of the Biblical teaching on God that need to be made explicit in the modern world. The God of the Bible is personal because His actions reveal the characteristics of a person. These may be listed as consciousness, individuality or selfhood, the power to act purposively, knowledge, communication, and goodness or love. Only persons are known to express these qualities in any high degree. Let us consider each of them briefly.

The God of the Bible is a conscious being. He is aware of Himself, His aims, His children and of His own experiences. An unconscious or impersonal deity would be totally outside the orbit of Biblical meanings.

The God of the Bible is the ultimate individual. He has His own unique being and is His own unique self. Just as no human individual is anything or anyone other than himself, so is it with God. But in the case of God, He is unique because He alone is the ultimate and uncreated individual. All this is clearly implied in the personalism of the Bible. This is not to suggest that God is there presented explicitly as a philosophical absolute. It is to assert, however, that the God of the Bible is in fact the ultimate uncreated Being who can be talked about philosophically.

Again, God acts purposively. Perhaps the key category for understanding the God of the Bible is purpose. This is particularly true if we include love as furnishing the content for God's aims. God is headed somewhere. He is dynamically operative. He is in process of achieving His aims. He created, creates, and sustains the universe to realize His ends. And human personality alone gives the clue to this basic characteristic of God. God is not some far-off static being; He is the ultimate volitional agent. The God of the Bible moves into an open-ended future. This is why He created and creates. This is why He makes covenants with His children. This is why He communicates His promises and calls men to move with Him into the future with hope.

Further still, the God of the Bible knows His world and all His creatures. As the psalmist said, "O Lord, thou hast searched me and known me!" (Psalms 139:1). This is a major recurring theme of the Bible. Jesus said, "But even the hairs of your head are all numbered" (Matthew 10:30). So God *knows* His children in all of the intimate details of their lives. The clue to this comes from our human experience of knowledge, limited though it is. One reason the prophets and Jesus could take God so seriously is that they knew He was ever aware of the tragedy and hopes of men. The assumption of the Father's detailed knowledge of individuals and communities is essential to the Biblical teaching on repentance and forgiveness, prayer, grace, assurance, gratitude, promise and hope. It is a primary presupposition of all levels of Biblical religion.

The God of the Bible communicates with men. He reveals Himself. He communicates His dissatisfaction. He makes His promises known so men can be aware of what to expect and how to respond. He spoke to Moses and the prophets. He communicated His nature and love through Jesus Christ. He made His presence felt through the Holy Spirit. The whole Biblical revelation rests on the assumption that God communicates with men. So the Bible is God's living Word. That Word is essentially in the form of vast cumulative promises that if men are open to Him and trust Him, He will move in and through them into a magnificent future that begins on earth and continues in community after death. Such communication is possible only on the level of personality.

The God of the Bible loves each human being. From this standpoint the whole Bible may be understood as a comprehensive epic of revelation of God's love for men.

In summary, then, the Biblical teaching moves in the opposite direction from two perspectives, namely, a crude anthropomorphic polytheism and a vague impersonal pantheism. The Biblical revelation, developing in keeping with its nature, presents a radical ethical monotheism that opens the way to the person-to-person relationships between men and God.

Modern man, who breathes the atmosphere of a new world created by science and technology, finds it difficult to think in terms of a personal God. It does not seem to fit into his contemporary experience. Consequently, the whole approach of the Bible seems unreal. Everyone who understands the Bible knows its personalistic teaching on God. But this, far from being a foundation for sound belief in the modern world, is a stumbling block to many. Perhaps we can do no better than to consider one by one some doubts about the belief in a personal God. Seven of these will be stated, each followed by a response.

Doubt   First, the belief in a personal God is not supported by science. Because, for some, the only road to truth is by way of scientific methods, it follows that the Biblical teaching on God as a person must be discarded.

Response   This is an honest doubt. Julian Huxley, in his book entitled *Religion Without Revelation,* goes so far as to say that science requires us not merely to doubt but to deny a personal God.

Nevertheless, the fact that the belief in a personal God is not supported by science is of no real consequence for three reasons. First, the sciences are not the only avenues to truth. Second, the sciences do not require men to affirm or deny any ultimate reality. They are neutral. They deal with limited aspects of reality and do not properly concern themselves with ultimate causal explanation or with the ground of all that is. Third, the confirmed generalizations of all sciences admit of a theistic interpretation. That is, there is no conflict between the sciences and the belief in a personal God rightly understood. And of course many first-rate scientists believe in God as the ultimate Mind. Therefore, it is arbitrary to pit science and the belief in a personal God against each other.

In the light of science, however, it becomes the duty of every-one who believes in a personal God to avoid crude ideas that bring God down to the level of man. This misses the Biblical teaching by cheapening the idea of God. The whole point is that we must think of God with the aid of the main person-alistic categories (conscious individuality, purpose, knowledge, communication, and love), which can express law, creativity, and open-endedness toward the future.

Doubt   Second, the modern mind wants to avoid the crude anthropomorphisms. If we are to think of God at all, surely we must free ourselves of the persistent tendency to make God in the image of man. To think of God as personal is to fashion Him after our own puny minds; and that does not fit into contemporary ways of thinking.

Response   This is a doubt that naturally arises from what modern man knows about the human tendency to think in pictures and to oversimplify. It rightly calls for the avoidance of crudity in the thinking about God.

In this the Bible itself joins the modern mind. For one of the major achievements of men like Moses and the prophets was precisely to overcome such crudities by the conquest of poly-theism and the triumph of monotheism. God is God. He alone is uncreated, unbegun and ending. God alone *has* to be. He is the necessary being. Therefore, He cannot be rightly understood merely after the pattern of the human mind. Those who still hang on to ancient crudities and speak of God as though He were "the man upstairs," or a glorified Santa Claus, are not in the line of the Biblical heritage. For the Bible in its developing teaching repudiates this as vigorously as any modern critic.

On the other side, is not modern man in danger of assuming a crude notion equally unBiblical and unwarranted? I have in mind the assumption that impersonal law and process are ulti-mate. No one can claim justly that human personality provides an adequate clue to the nature of God. God is far more than any human analogy can suggest. But men seek the best ways of talking about Him that are available. Is the model of impersonal law and process able to do the job? The question here is: Which option makes the most sense? Is it a mark of progress to use a category inferior to the best we know as a tool for understanding God?

The personalist suggests that the human mind or personality furnishes the best clue to understanding something about God. In saying this he does not mean to suggest that the weaknesses, foibles, and limitations of human personality give us the clue. Rather, the basic *universal categories* of personality furnish the best insights we have into thinking about God.

For example, a person is a conscious individual capable of acting purposively, of knowing, loving, and communicating. If we ask how there can be an ordered universe when there are infinite possibilities for chaos, the best answer moves us toward the ultimate Mind who coordinates His activities in producing the universe. If we suggest blind impersonal law and process as an explanation, we perceive that it cannot bear the freight. It does not really *explain* anything. What we require is *causal explanation* that is adequate. And we find this only by thinking personalistically in terms of the God who acts purposively as the ultimate causal agent. Here, then, the mind furnishes a clue that is not forthcoming if we assume that impersonal process is ultimate.

Such qualities of personality as purpose and intelligence are needed to explain what we find. And these presuppose other characteristics of personality, namely, conscious individuality and volitional agency. The term "unconscious purpose" has no assignable meaning. In so far as it is unconscious it cannot be purposive, and in so far as it is purposive it cannot be unconscious.

Illustrations of this kind of reasoning could be multiplied, but perhaps enough has been said to demonstrate that the belief in a personal God is a far more promising option than might at first appear. Moreover, when properly understood, it does not commit us to any crude anthrophomorphism.

Doubt　　　　Somewhat related to all this is a third kind of doubt. I refer to the doubt that arises from modern man's understanding of the rise and development of religion as an aspect of cultural evolution. Present day religious beliefs came originally from primitive beliefs. Crude beginnings often linger on in the advancing civilizations. This is no less true of Christianity than of all other religions. On this reading it is easy to drift into the idea that the Bible is a book of legends and myths with smatterings of history, touches of poetry, a few useful maxims, and some moral regulations. There is no reason why modern men should be bound to the idea of a personal God that is a legacy of primitive man.

Response　　　　Modern man has enriched the understanding of religion by putting it in the long winding river of cultural evolution. But he has often assumed without solid reasons that all religion is a mere human product.

Man has played a large role in the formation of his religions. But the real question is this: Is God at work in this historical development? Modern man tends to proceed on naturalistic assumptions, which lead him to interpret religious phenomena wholly in terms of cultural evolution. But the phenomena admit also of a theistic interpretation. Everything depends on whether or not there is in fact a personal God. If there is an ultimate Mind who involves Himself with men, then no historical-cultural analysis can be an adequate explanation of religious faith. This issue cannot be resolved by sociological studies.

Again, the origin of a belief has nothing to do with its validity. Therefore, the Biblical teaching on a personal God can be neither established nor undermined by studies in the development of religious beliefs.

Doubt　　　　Fourth, there are the doubts and arguments against the belief in a personal God that are drawn from psychology. Here the main thought is that there are valid psychological explanations of the religious experiences of the prophets and others. These ancient figures simply projected their ideas about

God into reality. Or, they extended their wishes by creating in their minds the kind of God who could satisfy their most insistent desires. So we ought not to believe in a God who is merely a projection of our wishes.

Response   The religious experiences of the prophets and apostles have been studied psychologically with much profit. But can their religious faith be adequately described in terms of such subjective factors as wishful thinking, projection, autosuggestion and the like? Only on the assumption that there is no personal God, or that man lives in a universe where impersonal process is ultimate. This assumption is often smuggled into the dialogue as though it needed no reasonable warrant.

Here again, everything depends upon whether or not there is a personal God. If there is, mere psychological descriptions of religious faith are woefully inadequate. They would be as pathetic as efforts to explain a marriage in terms of the psychological wishes and responses of the husband while ignoring the reality of the wife. The reality questions in life and in religion cannot be decided on the plane of psychology.

Doubt   Another doubt arises from man's contemporary experience of the absence of God. So it means little to speak to men now of a personal God.

Response   This doubt has the merit of arising out of contemporary experience. It has the merit also of arising out of the recurring experience of men in all eras.

There are no responses here that will satisfy everyone. Nevertheless there are some considerations that help us to explain why many men fail to experience the presence of God. Religion, like authentic love, requires the fulfillment of conditions. Men often experience the absence of love. But this does not mean that the experience is unreal for others. It means that they have not fulfilled the conditions for experiencing love.

Certain attitudes, moods, and habits shut out religion just as surely as they preclude love. The Biblical teaching as well as that of the saints assumes the organic connection between the fulfillment of conditions and living encounters with God.

For example, a cynical attitude long sustained has been universally known to leave men with the sense of the absence of God. Similarly, the sustained attention to the seamy sides of life, to tragedy, to man's inhumanity, tends to incapacitate men for faith. I do not mean that anyone should be insensitive to human suffering. Rather, I am speaking of a bitter hypercritical response that blinds a person to the total picture of the human situation. Chronic quirks, fears, and twists of mind and judgment make it almost impossible to experience the divine presence. Again, sustained doubts about the reality and effectiveness of God preclude the sense of His presence. A lack of genuine interest would also shut the door. The distractions of the modern world also make it very difficult for men to meditate and to be open toward God long enough to be aware of His presence.

Again, if a man is unwilling to seek and love God with all his heart, soul, and mind, he is not apt to sense the presence of God. The proud person will also miss out. So will the man who, complacently trusting in man and his achievements, does not bother to ask the deeper questions pertaining to life, sin, death and destiny. For it does not require the grace of God to meet the needs that come within the range of our own competence.

Christians have always urged that thinking about Jesus as the One who in a special way reveals God, helps them to sense the presence of God. When men have a clear apprehension of God's love through meditation on the life and mind of Jesus Christ, they find themselves responding to God's love and sensing His presence. This is especially true when men come together in the community of faith for worship that centers around Jesus Christ. Those who do not identify themselves with a community of faith often experience not only their absence from people but from God.

If contemporary experience did not reflect the absence of God, something would be wrong. This, for two reasons. First, many men do not in fact experience the reality of God. So contemporary experience reflects this fact. Second, men have not put themselves in a position to become aware of the living God. It would be as unreasonable to expect religious faith to thrive without the willingness to fulfill specifiable conditions as to expect love to thrive in a home without assignable attitudes and habits.

Another thought to be noted is that modern man's general perspectives often make it impossible for him to recognize the divine presence in his negative experiences. The sense of the absence of God is one of the surest signs of the presence of God.

In summary, a certain kind of world-view and certain attitudes and responses are indispensable conditions to the awareness of God's presence. Jesus said, "Ask, and it will be given you; seek, and you will find; knock, and it will be opened to you" (Matthew 7:7).

Doubt   Sixth, perhaps the main source of doubt about a personal God in contemporary experience arises from the antimetaphysical spirit of the modern world which removes the Biblical teaching from serious consideration. Men feel impatient with the search for ultimate reality. Hence, they have not considered carefully the reasons for denying a personal God. Instead, they have tended to let that belief be crowded out by more fashionable assumptions that merely reflect certain aspects of contemporary experience.

Response   What is required essentially is the steadfast willingness to question the prevailing skeptical and naturalistic assumptions of the modern mentality. Along with this there must be the continuing example of those who live the life of faith in the midst of the struggles and aspirations of men in need. For this too tends to lead some to consider the possibility of realms of reality which their skeptical orientations have missed.

In this era of the antimetaphysical spirit, one of the contributions of the Biblical teaching on God is to furnish the philosophical mind with an option about God. Though not philosophically developed, Biblical personalism nevertheless becomes a starting point for considering what it might contribute to the philosophical world as a way of thinking about God. And, when considered along with the other options suggested out of man's contemporary experience, it has much to commend itself.

Doubt   A seventh doubt about a personal God comes from theologians who are concerned lest we classify God among the creatures. They do not want to say even that God exists. For this suggests that He is another existing being along with all the rest. Similarly, to ascribe any personalistic category to God reduces Him to creatureliness. For example, Paul Tillich and others have suggested that the personalistic categories are symbols pointing toward God as the Ground of Being. They do not literally apply to God.

Response   The motive of securing the uniqueness of God in contrast to all other creatures is good. But this can be done without denying the literal reference of the personalistic categories to God. When we say that God knows us and His universe this does not imply that God is classified among the creatures. What does it mean to say that God knows us? What would it mean to say that He is beyond knowing? Either we affirm that God knows us or we lapse into impersonalism. So is it with the other personalistic categories. God is literally conscious, whatever else He may be. He acts purposively. He communicates or reveals Himself and His aims. He loves His children.

The best way to see this is by performing mental experiments in response to the question: What assignable meaning is there in supposing that God is beyond or other than each of the personalistic categories? For example, what does it mean to say that God does not literally *know* since He is really beyond knowledge?

Besides these intellectual consequences there are practical consequences here of first importance. The Biblical revelation with its entire heritage has been at work to realize a living relationship with God. Without the belief in a personal God, which is central in that revelation, prayer would be reduced to meditation, worship to self-searching and aspiration, grace to inner conditioning, and service to humanistic endeavor.

In conclusion, we may say that a brief outline of the main arguments for believing in God were stated in chapter 1. Personal observations on some of them may be in order here. Of those arguments, the most intellectually convincing is perhaps the argument based on the intelligibility of the world around us, including the universe. The more I reflect on this the more convinced I am that the only coherent explanation of this curious but everyday fact is that the Other Mind is at work throughout the universe making it a medium of communication.

Other very convincing bases for believing in a personal God begin with my inability to explain why there should be anything at all. Can anything less than Mind fill out the idea of Being? Closely related to this is the question as to why there should be an ordered universe. There are infinite possibilities for chaos. Obviously there is an ordering principle. But what is it? How can we think this through? The only direction my mind can move here with any sense of confidence is toward an ordering Mind, the clue to which is found in the ordering ability of purposive intelligent action. The arguments from esthetic experience and moral experience are to me strong also. The most convincing argument of a more practical sort is that which evolves from the lives of the saints. This seems to me increasingly irrefutable.

What we have in all of these arguments is not a neat set of proofs. Rather, we have the coming together from various quarters of many grounds for the belief in a personal God. Therefore, among the live options it is for me by far the most reasonable one. We shall consider some of these observations in more detail in the chapters that follow.

4

CREATION FOR A PURPOSE

From the earliest times men have thought about the origin of the universe. How did it begin? How does it continue? Where is it headed? To these questions various answers have been suggested.

There are at least six major theories on the creation of the universe. These can perhaps be stated best in historical perspective.

In the ancient world some said that matter is eternal and there is no Creator. Among the philosophers this theory was given classical utterance by Democritus and other Greek atomists who held that atoms are uncreated and eternal. Everything simply came out of the aimless motion of the atoms.

Others said that matter is eternal and uncreated but was originally in a chaotic condition requiring the ordering work of a Creator. The ancient Babylonian epic *Enûma elish* expressed the idea of an original watery chaos separated into heaven and earth. On the theory that this myth influenced the Biblical teaching, some have suggested that the idea of an original chaos awaiting the ordering hand of God is the real meaning of Genesis 1:2. Some Stoics also held to the idea of an original matter. Among ancient writers Plato gave it very impressive utterance in his dialogue called *Timaeus*. This, then, is the theory that the universe was not really created but given order out of an original chaotic stuff. According to this view matter is coeternal with God.

A radically modified Platonism in recent philosophy (which still contains much of this ancient perspective) is that of A. N. Whitehead and his followers. Whitehead uses the term "creativity" instead of "creation." He is strongly impressed with the unceasing emergence of novelty. But instead of holding that in the beginning God caused a nonexistent universe to come into being, he suggests that God has always been creatively at work in relation to things and processes other than Himself. Thus in some sense, for Whitehead, God and some kind of actual realm other than God are correlative factors in creative activity. Yet, for him, God provides the ultimate initiative. This cannot begin to do justice to Whitehead's important theory but it will at least suggest the direction in which it moves.

Another theory of creation was held by the many varieties of Gnostics who flourished among the early centuries of the Christian era. They stressed the evil character of the physical world and said that God is too good to have created it. So they came up with the idea that it was set going in its present form by a lesser deity. The more philosophical among them suggested that the Supreme God remained separated from this present world by a hierarchy of worlds. Each of these worlds produced a lesser one until the present universe was thought of as almost untouched by the hand of the Supreme God. That is, the physical universe at last came out of successive stages of degeneration until it was seen as something far removed from the perfection of the Supreme God. In this way the Gnostics tried to do justice to the goodness of God on the one hand, and to the evil character of the physical world on the other.

A fourth theory of creation is implied in pantheistic modes of thought. This way of thinking too goes back to ancient times and still thrives among some modern thinkers. According to it creation is the self-expression of God. It is not creation in the sense of causing to be what was not. Nor is God thought of as creating the universe by bringing order into an original chaos. Rather, He is simply giving concrete utterance to Himself. He creates "out of Himself." Creation is divine self-expression; for everything is an aspect of God.

A fifth view is somewhat related to pantheistic modes of thought and yet differs from them radically regarding creation. This is the view expressed in some Eastern religions that there is no world at all. The supposed physical universe is an illusion. Hence, there is no need for a doctrine of creation.

44

The sixth view is the Biblical perspective to which we shall turn next.

The question might be asked as to why no mention is made of certain scientific theories concerning the creation of the universe. Are not these too among the options? They are not included here because, strictly speaking, they are not theories pertaining to creation at all. They have to do with explanations of the present form of the universe after it got started. The real question here is this theological and philosophical one: What is the ultimate origin of matter and all that makes up the universe?

THE BIBLICAL TEACHING

The Bible teaches that God alone is self-existent and eternal.

> Holy, holy, holy, is the Lord God Almighty,
> who was and is and is to come (Revelation 4:8)!

By His own unique action He created the universe to realize His aims. This idea is maintained by the Biblical writers with amazing constancy. They seem to include in their perspective at least three major thoughts which are stated or implied throughout their writings.

First, there is the idea that God brought into being what was non-existent. Creation in the Biblical sense means to cause to be what was not. The traditional way of expressing this is by the Latin formula, *creatio ex nihilo*. That is, God created the universe "out of nothing." This means, among other things, that God did not have an already existing "matter," or "chaos," or stuff with which to create. He simply *created*. Some have thought that this really means that God created the universe "out of himself." But this is not an accurate way of expressing what the Bible teaches. The Biblical idea is that God, by virtue of His own mysterious powers, acted to form a realm of being that did not previously exist.

Implied in this teaching too is the idea that man has no insight into *how* God could have done this. Nevertheless, *that* He did it is the ultimate fact about the origin of the universe. Another way of stating it is this: God has the power to make any kinds of universes He desires, and He chose to make this one. How, we do not know. Why this one and not another out of the infinite possibilities, we do not know. Of course, there may be numberless other universes or realms of reality somewhere of which we are wholly oblivious.

Second, God created this particular universe to realize His aims. Once the *fact* of creation has been asserted, the emphasis shifts swiftly to the *purpose* of creation. The Biblical writers abhor the notion that the universe and man are the product of aimless processes. This is why purpose becomes a key category in understanding the Biblical teaching on nearly all topics. So this idea stands in the strongest possible contrast to certain modern options that stress impersonal process, and to some of the views of Eastern religions that emphasize impersonal being. Whenever men lose or minimize the sense of purposive movement toward an end, the Biblical teaching is lost and cannot be recovered without it.

This is not to suggest that all this is explicitly stated in systematic order by the Biblical writers. Nor is it to urge that they consciously singled out the category of purpose as a philosophical tool indispensable to their task. It is rather to say that this category was implicitly operative in their thinking of God in relation to man and the universe. From the standpoint of the present study we may say that when the Bible is read with the aid of the four principles of interpretation suggested in chapter 2, this is the direction in which the Biblical teaching necessarily moves. Creation means the beginning of an era and of a setting magnificent enough for God's aims. It is the opening curtain for a vast drama waiting to be enacted. It reveals God's refusal to withhold Himself in some far-off realm separated from the destiny of finite creatures.

Many of the aims of God in this mysterious cosmic drama are unknown to man. He can neither fathom the universe nor all of the aims of God in creating it. But the Biblical teaching is that man's part in the drama has been revealed, namely, to participate with God and men in the realization of values in

46

community. Creation was for the purpose of this divine-human involvement in interpersonal relations. It is therefore understood as organically interconnected with the continuing processes of the universe and of human history. A poetic expression of the continuity between creation and redemption is found in a well-known Christmas carol in these words:

> Ye who sang creation's story
> Now proclaim Messiah's birth.

The God who acted to create acted also to redeem; and this is all a part of the unified purpose of God.

This brings us to the third major teaching of the Bible on the creation of the universe and man: Man is given priority over nature.

There is a curious aspect of the Biblical teaching here, namely, that this present physical universe, which far outlasts man, will come to an end but the souls of men will not perish. This thought does not reach its summit point until the accounts of the resurrection of Jesus in the New Testament and in the subsequent interpretations of the meaning of that event. There is of course no hint here that man can guarantee his own existence after death or that he is by nature immortal. The idea is that the God who created him made him for an everlasting destiny. Everything depends on the policy and action of God. By the power of God the human soul will continue beyond death in another dimension of existence, that is, in a new universe of some sort.

This would explain in part why the Biblical writers were more interested in the creation of man than of the physical universe. They suggested that Adam was more important than the cosmos. They were interested from the start in the relationship between God and man in the drama of history; and they saw at last that this drama was designed to prepare the way for even greater adventures beyond death. The Biblical teaching here would suggest that anyone who thinks of this present spatio-temporal order as a permanent environment for the Kingdom of God has missed the way. On the other hand, anyone who overlooks the fact that God intends serious business in and through this present order is making an equally disastrous mistake.

The conclusion on this third aspect of the Biblical teaching on creation is that this universe and the present life of man were important enough for God to create and maintain for His aims. But far more than this environment is indicated, especially for the future of man beyond death. The physical universe was designed by God to be an instrument and means. It is the stage and setting, not the drama. Men are the experiencers and actors in this drama, which ever presses toward the realization of values in community. As a part of this drama, however, the physical universe operates as an enriching medium of communication. "The heavens are telling the glory of God" (Psalms 19:1). The world and the entire known universe evoke the sense of beauty and convey the sense of order and meaning. Therefore the Biblical teaching, in effect, calls upon every man to be a responsible person in his interpretation and use of the physical world. However inadequate this present setting and medium may be, it was made for a purpose. Man is to think of himself as essential to that purpose and to move with God toward a better world yet to come.

If there are other intelligent beings in other parts of the universe, it would be reasonable to suppose that God has called them also to be participants with Him in the ongoing creative enterprise. In the Christian church this Biblical teaching on creation has maintained its identity and continuity, despite encounters with many opposing perspectives, up to the modern world.

SOME MODERN DOUBTS AND RESPONSES TO THEM

During the modern period the doubts about the Biblical teaching on creation have been more pervasive and persistent than in any previous era of Christian history. These doubts have moved in four directions. First, there are doubts based on the limits of human knowledge; man cannot know about creation. Second, there are doubts that the universe was created at all. Third, there are doubts that there is any purpose back of the universe and man. Fourth, there are doubts that the teaching on creation should focus on man as central rather than on the physical universe. We shall consider these in that order.

Doubt   First, man cannot know about creation. Consequently, in all of his theories he should confine himself to what he is capable of knowing and so to what he can profitably explore. Some modern doubts about God as Creator arise, then, from the belief that man has no convincing evidence on the subject.

Response   This view was expressed long before the Christian era. We find it in principle in Socrates. It has been expressed by many others. Even Thomas Aquinas said that the belief in creation could not be derived from man's reason; it is based only on divine revelation. Kant also argued that we cannot answer the question as to whether or not there was an original act of creation.

This mode of thought is especially vigorous, however, in the contemporary world. We have already observed that the anti-metaphysical spirit pervades the modern mind. There is a built-in skeptical attitude toward all efforts to seek ultimate causes and explanations. This is particularly true when God is said to be the supreme principle of causal explanation. This built-in attitude is a nonrational assumption derived not from reason and experience but from the unconscious intellectual fashions of contemporary experience. So the general assumption is that whenever we seek an ultimate causal explanation of the universe we are going into waters over our heads.

Consequently, when scientists today speculate on the origin of the universe they do not concern themselves with its *ultimate* beginnings. They are thinking of how it came to be composed of galaxies, or of how our particular galaxy was formed, or of how our planetary system emerged. Granting the existence of a universe, how did it develop into its present form? That is the question they are asking. So they suggest various theories on the "origin" of the universe, including the "big bang" theory, the steady state theory, and others. Such theories are interesting as efforts to describe changes and developments in an already existing universe. In this respect they are exactly like the theory of evolution. They *describe* a possible succession of developments but do not *explain ultimately* why there should be a universe or an evolutionary process at all.

The best answer I know to the generally skeptical and antimetaphysical mood of the modern mind is this. Man wants to know. He finds a universe that is not self-explanatory. So he considers the various options. Though there is much data lacking, he takes the overwhelming evidence concerning the inability of the universe to explain itself and draws the inference that there must be the Creator. This appears in the Bible as intuitively plausible. To the modern mind there is no reason why, in the light of the options, the Biblical view may not be accepted as a reasonable inference. This will be elaborated on further in the responses to the second doubt. We may simply add here that the primary objection to the modern skeptical mood is that it tends to rule out the Biblical teaching in advance of serious consideration. That is, it shuts the door on the basis of considerations other than rational.

Doubt   Second, there is the doubt that the universe was created at all. The physical universe may be self-existent. It is just as easy to say that nature is uncreated as it is to say that God is self-existent and eternal. If something must be ultimate, why not call it nature instead of God? In this way we can keep everything within the bounds of natural law and natural processes. This fits more harmoniously into scientific approaches to the physical universe. It is also consonant with contemporary experience in general.

From an entirely different quarter, the denial that the universe was created is implied in the view that the physical universe is an illusion. Since it is unreal, there was nothing to create. This view has its vogue in some of the religions of the

East and in certain types of mysticism and pantheism in the West. It has little or no appeal to those who are influenced by science and technology on the one hand, and by an informed common sense on the other. This theory, though worthy of some notice, is so far removed from man's contemporary experience that we need not consider it here. We return to the view that nature and not the Creator is ultimate.

Response   It is easy to say that nature is ultimate. But can we *think* it? Here is where each person must perform a mental experiment. We seem to think of nature (do we not?) as having evolved out of previous things and processes. We can even think of a time when the physical universe might not have existed at all. This being the case, no matter what we say we are not thinking of nature as ultimate. The ultimate Being is the One who necessarily exists. If there were even the remotest possibility that He or It might not exist, He or It could not be ultimate. Therefore, nature is not properly spoken of as the ultimate causal agent. Moreover, it does not fit into contemporary experience to suggest that nature is ultimate because it seems to have come out of previous states and processes. The physical universe also seems to be running down in its energy. Nothing that can be thought of as even possibly running down can be ultimate.

In the case of God, however, we can think of Him as ultimate, that is, as the One who necessarily exists. Indeed, when we think of Him at all we mean that He is the self-existing or necessary Being. We cannot think of God as a being who might possibly not exist or as one who might possibly suffer any diminution of His energy. For to do so would be not to think of God at all. God alone *has* to be and He has to maintain His being and energy. Therefore He alone can be the ultimate creative agent.

There is another way of approaching this that shows we are not thinking soundly when we say that nature is ultimate. To do so merely misses the point. It obscures the *purpose* for suggesting the ultimate causal Ground of all things. Why does the human mind imagine an ultimate reality at all? Because the mind is so made that it seeks an ultimate causal explanation of the world in which it lives. The point, then, is not merely to recognize an ultimate of some sort but to affirm the kind of ultimate Being capable of explaining the universe and man. The objection to calling nature ultimate is not only that we cannot think of it as self-existent. Another difficulty arises when we ask: How can nature explain an ordered and interacting universe in which there are finite minds? It does nothing to say that nature or impersonal process is ultimate unless we can show that this is an adequate explanatory principle.

Here is where a mental experiment needs to be performed in which these two options are honestly considered with respect to their explanatory adequacy. It seems to me far more reasonable to believe that God alone is the ultimate causal agent than to believe that this universe could have originated out of blind impersonal process or nature. If it is argued that nature is neither blind nor impersonal, then "nature" is another name for God. For if "nature" performs all the functions of the ultimate Mind, including purposive action, the issue is merely one of terminology.

Another approach to this is to suggest that the mind of man requires the use of certain basic concepts or categories in its efforts to orient itself toward reality. A category is a concept that is necessary for understanding reality. The two basic questions about a category are: Is it relevant? Is it adequate to give man insight into reality? Against this background the options are clarified in the mind of man by means of categories. Which types of category offer man the best explanatory insight, those derived from mind or those derived from matter?

There is good reason to believe that the categories of mind, volitional agency, and purpose, are alone adequate and relevant in accounting for the universe and man. Matter, impersonal energy, and blind process explain nothing. The Biblical teaching on creation moves along this line by maintaining that anything less than the ultimate Mind is incapable of explaining how the universe and man came into existence. Though the Bible does not develop this by extended arguments, it recognizes that the human mind perceives intuitively that God alone could account for the world as we know it. For He alone can be thought of as the necessary Being.

Doubt   A third type of doubt regarding creation concerns the Biblical teaching that the universe was brought into being by the purposive agency of God. He created it for a purpose, or for a multiplicity of aims. There are many who are willing to say that the physical universe must have had a beginning. They might even accept the theory that in some way God created it. But when it comes to creation for a purpose, or for the realization of aims, they hold back. They have honest doubts because they do not see in the universe enough consistent movement coordinated toward the realization of worthy aims. Thoughtful men find it difficult to understand either the universe or human history as expressions of any over-all purpose. The universe does not seem to be headed anywhere. It goes through its endless rounds quite aimlessly. Or, so it seems. Human history, though rising to levels of purposive activity in individuals, does not appear to be moving toward any far-off divine goal.

Response   This kind of doubt must be taken seriously. For one thing, it has point. Nature is not merely an ordered universe: It is also "red in tooth and claw." It creates and destroys. All the facts pertaining to the problem of natural evils now come before us. There is also the curious indifference of the universe to human values.

This doubt is to be taken seriously also because the outcome of thought here bears directly on whether or not man's life is lived in a vast environment of blind impersonal things and processes.

The main argument for creation for a purpose, or for a multiplicity of aims, is that we cannot explain the emergence of human beings as the outcome of blind impersonal processes. The fantastic fact is that man has arrived as a creature seeking to realize values. Nothing less than Mind could produce minds

—or at least so it seems. From here it is but a step to the idea that the values man at his best seeks were included among the built-in aims of the Creator.

All this concerns the providence of God, which will be treated in the next chapter.

Doubt   A fourth modern doubt about the Biblical teaching on creation has to do with its focus on man rather than on the physical universe. The Bible gives priority to man over nature. In view of the insignificance of man both in size and in life-span, the Biblical perspective appears to be more of a projection of man's feeling of self-importance than a realistic understanding of things as they are.

Response   This too must be taken seriously. It is rooted deeply in man's contemporary experience. It will be given careful attention in the next chapter.

However, without attempting to argue the case here, I suggest that one of the most important contributions of the Bible to mankind is its stress on man as central in the purpose of creation. The relevance of this is increasingly clear in an age when life comes cheap and personality is dehumanized by the machine, by the computer, and by man's inhumanity. The problems here are so serious that men today must consider very carefully how they view man in relation to nature. There is good reason to doubt that contemporary man can come up with any way of giving dignity to human personality apart from a concept of his uniqueness under God in relation to the physical universe. This in turn takes us into the question of God's purpose for creating man. There is no way of moving from the idea that man is an accidental product of blind processes to the idea that he has dignity.

As far as the feeling of importance is concerned, a wide gulf separates those who believe that man came from an accidental collocation of atoms or chemicals in the oceans and those who believe he came ultimately from God. To be sure, God may have used any evolutionary processes He desired. He may have chosen to create man through physical things and processes. The Bible itself says He made man "of dust from the ground" (Genesis 2:7). This symbolizes the idea that God used physical things in the process of creating man. The only real issue arises when we view these physical processes as ultimate.

Upon reflection, then, it would seem that modern man would want to avoid easygoing denials of the Biblical teaching here for two reasons. The first is that this teaching does not deny any scientifically plausible theories on the origin of life. It simply goes beyond them to God. The second is that nothing less than the meaning of human existence is at stake here. All this will be reasoned in more detail in the next chapter and in other chapters that follow.

5

THE PROVIDENCE AND CREATIVITY OF GOD

Creation and providence go together. When we use the word "providence" we mean at least two things. First, we have in mind God's energy, which sustains man and the universe for the realization of worthy ends. God maintains what He began. Second, we mean God's continuing creativity. New things are constantly being formed. The universe is marked by the emergence of novelty. The things that already exist require God for their continuation. The things that are new or that are in process of being born require God as their ultimate causal Ground. In the last analysis these are two aspects of a single total process. For the maintenance of the universe as an interacting ordered system requires the constant creativity of God; and the emergence of novelty is possible only because of the continuity of God's energy in sustaining the universe. God moves toward the future through the past and present.

In the history of human reflection several major theories have been developed on how God is continuously related to the universe and man. Some have said that fate governs everything. Man is a puppet and the whole universe operates under inevitable forces. The universe expresses the iron decrees of nature rather than the providence of God. Our interest in this chapter is to consider only those views that affirm some kind of divine action in relation to the universe. Three of these may be noted here.

One such theory is called deism. This is the idea that God created the universe and left it to run by itself. The belief in God as Creator is affirmed. But the belief in God as presently at work in the universe is denied. God so transcends the universe that He has nothing more to do with it. For this reason the belief in God as realizing His aims by means of what He created is denied. So, on this view, God is considered necessary to explain the origin of things but not necessary for their continuation. This means also that the present creativity in nature receives its impetus not from God but from the built-in processes of the universe.

Another theory on how God is related to the universe is implied in pantheism. This is the idea that only God exists. Everything else is a part of God. The universe and man have no reality in themselves because they are expressions of God. They are as much a part of God as our thoughts and desires are of us. In deism God is wholly transcendent or above and beyond the universe and man. In pantheism God is wholly immanent or present in the universe and man.

In recent years, following Bergson, Whitehead, Teilhard de Chardin and others, there has been a special emphasis on creativity. Everyone is aware of creative energies at work in the world. New leaves are formed in the spring. New flowers bloom. New animals come into being. New babies are born. The vast energies of the universe are constantly moving forward in creative novelty. So certain thinkers have called us to pay more attention to these extensive evidences of creativity in nature. God is spoken of as the ultimate creative factor in the ongoing universe. Along with this comes the suggestion that God acts both in the immediate present and in the long run to realize worthy ends. God acts in the short period of springtime to bring new life on the earth. He acts in the brief span of a man's days to recreate the cells of his body and to enable him to reproduce his kind. Over much longer periods God acts pervasively throughout the universe to move toward new forms that emerge in the springtime of the cosmos, which might come every billion years or so. Whether in creatures whose lifetime is measured in seconds or in galaxies whose history is calculated in billions of years, God works creatively in them all.

This general perspective is informed by modern developments in the physical sciences. It takes into account the incredible vastness of the universe and the billions of years during which it has been in process. It recognizes in particular the gradual emergence of life-forms and the eons required in the evolution of the varieties of living creatures.

Providence and creativity are seen as organically interrelated. And God is thought of not so much as a far-off deity directing things by remote control as the ever-present deity whose energies work in and through the universe and man. Bergson calls this *elan vital*. Whitehead thinks of it as creative process. Teilhard de Chardin refers to it as the spiritual evolution of the universe. These views do not imply that God's energies are confined to the physical universe. They only suggest that, as far as this universe is concerned, God expresses Himself in and through it for the realization of at least some of His immediate and distant aims.

This third way of thinking, with its emphasis on the forward movement of God into the future, prepares the way for understanding the Biblical teaching. For as we have seen with respect to the idea of creation, the purposive action of God toward the drama of the future is at the heart of the Biblical vision.

The Bible teaches that God who created the universe is continuously at work in it. He created and creates. He ruled and rules. "The Lord is king for ever and ever . . ." (Psalms 10:16). Here the Biblical writers are poetic and imaginative rather than philosophical. God stretches out the heavens as a curtain (Isaiah 40:22). His energy touches the "highest heavens" (Psalms 148:4). He renews the face of the earth (Psalms 104:30), and in His hand are the deep places of land and sea (Psalms 95:4–5). He gives the sun for a light by day and the stars for a light by night (Jeremiah 31:35). The winds are His messengers, fire and flame His ministers (Psalms 104:4).

Three distinctive emphases are to be observed as the consistent Biblical teaching on the divine providence and creativity.

First, God transcends this present temporal order, yet at the same time he is somehow radically involved in it. That is, he is both transcendent and immanent. The Biblical writers held these two together in dynamic interplay. Plato could never get God and the world together. For God was thought of as eternally unchanging, timeless. He tried hard to bring the two together in his *Timaeus*. But he could never quite deliver his mind from the idea that the supreme being had to be free from the whole realm of energy and creative action.

In contrast to this, the Biblical writers urge that only a dynamic or active deity could account for a changing universe and for living creatures. These men make no effort to show how we can think through on this. They simply affirm that God, the transcendent Creator of man and the universe, maintains the most intimate working relationship with this present temporal order. They wanted it clearly understood that God is over and beyond all creation. In His transcendence He is to be likened to nothing other than Himself. As the Creator and Sustainer of the universe and man He alone is the Ground of being. The notion that God is totally present in the universe, so that He in no way transcends it, is abhorrent to the Biblical teaching. In its modern terms this is a reversion to pantheism in the interest of accommodation to secular modes of thought. At the same time the Biblical writers insist that God is the ultimate agent at work in the universe, sustaining it and acting creatively throughout it. To put this idea in theological-philosophical language, we may say that according to the Biblical writers the concepts of transcendence and immanence with respect to God are correlative categories. Both are indispensable in understanding God and His dynamic relations to the universe and man. Biblical writers affirm, in effect, that since God alone can explain or account for the universe and man He must be thought of as both their Creator and Sustainer. To sustain means to be continuously involved as the causally efficacious agent.

In summary, the transcendent Lord of all creation is also the ever-present creative agent at work in and through it. The power of God is so great and mysterious that He sustains the whole realm of creation without any loss of His individuality. And He expends Himself ceaselessly in creative action without any diminution of His energy.

The second Biblical emphasis is that God maintains the universe for the realization of His aims. Here again purpose is the basic category. Just as God would not create the universe and man without worthy goals, so He would not aimlessly continue to energize it and act creatively in it. God's providence and creativity are nothing more nor less than His purposive movement toward the future.

The physical universe is never thought of as an end in itself. It is instrumental. It is a means God uses to accomplish His purposes. God has not revealed to man all that He wanted to achieve in and through the universe. Some of His aims may include His immediate delight over the sheer glow and movement of the galaxies and of the infinitesimal universes in miniature. This is suggested in the Book of Genesis where we read that after the various stages of creation God saw that what He created was good (Genesis 1:31). Some of His aims lie out beyond the farthest reach of man's imagination, in worlds not yet ready for the formation of intelligent beings, worlds in

59

preparation for billions of years and waiting for the meaning that comes from the presence of finite minds. Of such a possibility the Biblical writers knew nothing. In effect they asked, who can fathom the aims of God? Yet they never wavered in affirming the instrumental character of the universe. Far from seeing it as an end in itself, they thought of it as a utensil to be enjoyed and used by God and to be discarded when He was through with it. It had no ultimate status. It is characteristic of the Biblical writers to suggest that this present universe is preparatory to another realm yet to come. Though this suggestion is not extensively developed by them, it is nevertheless a part of their total vision, in which God promises a future beyond this present temporal order toward which men may look with confidence and hope. Therefore, the teaching on the instrumental and temporary nature of the physical universe is not a basis for disillusionment. On the contrary, it is a basis for hope because the end of this present temporal order is a stage in the realization of a far greater realm promised by God.

The third distinctive emphasis of the Bible on God's providence and creativity fits harmoniously into the first two. It is the idea that man is central in God's purposive movement into the future. Whatever other aims God may be achieving, nothing is allowed to obscure God's purpose for man. We have seen that the Bible recognizes God as the Lord of the physical universe. But this theme is not central. Nature recedes into the background so that the drama of history in its moral and spiritual dimensions can be brought into full view.

The Biblical writers probably thought the earth was close to the center of the universe. Copernicus might as well have been a million years away. But this could not affect their essential idea, which was that man is central in the divine-human drama of history. What universe they knew was thought of as the stage or setting for this drama, a vast theater wherein God could act and man respond. It served God's ends and, by God's determination, it also served the needs of man during his brief pilgrimage on earth. Man was called by God to use the earth and its resources to meet his needs. But this was only to keep him going so he could respond appropriately to God.

The Bible teaches that God created and sustains the universe in order to provide a setting for the concrete realization of ideal values in community. The Biblical writers do not exclude the possibility that God has innumerable other ends in view as He maintains the universe. They simply regard it as their mission to be bearers of the divine revelation pertaining to man and his destiny with God through this present physical environment. Therefore, regardless of God's other aims, which are largely unknown to man, His providence and creativity come to their clearest visibility in His acts that are especially beneficial to man. Creation and providence are seen in the Bible as they bear on man's participation with God in realizing the Kingdom. The physical universe, then, is understood in the Bible as having its primary meaning only in relation to man as the unique finite bearer of moral and spiritual values. Man is the one order of being who is central in God's desire to realize a community where moral and spiritual values obtain. In this sense man is the only known creature in whom the deeper moral aims of God come to clear focus.

Here again it is of first importance to keep steadily in mind the Biblical vision of man as a creature chosen to participate with God in the movement toward the future. God is headed somewhere and He created and sustains man to go with Him into the Kingdom yet to come. This forward movement, however, does not take the form of a withdrawal from this present life and universe. Otherwise, these would lose their significance. There is a divine meaning in the immediate energies of the universe, in the blooming of the flowers, the shining of the stars, and the movements of the galaxies. There is a divine meaning too in the immediate glow of experience, the laughter and tears, the daily routines and satisfactions, and in the passing moments of friendship and illumination. None of these is lost for God.

Nevertheless, the Biblical vision is also that God never intended these events in this passing universe to furnish any final stages of satisfaction and achievement. They are both presently meaningful and preparatory for what is to come. We experience what the Biblical writers knew when we become increasingly aware of the curious ineptness in this present temporal order to satisfy the deepest longings of the human spirit. The full ranges of our experiences in this world leave us haunted by the desire for more, for further dimensions of reality and meaning yet to be explained. The Biblical writers brought together this profound human discontent with the God-given vision of a magnificent future to come. Their call was therefore to the men of faith to move into the future on the promise of the coming Kingdom.

SOME MODERN DOUBTS AND RESPONSES TO THEM

Concerning this Biblical vision of the providence and creativity of God the modern mind experiences serious doubts. For the purpose at hand these may be expressed by three questions. First, the Biblical teaching may be emotionally appealing, but how do we know it is true? Second, can we really think through the idea of God as both transcendent and immanent? Third, does the evidence, including the innumerable diseases, deformities, and catastrophies of nature, permit us to believe in the Biblical teaching on the purpose of God for man? We turn now to a consideration of these in that order.

Doubt   The first doubt, concerning how we can know all this, is characteristic of modernity, where the stress is on method and verification. One of the most useful questions anyone can ask about a belief is simply: How do we know it is true? This doubt, so frequently arising from contemporary experience, has to be faced again and again.

Response   It is often supposed that in the quest for truth man starts from scratch. He knows nothing and moves by scientific procedures away from the naïve perspectives of common sense to the enlightenment of the more sophisticated perspectives of the modern world. The truly modern mind, it is supposed, will begin without assumptions and metaphysical presuppositions. My contention is that this is a pet delusion of the new breed of modern dogmatists. The fact is that before we can analyze how we know, we have to experience what it is to know. So the task of the thinker who deals in epistemology is not to construct knowledge artificially but to analyze what it in fact means to know. He recognizes knowledge as a given fact of experience. Men know and they know that they know.

The psychologist does not construct his idea of human personality first and then study it. He seeks to understand man as he finds him. The social scientist studies societies as they are. In medicine the scientists begin with the given facts of disease and health and proceed accordingly. Similarly, in understanding the nature of knowledge we begin with the incontrovertible fact that men know and know they know. In primitive times a hunter did not ask, "How do I know I see a deer?" He saw it and knew he saw it. He ran with it, drove it into a trap, killed it and ate it. If it got away, he knew that too.

What has all this to do with our knowing the Biblical revelation on the providence and creativity of God? Several things. First, it suggests that the modern mind is not nearly as free from its own unexamined assumptions and presuppositions as men may suppose. A man may say that he has no metaphysical assumptions. But let him try to maintain his position in the light of careful analysis. He assumes that the external world and other people exist. He assumes an ordered universe. He assumes that causes precede effects. Regarding his own mind and its activity in gaining knowledge, he assumes that sense experiences give authentic clues to the external world, that memory is essentially reliable (for he accepts his remembered experiments and observations of yesterday and of the past moments), and that reason can be trusted. All of these are among the many presuppositions of experiments and of common sense.

But modern man tends to go even further into metaphysics by assuming that nature or blind impersonal process is the only kind of energy there is in the physical universe. This is a metaphysical theory that needs to be examined with care. If it is true, it makes the Biblical teaching on the purpose of God a mockery. If it is inadequate or essentially false, the Biblical teaching may stand. The point here is that modern man has been incredibly heedless in his acceptance of naturalistic pre-suppositions. He needs to clean out the Augean stables of his categories. He needs to ask elemental metaphysical questions. How can blind purposeless process explain what we find? How can it account for existence? How explain an ordered universe when there are infinite possibilities for chaos? How can it illuminate the almost unbelievable fact of the intelligibility of the universe? How does it serve in interpreting creatures who experience values?

So the basic issue, again, has to do with which of the options makes the most sense. The Biblical writers had the vision of God who acts purposively. Does not this make more sense than modern man's vision of a universe pervaded by aimless energy?

Doubt   A second doubt concerns how we can think of God as both transcendent and immanent. Here it is supposed that because the energies of the universe seem to be *within* it we can find no assignable energy that could come from a being who transcends it. If all the energy expresses itself from *within* nature, the idea of an external causal efficacy is ruled out from the start.

Response   This, of course, is an age-old philosophical and theological problem. No new developments in the modern world have changed the issue or given more weight to one view than to another. We have no recourse but to try to reflect on this as best we can. The idea that all reality is in process began to emerge in the ancient world with Aristotle and others. This theme has been accentuated in the modern world by extensive advancements in the physical sciences which suggest that matter is a form of energy. This energy seems to arise wholly from within. So the idea of a transcendent God is thought of as not speaking to man's contemporary experience, which leads him to think of all energies as internal only.

Against this background it is easy to understand the sudden popularity of the thought of certain theologians who rose rapidly to prominence only to recede again into the background. We may mention Bishop Robinson's *Honest To God,* the various writings of those involved in the "death of God" ferment, and those who have made their claims for the radical secularization of religion. These have all shot up like rockets, exploded, and exhausted their resources. They share in common one major emphasis, namely, the idea of the divine immanence. Whatever else God is, He is not to be thought of as "up there," "out there," "over and beyond." God as transcendent is dead; God as immanent is alive. For God is within. He is the life-process wherever it is. God is process as found both in nature and man.

The inadequacy of this half-truth is nowhere more clearly seen than in the fact that it cannot stand up under the initial shock of serious questioning. It is no accident that these various "new theologies" are already old within ten years after they got started. All that was needed was for competent thinkers to show their imbalance and the ineptness of their authors at causal explanation.

We have seen that the mind, by a kind of gravitational pull, seeks adequate causal explanation. Upon careful reflection the mind seems to sense clearly that mere process explains nothing. There are several reasons for this. First, no one can think of any mere process; always there is *something* in process. This means that when taken by itself, the category of process (or flux, or energy) is wholly inadequate as an explanatory principle. Something more is required. Second, what we require, then, is to think of *being-in-process.* But "being" also is an abstraction. There is no assignable meaning here unless we think of particular beings. "Being" apart from concrete individuality is nothing. So we come to the idea of individual-being-in-process. And here, if we seek adequate causal explanation, we look to God as the ultimate Being or Individual whose nature, among other things, is to be dynamic and creative. Third, if God's energies totally exhausted themselves in the flowing processes of the universe (as the immanentalists must affirm), then there is no way of explaining how the past events can cause future events. For they would be wholly exhausted in their own processes as are fireworks, and hence would have no energy left to initiate any future events.

Therefore, what the mind requires is the idea of an ultimate reality who, though ever active and creative, never suffers any loss of his own being and energy. William Ernest Hocking expressed this general theme philosophically in his lecture on "History and the Absolute":

> It is the thesis of the present course of lectures that this philosophy of Flux has run its course. It has done important service in showing that Time cannot be exhausted into its mathematical properties, but has an inner complexity of structure. . . . On the other hand, Time is not capable of independent existence: without Being and its degrees of Change-and-Changelessness, no Time. And the very meaning of these rates of Change, whose reciprocal is the degree of Stability, implies a Substance.

He adds:

> It is largely the business of science to classify and measure types of change, and to bring specific types of change under more general laws, such as the law of entropy. But the ultimate explanation must be in terms of a Being, for which *to be* is *to change*. The Self is such a Being: Time and Change are implied in the very existence of a Self: to be is to become.

The God of the Biblical writers, though not spoken of in such philosophical terms, nevertheless fills out the basic categories of which Hocking speaks. For He is the Creator and Sustainer of the universe whose nature, as the ultimate Self or Mind, is to energize without any loss of His being and causal efficacy.

But the question still remains as to how we can think of

God, the transcendent Being, as causally efficacious within the universe. That is, how can we think of him as both transcendent and immanent?

If we try to think this through theoretically, we get nowhere. For if God is outside the universe, He cannot be in it. And if the energy of the universe works from within, how can God affect that energy from without? Theoretically speaking, this is the question concerning whether or not all causal forces are internal. Are there no external causal forces? If there are not, of course, we would have to be pantheists and immanentalists. How God can be other than the universe and at the same time its causal Ground, we do not know. We only know that our best thinking requires this.

Nevertheless, we gain some insight when we turn from theory to experience. We know as a matter of fact that many external forces affect us. I am not you; you are not I. Yet, I can influence you from without and you can influence me from without. I am not my body, but I make my body do things. I make it walk, or run, or drive a car, or eat, or rest, or talk, or hold a book. So my mind, which is not my body (though it is intimately connected with it) affects my body and in turn is affected by it. I am not my environment. The trees, grass, sidewalks, streets, cars, traffic lights, buildings, and other people are all around me; and they affect me without losing their own uniqueness and identity. And when I am influenced from without I do not lose my identity. The conclusion from practical experience, then, is that external causes do in fact operate in the real world. The key to insight here is found only when we use the categories of personality as the models for understanding God's dynamic purposive action in relation to the universe.

Similarly, we assert in keeping with the Biblical writers that though God transcends the universe which He created, He nevertheless affects it at every point and in every process with His continuing providential care and creativity.

Doubt   Once more, there are the doubts about the providence and creativity of God that arise from the fact of natural evils. Thomas Huxley spoke of the unfathomable injustice of the nature of things. Some would add to this the sum total of the misery man has brought upon his fellowmen. Taken together these become for many people a formidable barrier to the belief in the divine providence and creativity. The questions inevitably arise: Why all these evils in God's universe? If God is acting to realize a significant future, why is there so much needless pain in the process?

Response   Such questions are neither modern nor ancient. They are ageless. To them has been given a wide variety of answers which may be briefly summarized. Before doing so, however, we must clarify the problem itself. The problem of evil, as generally discussed, concerns only those evils produced by natural things and processes. We are not here dealing with the evils and tragedies caused by man himself. These two dimensions of evil are interrelated, but there is this difference, that the latter can be accounted for as products of man's freedom and consequent responsibility. In the case of natural evils no such explanation is possible. And if God is so much in charge of the things and processes of the physical universe, it becomes a question of utmost seriousness as to why God should either cause or permit these natural evils.

The kinds of natural evils we have in mind here are these: (1) tornadoes, hurricanes, storms, floods, earthquakes; (2) deformities of body and mind; (3) diseases of all sorts and particularly those caused by tiny creatures such as microbes and viruses striking against the human body and against that of other animals; and (4) to these we may add the pathetic imbalance in human nature that brings together in one individual a strong body and a weak intellect, or a keen intellect with a frail body, or any of the various other unhappy combinations that appear to result in natural handicaps.

Many thinkers have found it impossible to ignore the theological problem posed by the recurring presence of these natural evils. Some of them have devoted their best thinking to this problem. We may now consider certain representative theories that have been developed in answer to it.

Broadly speaking, there are six theories whereby men have attempted to account for the natural evils in God's universe. First, natural evils are unreal, they are illusions. For example, Augustine thought of evil as the absence of good. The main objection to this view is that it defies obvious experience. Everyone with a toothache knows that it occurs. Similarly, everyone is aware of the reality of the evils described above whenever they strike a community or an individual.

Second, natural evils are not really evils at all because the only genuine evil is a morally bad will. Natural evils may cause pain but this is not what counts. Therefore, there is no real problem because it does not matter what happens to the body or mind outside the moral dimension. The chief objection to this view is that while seeking to give glory to the unique moral dimension it actually undermines it. Why? Because morality seeks to overcome everything that tends to strike against human well-being. This view does not even permit us to regard evils as really bad. Another decisive argument against this view is the universal value judgment that such natural evils as those mentioned are really evils. This is seen in the plain fact that they are universally regarded as unwelcome and to be avoided or guarded against, if possible. So there are moral evils and natural evils. Both are bad.

A third effort to solve the problem of evil runs like this: Natural evils are necessary to virtue and goodness. Men would be able neither to know the good nor to achieve it without these evils. For to know the good they must see it in contrast to evil, and to achieve the good they must encounter evil. On this reading, it is better to have these evils than to be free from them. The major difficulty here is that this too confuses the human mind in its values. If we do not know that natural evils are really bad, how can we know the good? Here diseases and other evils are viewed as sparring partners. Virtue is possible only because of the encounter with these evils. But the goal of morality is not to spar with them. It is to overcome them.

Fourth, natural evils are a necessary stage in the development of character and of the ideal society. This is the most popular theory. One reason for this is that it is informed by the theory of evolution. The view here is that natural evils have been and are necessary as stages in the long processes of evolution. They are like the bitterness of the unripe apple. Since the final outcome is supremely worthy, the process leading up to it, though in many ways marked by evil, is fully justified. God is using all these means to bring about His good ends. The basic trouble here is that this theory misses the point. Why should an all-powerful deity have to use such means as hurricanes, tornadoes, cancer, and insanity to bring about His good ends? If it is said that this is necessary as a stage in the development of character, I ask that we stop and think. Is cancer necessary for character? If we want to know what a man's character is, do we ask how many diseases he has had? As far as we know Jesus was never ill. Would it change our estimate of His character if we were to come upon some new document stating that as a youth Jesus had smallpox? This theory, then, says in effect that evils are goods in disguise. We hope some day to rid the world of diseases. Will men then be worse off?

A fifth kind of theory seeks the answer to the problem of evil by suggesting that God's power is so limited He cannot control everything that happens in nature. God is supreme, He acts purposively, but He still cannot prevent these natural evils. This theory, developed by Edgar S. Brightman and others, has the merit of facing the fact of natural evils and of regarding them as really evil. They are not goods in disguise. Since God is good and evils are evil, God must not be able to prevent them. The chief objection to this view is that it implies such a drastic limitation of God's power we have no adequate basis for affirming that He really controls the universe as a whole. If God cannot control cancer, or could not even though He wanted to, how can He be the God of the universe?

A sixth theory is that God delegated to the physical universe a certain spontaneity, as He did in endowing man with freedom, in order to realize higher values in the physical universe as well as in history. The most able spokesman for this theory is F. R. Tennant whose work on philosophical theology is still worthy of careful study. His view has the merit of recognizing evil as really evil. At the same time it suggests that God made the universe in such a way that natural evils, though bad, are permitted because of the larger values which could not have been possible without a delegated spontaneity in nature. Just as moral achievement in men required freedom and the consequent possibility of sin, so is it regarding the spontaneity in nature and the consequent natural evils.

My own view tends to move with this last one, though I do not think we have any clear theoretical solution to the problem of evil. Martin Luther once said, "Anyone who tries to bite that file will only break his teeth." Nevertheless, there are at least five points to be made.

1. The belief in the existence of God cannot be overthrown or placed in serious jeopardy by the evidence of natural evils. This is because, as we have seen, there are solid reasons for believing in God. These reasons, based on pervasive evidence from the universe and human existence, cannot be laid aside or overturned by this problem. Evil is not the basic reality in the universe. We must not exaggerate the quantity of natural evil. It is a real but minor factor, relatively trivial compared to the existence, orderliness, interaction, and creativity manifested throughout the universe. The problem of existence, order, and goodness without God is far more difficult than the problem of evil with God. Theism stands.

2. Granting this, the question is: How must we think of the evils in God's universe? The answer must move in this direction: God had in mind valuationally justifiable goals for permitting natural evils, but we do not know what those goals are. This does not imply that the evils are good, any more than that sin is good in God's sight. Rather, it means that (as in the case of sin) God had some authentic basis for allowing natural evils even though He opposes them. One reason why we cannot say more is that we do not know enough in detail about the universe as a whole. It has been in existence for billions of years.

If we could know enough to analyze the movement of things across those many years, we might find empirical confirmation of some vast value-realizing divine operation. This sort of thing has been suggested by Teilhard de Chardin and others. But, at the present time, there is no way of taking this out of the realm of a magnificent vision and bringing it into the sphere of a concretely elaborated theory.

Another reason why we cannot say more is that we do not understand the precise relations between God and the universe. The universe might conceivably be a living creature, as Plato surmised. Or it might be an intricate system of finite living creatures, as the panpsychists suppose. Hence, the delegated spontaneity could be understood. For, in either case, innumerable values (many of them beyond the human wavelengths) might be constantly realized both in the experience of God and in the so-called physical universe. There would be the extensive interplay between the living creatures and the divine experience. And if there are values to be realized only by means of the delegated spontaneity in nature, the whole enterprise would seem to be justified.

3. The apparent indifference of nature to us is not a part of the problem of evil. It is the impersonal and neutral character of the physical world that makes it suited to our needs. If every time a sculptor used a chisel on a rock it would cry out in pain, he would carve no statues. If a tree pleaded in agony as the woodman sawed it, it could not be readily used for building houses or making paper. So it is this impersonal and neutral character of physical things that makes them useful for human ends.

4. This is a many-sided problem. Looking at it from another side, there is a sense in which the physical processes are not neutral or indifferent toward man and ideal values. For the universe was God's instrument in producing and sustaining man. Again, the "steadfast ordinances of the world" make it possible for man to anticipate the future accurately. He sows knowing he will reap. He can carry out his plans only because nature faithfully expresses a predictable order. Besides this

the physical world enriches man's experiences with its colors, shapes, and beauty. Again, it supports the moral life by giving man materials with which to build institutions for human well-being, by enabling him to move from place to place, and by offering innumerable aids to communication through sight and sound. Once more, man's churches and religious symbols are made of physical things. And the whole visible universe awakens in him something of the sense of God's presence. Jesus could teach in parables on the Kingdom because nature lent its helping hand.

5. Turning from the theoretical to practical considerations, men have learned from the life of faith in God that there are divine resources for creative living in the midst of their encounters with natural evils. God does far more than help men in their times of disaster. But He does that too. At any rate, this has been the report of numberless men and women across many centuries. The general providence of God in nature is supplemented by the providence of God made available through grace by faith. Consequently, men can look to God in faith and know that He goes with them into every encounter with evil and that He gives them the power to see life through.

Part III

On God and Man

6

GOD AND THE MORAL ORDER

God maintains the physical universe as an appropriate theater of the moral life. Therefore, the Bible moves from nature to human history. And it proceeds rapidly from general history to man as a creature of moral responsibility before God. If, as we have seen, God created the universe and man to realize moral and spiritual values, then there must be some kind of moral order maintained by God. Here again the Biblical teaching has had to make its way through encounters with a number of perspectives that have attracted wide attention.

THE MAIN ALTERNATIVE VIEWS

Men have tended to think in at least five ways about the moral order. These stand in varying degrees of contrast to the Biblical teaching.

First, some have denied that there is any moral order at all. Nothing is really right or wrong. According to this view, known as ethical relativism, there is no universal basis for recognizing the difference between right and wrong. Consequently there are no fixed moral principles. This ancient theory comes back in every generation in somewhat new styles.

Some say that right and wrong are relative to a particular community. In Rome do as Romans do. The idea here is that right and wrong are merely human devices for controlling the conduct of people in society. Moral principles are created by men for men. Karl Marx and the communists have contributed heavily to ethical relativism. According to them, so-called moral distinctions are in reality the man-made products of the ruling classes for suppressing the have-nots. Far from being principles to be obeyed, they are to be repudiated at will in the interest of the masses. They have no ultimate moral status.

Ethical relativism is often supported by impressive sociological studies suggesting that moral regulations have simply been learned and developed by men to meet the needs of the times. They differ from age to age and from society to society. What is considered right in one group is called wrong in another. Therefore, moral regulations have no universal validity.

Sometimes ethical relativism is supported in one way or another by psychology. For example, it has been supposed that moral principles are artificial and unreal because they impose needless restrictions on the dynamics of personality. Man needs to express his vital impulses without the cumbersome or restrictive regulations of some imaginary moral order. The experience of guilt is interpreted as a psychological complex rather than as an authentic instrument for right living. Another type of psychological analysis leads some to suppose that the moral order is simply a projection of the human mind. Few competent psychologists would say that their studies *imply* ethical relativism. But it is often assumed that moral distinctions, being open to psychological scrutiny, are *merely* subjective. Their apparent objectivity is just another instance of the familiar practice of projecting our feelings and thoughts into reality. There is no such objective order. It exists only in man's thought for "there is nothing good or bad, but thinking makes it so."

A second theory on the moral order is known as hedonism. According to it, man is so made that he welcomes pleasure and shuns pain. So it comes easy to measure good and bad, right and wrong, by the pleasure-principle. Since ancient times some have thought of pleasure in terms of sensuous physical gratification while others have looked toward the satisfaction that comes from the higher pleasures of the mind. But all forms of hedonism share the view that pleasure in some form is the supreme good, and consequently, the measure of right and wrong. It alone is the real basis of the moral order. Anything that produces pleasure is good, and the more pleasure the better. Anything that produces pain and suffering is bad, and the more pain the more evil.

A third way of thinking about the moral order is to view it as grounded in nature. There is a difference between right and wrong but, instead of being grounded in God, it is based on nature. We are not here thinking of the ethics of natural law which may be harmonized with the Biblical teaching. A popular way of stating it would be this: If you want to know the difference between right and wrong or good and bad, you ask, Is it natural? or, Does it express natural impulses? Here of course there are many theories as to what nature requires. The standard of right may be thought of as what makes for health or long life; or it might concern the full expression of all the major natural impulses; or it might have to do with adjustment to human nature or to the natural environment; or to the direction of evolution; or it might concern the inborn will to power.

Nietzsche used this mode of thinking in his attack on Christianity. He said that Christianity praises the weak and womanly virtues to the neglect of man's more vigorous impulses. The will to power is natural and it should express itself without the stultifying restraints of altruism.

Closely related to this kind of ethics of nature is egoism. As we are considering it here, this is the view that the only kind of motives a man can entertain are selfish. Nietzsche recognized that a man could be unselfish, and he deplored the fact that Christians believed in acting in behalf of others. But there are some who deny that man can be altruistic at all. They urge that all motives originate in a self, so it is reasonable to believe that they are directed toward the self. They reason also that many motives are obviously selfish and the rest can be interpreted as selfish. Even a mother's love as she makes sacrifices for her children is interpreted as consciously or unconsciously aiming to satisfy some selfish goal. The scientist carries out research programs to conquer a disease because of the money, or the honor, or the self-satisfaction.

Fourth, there is the idea that the moral order is grounded in man. Man is a moral being. Right and wrong, duty and obligation, goodness and virtue have an enduring place but without any reference to God. Immanuel Kant did much to give this view an exalted position among ethical theories. He said that morality is autonomous. It stands in its own right without being dependent on religion, or science, or custom, or society, or anything else. It is based on man's moral nature. The moral law is absolute whether men are religious or not.

Others hold that Kant was too individualistic. They agree with him that the moral order is grounded in man. But they suggest that it is based on the demands of society rather than of the individual. Moral regulations, they say, were established to serve the group. Men, in the demands of their social life, simply require rules with a moral sanction. Therefore the moral standards and values are derived not from God but from man in community.

A fifth way of thinking about the moral order is seen in the so-called new morality. This is sometimes referred to as situational ethics, or contextual ethics. As we are discussing it, it has been developed as a form of Christian ethics, and it brings together elements from a wide variety of themes.

There are several different approaches to it, but it will be sufficient here to indicate its nature by reference to four basic ideas. 1. There is only one ethical absolute, namely, love. 2. Rules, moral regulations, commandments other than to love, have some importance, but they may be broken at any time, for they are not absolute. 3. The *situation* for action must be taken with utmost seriousness; for in one situation love requires us to follow one course and in another situation it may call for something else. 4. The best use of the mind is necessary to identify the kind of action that love requires in a given situation.

According to the new morality, then, the moral order consists almost entirely in God's love for us and our love for God and our fellowmen. It seeks to free men from networks of rules, maxims, commandments, and from fixed policies—except for the enduring disposition to love our fellowmen.

Against the background of these various approaches to the moral order, the perspective of the Bible may be seen and understood more clearly. It teaches at least four things on this theme.

First, it affirms that the moral order is ultimately grounded in God. Prior to the creation of man there was in God Himself the final basis for distinguishing between right and wrong. He does not wait for men to make up their minds about what they ought to do. For He is the fountainhead from whom all moral standards flow. Being good, He requires goodness.

Occasionally in the Bible the goodness of God is obscured by His arbitrariness (1 Samuel 6:19–20; 2 Samuel 6:6–7, 24:1–17). And His goodness is made available only or chiefly to the people of Israel. But beyond all the ambiguities, there is the persistent movement of the Biblical teaching toward the absolute righteousness of God, which comes at last to be seen in its universal proportions. This fact stands in amazing contrast to the gods of the people surrounding Israel.

God takes the initiative in seeing to it that His covenant with Moses and the people of Israel is *ethically* conditioned. Moses knew this. But it was not until the eighth-century prophets that it came to fuller clarification. Then, after the collapse of Israel as a nation, some of the prophets envisioned the God whose goodness reached out toward *all* men everywhere (Malachi 1:11, Jonah 4:11, Isaiah 19:19–25; also Psalms 22, 65, 86, 87). At length this understanding of God as the Ground of all goodness reached its supreme utterance in Jesus of Nazareth who expressed it in terms of a self-giving love. For God is love.

It is interesting that the Biblical writers stressed God's ethically conditioned interpersonal relationships above other possible divine manifestations. For example, they might have placed the main emphasis on feeling or esthetic experience. Or, they might have stressed the revelation of God through intellectual pursuits. Again, they might have called upon men to find God by withdrawing into a world of mystical union and ecstasy. But they did not do this because God revealed Himself to them as the Ground of the moral order. To be sure, they knew God as the ultimate Source of beauty and esthetic feeling. They knew him also as the God of truth. And they spoke of the ecstasy of enjoying the presence of God. But the central emphasis of the prophets and others was on the ethically conditioned covenant relationships between God and man.

Second, the Bible teaches that man was created by God to participate in the moral order. He was made to be a bearer of the moral law.

The moral order is the first level on which God's purpose for man becomes clearly visible. For example, in the story of Cain and Abel, Cain asks, ". . . am I my brother's keeper?" And God says, ". . . The voice of your brother's blood is crying to me from the ground" (Genesis 4:9–10). This suggests that from the dawn of history God saw man as morally responsible. The built-in capacity for moral responses awaited the development of continuing societies to come to expression. So prior to the Ten Commandments or any other specific moral regulations there was in man the capacity for making moral distinctions. God made man in the image of His own goodness and thus called upon him to be a finite bearer of the moral law. For this reason Paul writes of the law written upon the hearts of men (Romans 2:14–16).

Among all known finite creatures man alone has the ability to participate significantly in the ethical sphere. In the Bible this fact becomes the first sign of God's determination to realize a moral order. So it is no accident that this theme is summed up, as far as the Old Testament is concerned, in the words of Micah:

He has showed you, O man, what is good;
    and what does the Lord require of you
but to do justice, and to love kindness,
    and to walk humbly with your God (Micah 6:8)?

This leads to the third factor in the Biblical teaching on the moral order, namely, that it comes to expression in community through moral regulations or commandments. It is an important theme of the Biblical writers that men must be sincere in their desire to do what is right before God and man. No external forms or ceremonies or deeds can take the place of inner rightness toward God and man. At the same time these writers are aware of the concrete realities of man's existence in society that require publicly recognized regulations and commandments.

This is best illustrated in the Old Testament by the Ten Commandments as seen in their historical significance. Though listed in only two places (Exodus 20:1–17; Deuteronomy 5:6–21), they play a central role in the Old Testament. They are at the heart of God's ethically conditioned covenant with Israel. To break them was to repudiate that covenant. It is true that the Commandments are not merely ethical. First and foremost they are religious. But because they are religious they express also the moral order. Picture the historical situation in which Moses and the people of Israel found themselves. Under his leadership they escaped from their enslavement to the Egyptians. They fled from Pharaoh's approaching army across the Red Sea onto the peninsula of Sinai. After many hardships, grievous murmurings, and a fierce battle with Amalek, they reached the wilderness of Sinai (Numbers 33:1–15). In a word, they were an uprooted people.

Moses found his responsibilities too much to bear. He reminded the people of God's laws, which had already been taught them and which doubtless included elements of the Ten Commandments. But this was not enough. For many came to Moses with their problems. Children were disobedient. Now and then someone would commit murder. Thieves did their contemptible work. There was sexual looseness. False witnesses added to the troubles. Besides all this, Moses had to deal with idolatry. Troubles were heaped one upon another. And Moses faced the dreadful spector of an entire people being reduced by inner decay to a mass of irresponsible folk without identity.

With these burdens on him, Moses went up on Mount Sinai

for divine guidance. Out of his encounter with God he confronted Israel with the Ten Commandments, which were to measure their trueness to God. There had to be a convenient number of divinely sanctioned rules everyone could understand and easily remember. Otherwise, chaos. The people had to be made subject to a *moral* order grounded in God. For this reason the last six of the Ten Commandments reveal God's concern for moral values in society. And, once the Commandments were given, the prophets held them up to remind the people of God's covenant and their call to obedience.

Not even King David could get away with adultery and murder. For God spoke through the prophet Nathan saying, "Why have you despised the word of the Lord, to do what is evil in his sight? . . ." (2 Samuel 12:9). The idea that God's moral order is reflected in the Ten Commandments and in what they imply for the covenant relationship is a major assumption of the prophets.

This radically serious interest in specific commandments moves toward fulfillment in the New Testament. There, in Jesus, and in Paul, all Commandments are brought together under the two Commandments to love God and men. Jesus did not deny the crucial role of specific regulations except as they were man-made devices that cluttered up life and hence obstructed the will of God. He was fully aware that love implies specific duties, which are implicit in nearly all of His parables and teachings. He opposed any and all rules or injunctions that had lost their relevance to life.

In the teaching of Jesus, moral regulations are not viewed as artificial intrusions upon the moral order or merely as guides to insight. They are seen in their life-subserving function. They are indispensable in the expression of love. A love that does not express itself through specific *ways* of living in relation to others is little more than sentimentality. For love is not merely a feeling toward those in need. It is a policy. Moral precepts and regulations are primary instruments in the work of the Kingdom of God.

Jesus did not come to destroy the law or the moral order.

He came to fulfill them. His clearest statement, which summarizes the whole point, is this: The sabbath was made for man, not man for the sabbath (Mark 2:27). Therefore, regulations as well as institutions are to be considered as valid or invalid on the basis of what they do to people in community. Jesus opposed certain religious leaders of His day because they held fast to many regulations that did not serve the unique purpose of morality under God. This is the perennial basis for the Christian call to personal and social renewal. In this the teaching of Jesus gives the most exalted utterance I know to the deep-lying purpose that is not only back of the Ten Commandments but also back of the moral regulations of all civilized societies. Jesus brings to fulfillment the dim and confused gropings of mankind for a moral order. For their true meaning is to serve the interests of love. As Augustine wrote, "Every commandment has love for its aim." Similarly, every authentic moral regulation has the well-being of men for its aim.

This account would be wholly inadequate without another characteristic of the Biblical teaching on the moral order. I refer to the essentially religious understanding of moral responsibility. The Bible has no place for morality unrelated to God and to His concern for a kind of goodness that is concretely realized in and through men. For it has to do not with man's trueness to the Commandments as merely moral injunctions but with his faithfulness to the *God* of the Commandments. The point is that the Biblical writers are first of all trying to draw men into ethically conditioned relationships with God.

Here is where the personalism of the Bible comes in again. For God is not striving to promote a morality disconnected from faith. Faith and morals are organically interrelated because obedience to the Ten Commandments is understood as obedience to God. This is why the covenant idea is central. For in a covenant there is a person-to-person encounter. And the Biblical covenant is an ethically conditioned person-to-person encounter. The goal is to obey the Commandments as an expression of faith in God. Faith has priority over morality in the Bible. But there can be no authentic faith apart from the moral order. The prophets and others saw that what comes closest to the very stuff of the soul as a responsible agent is the moral life under God. Therefore, with astonishing consistency across many centuries those ancient writers refused to separate these two spheres that God had joined together.

This organic union of the ethical and the religious through the faith-relationship to God reaches its fulfillment in the New Testament where love becomes the new law and where God gives sufficient assistance to help men to live the life of Christian love. Of this, more will be said in the chapters that follow.

SOME MODERN DOUBTS AND RESPONSES TO THEM

Modern man finds it almost impossible to avoid doubts about the moral order. Among his specific doubts are four that call for special notice here.

Doubt   First, the most serious doubt is that there is a moral order at all. The very term "moral order" seems vague. What assignable meaning does it have? Does not the language itself trick us into supposing we are dealing in reality when we are actually dealing only in imagination? Besides, what steps can we take to verify the objective reality of a moral order?

Such questions are all the more pertinent when we consider how extensively the modern approaches to reality have been affected by psychological and societal studies. There are so many different temperaments in people, there are such varieties of personality types and of personality problems, and there are such diverse cultural and environmental situations that it is no simple matter to say what is right and wrong for everyone. The quest for a universally valid order seems beyond our reach.

Response   Let us begin with a definition of the term "moral order." First, by this term I mean that there is an objectively valid basis for distinguishing between right and wrong, for recognizing *obligation,* and for identifying the *good* and expressing *virtue.* These are the main categories, and they are unique in the moral experience of mankind. This basis goes far

83

beyond our wishes and imagination. It is not merely the product of human society. If a totally new community of people were suddenly formed on Mars or on some presently uninhabited part of the earth, a moral order would reveal itself in due course. It is not so much created by men as discovered by them.

Second, I mean by "moral order" that there is a kind of cosmos of interconnected ideals and values with which men must reckon. These interconnections of ideals and values are not merely produced by men, they are found to be interrelated in networks or systems of values.

Third, I mean by "moral order" a unique realm that can be recognized and appreciated only by persons. Right and wrong, duty, virtue, ideals and values, all of these unique categories have their meaning and relevance only for conscious selves on the level of human beings or of higher beings than man. Except possibly on the most rudimentary levels, monkeys and other primates cannot think and act morally. But persons can.

What is the basis for believing that such an order or cosmos of values exists independently of man's wishes or imagination? Here there is no mathematical proof, nor is there any scientific verification. I suggest that we proceed by giving honest consideration to eight concrete types of cases that represent large areas of life.

1. Suppose a person says, "I do not think any act is better than any other act; there is no basis for distinguishing right from wrong." He might be asked a question involving specific options: Is it better to slap your grandmother on her birthday or to give her a present? (If a person answers, "That depends on what kind of grandmother she is," he only shows that he is not trying to follow the issue honestly. There are of course rare circumstances—as of a grandmother who is a part of a gang of criminals—that are no part of the question here.) Jesus told the story of the Good Samaritan in answer to the question, "Who is my neighbor?" The assumption of the questioner seems to have been that we cannot really know who the neighbor is. But when Jesus finished the story, all He needed to do was ask

which of the men showed himself to be the good neighbor. The answer was self-evident.

2. Again, if a person says, "There's no such thing as right and wrong," he might be asked: "Should a man keep a solemn promise or break it?" (I am assuming that nothing interferes with keeping his promise.) Everyone who answers this with moral motivation in mind will see that a promise should be kept. So in this kind of case, of which there are numberless instances in human relations, the answer points toward the belief that we do recognize a solid basis for distinguishing between right and wrong. It is right to keep promises and wrong to break them. The plain fact is that even when we deny a moral order we still know that some acts are right and others wrong, or more right than wrong. We catch ourselves expressing moral judgments about what is fair and unfair, just and unjust, good and bad. So the man who denies the moral order repudiates in practice what he affirms in theory.

3. Consider the strange experience of praising the noble actions of men long dead and of condemning the unjust deeds of those in centuries past. Why praise Socrates for his courage and integrity in teaching what he thought was true even though it led to his death? He lived long before Christ and has no influence on us as a living person today. Or, on the negative side, why do we condemn as wrong the act of Judas in betraying Jesus? Is this merely subjective preference? Again, why do we praise Schweitzer as good and refer to Hitler as one of the worst men that ever lived? Is this mere whim or fancy? Is there no objective basis for it?

4. Why do we experience remorse or guilt? The cynic is apt to say, "Because we get caught." But the question goes far deeper than that. A soldier lets his buddy suffer and die on the field of battle to save himself. Perhaps he did the best he could, perhaps not. Here I am supposing he did not do his best. His buddy dies. Nobody else knows the facts. None will ever know them unless he tells the full story. Why does he feel remorse and guilt? Is it a matter of getting caught? Of course not. Rather, it is a case of having to live with one's self.

85

5. Again, why is it that in nearly every novel or play of any consequence there are heroes and villains who come to be recognized for what they are and are responded to accordingly? Why should even children respond to the heroes and oppose the villains? Is this mere fantasy? Recently some writers and producers for television programs have attempted to confuse the values of men by letting the heroes champion the causes of evil men. But the programs fell dead. Why? To be sure, there are admirable traits in morally bad men, as there are in Milton's Satan. But this has no force against the point here made. All life and drama presuppose a basic difference between the good men and the bad. We know, of course, that no men are wholly good or bad.

6. Another consideration comes from asking a question: Why do people in all ages tend to respond almost intuitively to the ideal whenever it presents itself? William James, referring to saints and spiritual heroes, writes in *The Varieties of Religious Experience,* "They show themselves, and there is no question; every one perceives their strength and stature."

7. Again, the universal recognition of the moral order is seen in the way men respond to tributes of praise given them for their moral character. This shows that there are pervasively assumed moral standards and values in the community. The virtues of men can be announced in the news media without any fear of libel. No man sues another for praising his noble qualities. For virtue is universally regarded as good. Or, suppose a man in public office is involved in scandal pertaining to money, or sex, or intrigue. As soon as the facts become clear there is the inevitable emergence of moral judgment. On the other side, though the virtues of men are often accepted as a matter of course, they are still constantly or at least latently regarded as worthy of imitation.

8. Once more, people do in fact ask moral questions. "Was I right in what I did?" "What responsibilities do I have for the communities in which I live?" "What about my family obligations?" "Should the color of a man's skin have any bearing on

his rights as a human being?" These and many other moral questions are raised by men.

The conclusion of all this is that the moral order is an inescapable feature of man's life in community. While men may repudiate it in practice (just as they may spurn the pursuit of truth) they cannot do away with it.

"But," says someone, "you have not yet dealt with the psychological, cultural and environmental factors. Is it not still true that men of different types and from different cultures have differing moral standards and values?"

A point needs to be cleared up before going directly into this problem. Men have many motives. Some motives are essentially moral, others are not. A man may, by temperament, have an intense interest in music, or art, or athletics, or money, or power, or science, or religion, or in being a drifter. These special interests, which come from a combination of psychological make-up and environment, lead to many individual differences that are not moral in nature. Yet such varieties of interests do affect the moral life. This is a complex matter that could be discussed profitably at length. But for the purpose at hand I merely call attention to it to suggest that many differences among people are not essentially moral even though they affect the responses men make to the moral life. For example, if a tyrant or a robber baron repudiates moral standards and values to accomplish his immoral aims, this has no force against the objective validity of moral truth. Similarly, if a whole society or a period of history is marked by moral decay, this has no more force against an objective moral order than pervasive ignorance and prejudice have against science. Therefore, differing interests and conflicting preferences among men do not imply ethical relativism.

Turning to the issue directly, the first comment is that the differences in moral standards among men are both exaggerated and misunderstood. I suggest that in all civilized societies there is essentially the same *moral* foundation on its human side. The universal character of morality can be seen not so much from a study of the various ethical theories as from an examination of concrete moral regulations. These operate in all societies.

Here I refer to the written and unwritten black lists of bad deeds and white lists of virtues. The brightest light is thrown on these when we discover the *purpose* they were designed to fulfill.

For example, we understand hospital regulations concerning quietness and visiting hours when we note the purpose behind them. They are established for the well-being of the patients. Traffic regulations about stopping and going, rights of way and the like, are designed to help all the motorists. Moral regulations have a more exalted place than these rules. But they are similar in that they too are aimed toward the well-being of people in community.

Two things are to be said about moral regulations, that is, about black lists of bad deeds that carry moral sanctions and white lists of virtues that carry moral approval. First, they are found in all societies and particularly in civilized societies. Second, the *purpose* back of them in all societies is the same, namely, to guard and foster the well-being of the people in the community. Everyone is aware that often tyrants have laid down certain rules that are far from life-subserving. But this has no force here because, as we have seen, men may have other than moral motives for doing anything. Moreover, it is also true that there were often moral regulations which, though originally designed to protect and promote social well-being, either were not contrived in wisdom or have outlived their usefulness. Superstitious taboos have often been of this nature.

The most famous of all moral regulations are probably those in the Ten Commandments. The *purpose* behind them is clear. Why say, "You shall not kill"? To protect life. Why, "You shall not steal"? To help people make free use of their tools and possessions and to prevent the commotions in society caused by stealing. So is it with the others. They are designed for human well-being. This is true not only of the moral regulations in the Ten Commandments. An examination of the deeper reason behind all *moral* regulations in human societies reveals their life-subserving import.

The point is that there is in fact a universal basis for morality in all societies and this goes a long way toward destroying the arguments for ethical relativism based on the supposed diversities of customs and rules. There are of course many differences. But all men, in so far as they are morally motivated, aim for the well-being of people in community. Though they may go about this in various ways (sometimes even with foolish rules and regulations) the universal aim is there. And, on the human side, this is a most important clue to the uniqueness of the moral order.

What is done by the Biblical writers is to connect the well-being of those in the community with the concerns of God so that moral regulations are given far greater force by grounding them in God.

Doubt   Another question posed by many modern minds is this: If there is a moral order that seeks to promote human well-being, why not find the key to well-being in the pleasure-principle? This view has been given some support by Sigmund Freud and his followers who insist that moral regulations often have a stifling effect on personality development. So they call for a more free expression of the basic pleasure-giving impulses. Hence, the formula: Express yourself!

Response   No civilized societies have been willing to make this more than an aspect of the moral life. Their moral regulations were not and could not be aimed merely to protect men against pain and to promote their opportunities for pleasure. Yet this has always been a factor in the purpose of those regulations. The point here is that hedonism has not in fact been made a prominent feature of the actual moral regulations, written or unwritten, as they have functioned in communities. Therefore, it is phoney and unreal except as it expresses an aspect of life.

Again, we see the inadequacy of the pleasure-principle when we realize that human well-being can never be secured apart from hard work, self-sacrifice, inconvenience and suffering, which is sometimes deliberately accepted. Hedonism does not adequately take into account the fact that men are sick and need help. They need the kind of help that comes only when somebody abandons his own interests and seeks more than the life of pleasure for others. Hedonism fails to see that, for example, at least a few men are lawless, vicious, and inhuman, and somebody has got to undergo danger, struggle, and even death to keep the community going at all.

Another important consideration here is that whenever we actually seek pleasure as the supreme good for ourselves and others we sense that something basic has been overlooked. Man himself is dissatisfied with the pleasure-principle. This is why the four classical virtues of wisdom, courage, temperance, and justice require far more of him than even the highest levels of pleasure. Similarly, the Christian virtues of faith, hope, and love move man into far more meaningful dimensions of experience and achievement than the pleasure-principle can offer. All men of vision would rather abandon innumerable pleasures to gain more worthy objectives for God and man. This idea was given graphic utterance in the Book of Hebrews where we read of Moses that he chose "rather to share ill-treatment with the people of God than to enjoy the fleeting pleasures of sin" (11:25).

The conclusion is that hedonism in all forms has been too superficial to become the basis of the moral regulations of mankind.

Doubt   What about the ethics that base the moral order on nature? Why not say that if a course of action is natural, it is morally right?

Response   Many natural impulses are good. They are therefore to be included in the moral order. Moreover, natural responses, in contrast to artificial ones, are good.

But this view in general fits well into the mediocre ways many people actually live. It is used therefore to justify them in their commonplace and even inhuman deeds. They get and grab without regard to the general welfare. This is quite natural, but it is against the central purpose of morality as found in human societies. Lying, cheating, sexual promiscuity, ruthlessness in making money, these and other activities have a strong basis in man's natural selfishness. Uncontrolled anger is natural and evil. People do not *learn* to feel anger and hostility. They simply do so naturally. Many natural impulses are as destructive as they are natural. Plato had one of his cynical characters define justice as the interest of the stronger. Might makes right. "In this world," say many, "it is dog eat dog and those who do not agree are either liars or fools."

One of the most convincing arguments against this view is simply that the moral regulations of all societies have been aimed toward protecting men against this very approach.

Another convincing argument is simply that natural impulses often conflict with each other. It is natural to love and to hate, to seek friends and to make enemies, to lie and to tell the truth. And so it goes.

The conclusion would seem to be that men, in their moral thinking, have seen the need for regulations, not so they can imitate nature but to rise above it.

Doubt   What about the "new morality"?

Response   It is not new. At its best it seeks to bring morality to bear on man's life in ways that are realistic and relevant. At its worst it is little more than a crude type of hedonism.

The chief contributions of the "new morality" may be briefly stated. It seeks to free men from a stifling legalism. It makes for a certain openness in responding to human needs. There are new situations and new problems that demand new answers. Moreover, the call for intelligence in handling life situations, though not new, is often neglected. It rightly stresses love as the master impulse back of all authentic morality.

The "new morality" fails at a number of points. It does not adequately recognize that written or unwritten moral regulations are inevitable in all civilized societies. They function and will continue to do so. The main reason for this is that human vitality has to be restrained and directed. This fact puts the "new morality" in a largely unreal relationship to the concrete morality that actually operates in human society. Therefore, any theory that tends to weaken the sense of the importance of appropriate moral regulations has the effect of abandoning the moral order. This is why the great prophets as well as Jesus took the law seriously even while they emphasized such virtues as justice and love.

Moral regulations are implied or explicitly stated on nearly every page of the books of those who expound the "new morality." If the story of the Good Samaritan illustrates the one absolute of love, it also ends with the *rule* to go and do likewise. Rules are far more important than they are made to appear in the "new morality."

Moreover, man needs to respect the main moral regulations because they express in shorthand what has been discovered in the history of mankind. They are moral generalizations from experience that are designed to equip men for decision-making in the situations of life. For this reason the "new morality" does a disservice to humanity. It leaves the false impression that all we really need is to go into each situation with a good heart and a sound mind. There is no need to take rules and regulations with utmost seriousness. I know, of course, that the devotees of the "new morality" have a place for rules in their thinking. But their categories and their ways of developing their thought leave the impression that rules and policies are not to be taken with radical seriousness. Their emphasis is on "rules are made to be broken" rather than on "the exception proves the rule."

A good case can be made for the idea that love alone is the absolute principle. Nevertheless, it does damage psychologically and morally to suggest that rules and regulations are to be reconsidered in the many situations of life. In one situation tell the truth, in another a lie. In one situation commit adultery, in another not. There is something about this that is alien to the Judeo-Christian heritage, as well as to the morality that is present in all civilized societies.

Again, the "new morality" tends to presuppose that everyone

is an expert in the case method. Each situation is new and everyone is to be motivated by love and guided by intelligence. This is too much of a burden for even the wisest men. The plain fact is that we do not have time to reason out the best course of action in every critical situation. The person equipped with habits, who swiftly recalls previous situations, and who takes basic rules seriously is likely to do the best job morally. In the case of an immature person it is almost self-evident that he would be acting more reasonably to take proven rules and regulations seriously than to play each situation by ear as he goes into it.

Experience teaches also that rules and regulations are necessary in the formation of the kind of character that can handle life-situations. In minimizing them the "new morality" tends to encourage an easygoing attitude toward right and wrong. This leads inevitably toward mediocrity.

Experience teaches also that unless we go into a critical situation already well prepared by moral regulations and habits, we are very likely to fail. The memory lapses, intelligence often blunders, time is short, and selfish impulses exert their downward gravitational pull.

Again, love itself requires moral rules and regulations. How can we love a neighbor if we do not keep promises, tell the truth, and make it a rule to consider his dignity and well-being? What are authentic rules but fixed ways of expressing relationships among people? Hence, love demands them. They are structural features of what it means to love one's neighbor.

Finally, the "new morality" leaves much to be desired in a world that cries out for order and better management of human affairs. The threats of mass starvation, of overpopulation, of war, and of dehumanization do not suggest the need for the "new morality." They suggest rather the need for the love of God, which expresses itself through built-in rules and policies.

The Bible brings together three important truths about the moral order that are often separated or only loosely connected. These are faith in God, love for all mankind, and the expression of faith and love through moral regulations that become habits and policies of life.

It is not possible to have an authentic faith in the God of whom Jesus spoke without being moved to love our fellowmen. If we put our trust in God for life, we seek what He seeks, namely, the well-being of people. So faith awakens love and, in turn, is strengthened by it. Jesus taught this organic interconnection between faith and love in nearly everything He said and did. One of His clearest and simplest statements concerns forgiveness. He said, "For if you forgive men their trespasses, your heavenly Father also will forgive you; but if you do not forgive men their trespasses, neither will your Father forgive your trespasses" (Matthew 6:14–15). In effect Jesus was saying that if we are unconcerned about others, our Father will withhold from us the full benefits of His love. He still loves us, just as He is always ready to forgive. But His love and forgiveness are not made available to us unless we love our fellowmen.

This brings us to the factor that has been too often placed in a compartment by itself, namely, the function of moral regulations in the Kingdom of God. The faith that breeds love necessarily expresses itself through moral rules and regulations. These become built-in habits and policies that make the Christian man a person who strives, however imperfectly, to meet the needs of men. This approach changes our feeling toward moral regulations. Instead of regarding them as schemes of stifling "do's" and don'ts," we see them as expressions of the life-giving love of God who is concerned to meet our needs. Nietzsche used the words "moralic acid" to describe his cynical feelings about moral precepts. Jesus showed their life-subserving function and their built-in power and so gave us a new feeling toward them.

Those who teach men to loosen their grip upon the moral rules and regulations of society in general and of the Christian community in particular are moving outside the orbit of the Biblical revelation and its heritage. For in the Hebrew-Christian stream love and justice on the one hand, and laws and regulations on the other, are organically connected. Rightly understood, they are two aspects of the same thing. Both are necessary in their own ways to share the life formed by faith in God. Dynamic love expresses itself through order.

7

MAN AS RELATED TO GOD

The understanding we have of man affects every aspect of thought and life. Our interpretation of history is basically governed by what we think of man. All theories on reform depend largely on views of human nature. Our ideas of the future and its possibilities rest largely on our thoughts on man. Even our understanding of God is shaped to some extent by our views on man. Therefore, Christians have devoted a large amount of thought to understanding the nature and destiny of man. As is the case with all major topics, there are many contrasting approaches to the study of man. This is particularly true of the modern era with its psychological and societal studies. Here I wish to concentrate first on the various ways in which modern man has looked at himself and next on the Biblical teaching. Then we shall be in a position to consider some modern doubts about that teaching.

THE MAIN ALTERNATIVE VIEWS

Modern thinkers, like their ancient forebears, have understood man by seeing him within a network of relationships. But in recent times the network has become far more complex than anything known in the ancient world. Broadly speaking, modern man has viewed himself in three relational settings: (1) in relation to nature, (2) in relation to society, and (3) in relation to psychological, psychophysical, and subconscious processes. Other approaches might be noted, but these are the predominant ones. Each of these will now be considered briefly.

First, the efforts to understand man in relation to nature move in various directions. Some think of him primarily in relation to the known physical universe. He is an infinitesimal item on the agenda of an unbelievably vast scheme of things. Astronomically speaking, man is almost unworthy of notice. Somehow he belongs in this spatio-temporal realm. His body seems to be composed of elements found throughout the universe. Someone has said of him that he is but an episode in the history of carbon. His life in this present order is as precarious as it is brief. Compared to him stones and stars have far more capacity for endurance. In size and staying power he is little more than a nonentity. Yet, modern man sees himself as having certain advantages over the physical universe because he is the astronomer, the space explorer, and the knower. He alone among known creatures is capable of intellectual comprehension.

Others have studied man in relation to nature by seeing him as a higher development of animal life. They have noted in exhaustive detail how he is related to the lower animals in origin and structure. The various theories of evolution were inevitable. For these detailed comparisons were sure to suggest a common origin of all animal life. So man is placed in the thick of the biological order and examined as the most gifted of its products.

Second, modern thinkers have studied man endlessly in his associational relationships. The rise to prominence of sociological or societal studies is one of the signal achievements of the past hundred and fifty years. These have taken scholars into economics, political science, cultural anthropology, sociology, sociology of religion, and innumerable other specialized studies of man in rural areas, man in urban centers, and man in other specific social environments. Communist theorists have attempted to understand man primarily in his relationships to other men in the processes of overcoming material scarcity. For them his role in the economic structure is the primary source of insight into human nature. It is also the key to social revolution, which is their primary interest.

The third main way modern man has sought to understand himself is broadly psychological. It ranges all the way from physiological studies to experiments in extrasensory perception and telepathy, from the study of consciousness and its interrelationships with the body to the probings into subconscious processes and personality malfunctions. All this represents one of the outstanding accomplishments of man's search for truth about himself.

As these three approaches of man have progressed during the past two hundred years they tended to suggest that any reference to man in relation to God belongs to the occult or esoteric. Consequently, at no point do the doubts referred to in chapter 1 become more explicit than in the modern studies of man.

THE BIBLICAL TEACHING

In contrast to these approaches the Biblical writers see man almost entirely in relation to God. For this reason when we pass from these modern ways of looking at man to the Biblical teaching and its heritage in Christianity, we feel as if we were moving from one climate to another. There is no inherent conflict between them. But there are fundamental differences.

The Biblical writers do not present a systematic account of man as related to God. Nor do they agree fully in their emphases. But all of them come together on one assumption, namely, that the God-man relationship is basic. Biblically speaking, the thought that man could be anything apart of God is ridiculous. We might say, then, that in the Bible man is involved in a network of relationships to God that suggest the measure of his greatness and tragedy. From God's side man is seen as created and sustained by God, as known and loved by God, and as called and judged by God. Within this system of interconnectedness we may lift up for special comment six relationships between man and God that define the Biblical understanding of man.

First, man is related to God as a creature to the Creator. This means that, like every other creature, he is wholly dependent on the divine energizing. Without God's continuing creativity he would instantly perish. When this fact rises to consciousness on the level of religious experience it becomes what Schleier-macher called the feeling of absolute dependence upon God. In the setting of the Bible this creature-Creator relationship includes two important emphases. First, the Biblical writers do not want man to forget that he is a finite creature along with all other living creatures. He is here today and gone tomorrow. He is an animal among animals with all the physical properties that doom him to die. He may prolong his life by foresight, but he cannot guarantee or insure his being. This is the universal idea of the transciency of life that comes home to every man who confronts death. Second, along with this the Biblical writers want man to know that he is *God's* creature. God wanted him to be. Thus his creaturehood does not lead to that brooding sense of pathos so characteristic of all whose thoughts keep returning to man's finitude and death. For he came into being not out of the aimless processes of nature but out of the deliberate purpose of God.

This suggests a second relationship to God of which the Bible speaks, namely, man's unique kinship with God. God made man a special kind of creature. That is, God chose to make him the kind of creature through whom the moral and spiritual meaning of creation could be realized. This implies that, unlike any other known creature, man is a living soul. Though he is a psychophysical being, as the Bible suggests, he is also a soul created for meaningful ties with God. God made him in His own image. Of course, this has nothing to do with man's physical make-up. Idols were fashioned to represent God in the image of man, with eyes, ears, hands, feet and the like. The Biblical writers carried on an unceasing warfare against such idolatry.

To understand the Biblical teaching on the image of God we must move from the physical to the spiritual. More particularly, we must move into the sphere of moral and spiritual values. Here the unique kinship between man and God can be clarified and given concrete meaning.

In the long history of prophetic insight and human reflection the wisest and best men have said that there is a difference between what is good and what is bad, between the beautiful and the ugly, between truth and error, between worship and blasphemy. In other words, they have said that in addition to the physical universe there is a moral and spiritual cosmos. In this sphere man's kinship with God becomes real.

God is good. God is the author of the beauty and glory of the heavens. God is the Lord of truth who, as the psalmist says, "hates every false way." God alone is holy and worthy of worship. This God has given man the capacity to grow and adventure in goodness, beauty, and truth. So what God possesses in His infinity man possesses in his finitude. This can be said of no other known creature. One would guess, on theological grounds, that there are other intelligent beings on planets throughout the universe. But of them at present we know nothing. Man, then, has a unique kinship with God whereby he can participate with God in the activities within the moral and spiritual cosmos. This is why man can worship God, adore Him, and seek to move with Him toward the realization of His aims.

The idea of man's kinship to God reaches its highest utterance in the New Testament where Jesus speaks of God as Father and of men as His children. Here the analogy of the intimate interpersonal ties of the family is used to express this mysterious kinship between man and God. Thus the idea in the Old Testament of man as created in the image of God is fulfilled in the New Testament where man is thought of as belonging in the family of God. This is the sphere of interpersonal relationships in their intimacy and depth.

Theologically this idea of kinship between God and man has been elaborated under the concept of the I-Thou or person-to-Person relationship. This is true to the Biblical teaching. It is the basis too of the Biblical teaching on the dignity and value of the human soul. The soul was made by God to be a creature of special worth because of its ability to participate with God in the realization of moral and spiritual values.

Implied in all this is a third relationship between God and man, namely, that of intercommunication. The Biblical writers insist that God has spoken to them. In fact the whole idea of the Bible as God's living Word presupposes that God takes the initiative to reveal Himself and to communicate with men. A word is a vehicle of communication. One person shares what is on his mind with another person primarily by means of words. Men enter into the inner life of a community by means of language. So it is no accident that in Christianity the Bible is referred to as God's Word and Jesus Christ as the Word made flesh. For all of this has to do with God's initiative in communicating with men through men.

But this is not a one-way process. Man is kin to God. Therefore, he not only can receive and understand to some extent God's message of love, he can also share what is on his mind and heart with God. This is why prayer plays a central role in all high religion. For there man becomes aware of the divine presence and realizes that he is known and loved by God. At the same time his mind is illuminated by the Word that is communicated to him. In public worship too there is the sense that God is reasserting His love and concern for His children while they are expressing their praise, gratitude, sorrow, need, and faith in God. Thus worship too is an instance of divine-human intercommunication.

In the New Testament this range of man's kinship to God is particularly conspicuous both in the interpretation of Jesus as the Word made flesh and in the understanding of the Holy Spirit as the divine presence intimately at work in men. Among other activities, the Holy Spirit illuminates men's minds. He communicates the love of Christ and enables them to comprehend the living Word of God mediated through Jesus Christ. There are passages in the Bible that suggest God guides men by giving specific information about men and events. Paul had a vision of the needs in Macedonia and went there instead of to Bithynia (Acts 16:6–10). There are other instances of this type of guidance (Acts 20:23, 21:4, 27:23–24); but, although these occur they do not express the main Biblical teaching concerning the initiative of the Holy Spirit in communicating with men. The major thrust of the New Testament is that the Holy Spirit communicates to men the love of God in Christ and makes them aware of their need of repentance and faith. In any event,

God communicates with men and they communicate with Him.

A fourth relationship between man and God is made possible by man's freedom. This is the relationship of being in dynamic harmony or disharmony with God. God has created man with the power of contrary choice. In a finite being like man this power is radically limited. But it is real and far more extensive than many thinkers are willing to recognize.

Without freedom the Biblical teaching on the person-to-Person encounters between God and man, including the whole covenant idea, would be reduced to poetic fantasy and mythology. For man would be a puppet with no insight whatever into the decisions, policies, and aims of God. Decision, response, and agreement would have been out of the question. The Bible teaches that the universe was created by divine choice. God made it for a purpose. But this can be understood by man only because he too can choose from among alternative courses of action. In fact, at the heart of Biblical religion is the divine call to choose, to respond to God's aims, and to seek out his ways. Unless man could act purposively on his finite level as God does on His infinite level, this call of God would be meaningless. Man could neither understand it nor respond to it. Here again this fundamental kinship between God and man makes possible the person-to-Person encounters and the all-important covenant relationship of which the Biblical writers speak.

In opposition to this there have been influential theologians who have said that the Bible teaches absolute determinism. According to them man has no choice. Only God's action can save him. So everything depends on whether or not God chooses an individual for His Kingdom. If so, he is among the elect; if not, he is among the damned. And there is nothing he can do about it. Augustine, Luther and Calvin affirm this type of rigid theological determinism. In the Bible too there are statements that tend to support their interpretation (Genesis 19:24–25; 1 Samuel 2:2–10; Psalms 46:8–9; Isaiah 10:5–6, 44: 21–28; Jeremiah 50:40–46; Ezekiel 36:16–28; Romans 9:12–24).

But this perspective is not true of the Bible as a whole. Throughout, there is the recurring presupposition of man's responsibility before God. The assumption of human responsibility is stated in the story of Adam and Eve (Genesis 3) and it maintains its identity through the varied events of Biblical history until it reaches dramatic utterance in our Lord's account of the last judgment (Matthew 25:31–46). Man was given a lordship over the earth which clearly implies responsibility (Genesis 1:28, 9:3; Psalms 8:6–8). The Ten Commandments, as well as the covenant relationship implied in their use, presuppose that men can obey or disobey God. Moses, assuming man's freedom of choice, challenged those who were on the Lord's side to stand forth (Exodus 32:26). The moral defections of kings, from Saul and David to Rehoboam and Jeroboam and all the others who "did that which was evil in the sight of the Lord," leave no doubt of their accountability. The prophets addressed men as if they had freely chosen to disobey God and to strike against their fellowmen (Isaiah 1:16–23, 5:8–25; Jeremiah 7:8–11; Ezekiel 18:1–23; Amos 2:6–8, 5:21–24, 6:3–6; Micah 3:1–3, 6:7–8).

Jesus also made it clear that man bears a primary responsibility for his life in relation to the Kingdom of God. His teachings assume this throughout. He denounced certain Pharisees because He assumed they were responsible for their misguided actions. Jesus Himself felt the awesome responsibility of choice. He was tempted as we are. He set His course toward Jerusalem to complete His mission. In a moment of the highest expression of freedom, when He wanted to be released from His agony, He prayed, ". . . not my will, but thine, be done" (Luke 22:42). God could not have revealed His love through a man who, before the choices of life, merely went through the forms of freedom without the reality of it.

The language of the New Testament from beginning to end, with minor exceptions, clearly implies this momentous fact that man is a creature free to accept or reject God's gracious gift of salvation. Consequently, he is constantly called upon to respond, to choose, to trust, to obey. Almost every key word in the New Testament vocabulary of the Christian life implies the power of saying "yes" or "no" to God. The Christian is to walk, run, keep awake, put on the whole armor of God, fight the good fight of faith, strive to excel, pray, and return good for evil. The speeches, sermons, and admonitions of the apostles and others all imply this same freedom of response.

We are not saying here that man's freedom functions as the principle of salvation. We are merely stating that it is a factor in this and all other processes in which man is involved. And, again, it is this primal fact that makes possible man's participation with God in the moral and spiritual cosmos.

This leads to a fifth relationship on which the Bible concentrates heavily. The misuse of man's freedom leads to his moral and spiritual wrongness with God. Man is the only known creature who can be thus alienated from God. Man alone can be a sinner. This topic will be treated in the next chapter, so it requires no further elaboration here.

Another important relationship here is that man is known and loved by God. This is an ineradicable feature of the Biblical revelation and its heritage. God knows man as obedient and disobedient, faithful and unfaithful, selfish and unselfish. And He loves him. Knowing all these things, God has still shown His love by acting redemptively and creatively in behalf of all men through Jesus Christ. However much He knows about them His love never fails. He seeks their favorable response and longs for their total well-being. This theme too will be elaborated upon further in later chapters. But it requires special notice here because it is essential to the Biblical teaching on man and also because in some prevalent modern perspectives this note is tragically absent.

These six relationships between man and God constitute the central teaching of the Bible on man. Their importance is seen further in the fact that they apply to all men everywhere. With the exception of a few passages in the Old Testament this awareness of the solidarity of the human race in relation to God was not made clear. Even in the New Testament the essential direction of the Biblical revelation is not at all points visible. Nevertheless, in the developing interpretations of the mind of Christ and of the implications of His teachings, this affirmation of the solidarity of the human race has come to the fore.

Three pressing doubts arise about the Biblical teaching on man. There are others, but these have a kind of priority.

Doubt   First, modern man finds it difficult to think of these relationships between man and God as dynamic and real. They seem more like mythological constructs than the outcome of a realistic analysis. We can see clearly what is meant by saying that man is related to nature, to lower animals and to galaxies. We know also what it means to speak of man in his social relationships. Similarly, psychophysical, psychological, and subconscious processes have the marks of concrete reality. But this network of interrelationships with God seems to lack a basis in experience.

Response   Everything depends on the reality and nature of God. If God is, and if He loves human beings, nothing is more reasonable than the Biblical teaching on man. If not, then it is all a rope of sand. We have already considered some of the grounds for believing in God, but we need to reflect on the experience of those who have been aware of these relationships. Man's creatureliness has been sensed in his feeling of absolute dependence on God. His sense of kinship to God has been experienced in prayer and communion with God. His sense of wrongness has been found in the experience of guilt, remorse and alienation. His sense of being known and loved is experienced whenever he has approached God in true repentance and faith. He has sensed God's love in the new resources for creative living experienced in the life of sustained trust. So it is simply not true to the realities of religious history to suggest that these relationships between God and man have no basis in experience. Many people never enter into the religious dimension on any high level. But this does not entitle them to

104

rule out what others have experienced. Some men never enter the world of science, but this does not minimize the truth and value of scientific discoveries.

Another comment is this. Doubts can go both ways. We may have serious doubts about the Biblical perspective on man-as-related-to-God. We may have serious doubts also about the adequacy of the approaches of modern thinkers to man. It is not that all these studies of man are without value. Far from it. Rather, it is that they are inadequate; and their inadequacy is not due to insufficient numbers of scholars and investigations. It is inherent in the approaches themselves. For the basic question is, Can man have any ultimate meaning if we understand him apart from God? Is there any way to move within these scientific studies of man to an adequate philosophy of the meaning of human existence? The answer would seem to be clearly that there is not.

This places modern man in the curious position of wanting to affirm the democratic idea of the dignity of man while at the same time he assumes a perspective in which man has no enduring significance. So modern man's ways of looking at himself are hopelessly schizophrenic unless they can be supplemented by an orientation toward God. The Biblical teaching, then, far from being irrelevant, is needed to help modern man avoid nihilism. There seems to be no possible way of affirming the worth and dignity of this finite creature, man, apart from the God who created him, sustains him, knows and loves him. Otherwise, he is cut loose to drift for a time in an alien universe. Like an iridescent bubble he is soon to burst into oblivion. Without God man is an unknown entity in an unconcerned universe. In such perspectives as nontheistic humanism, naturalism, Freudianism, and certain forms of existentialism, man is—despite all the talk to the contrary—a "passing whiff of insignificance." He is headed for zero. And what comes out at zero cannot be very important. Endurance and value must go together for there to be any authentic dignity and enduring meaning in man's passing life on this planet.

Doubt   A second doubt concerns whether or not man has a soul or is a soul. If not, how can he be related to God at all? This doubt is apt to take two forms. Some think there is no soul because everything man is can be reduced to his physical body and its actions. Hence, the so-called soul is nothing more nor less than certain aspects of the body and its functions. Others, following Buddhists and other thinkers, say there is no soul because all a man is, in addition to his body, is a succession of moments. These moments may be conscious states, or decisions, or feelings. But there is no real self or mind or soul that abides in and through the succession of moments. This doubt arises in the minds of those who follow the mystical religions of the East where the category of individuality is generally obscured. For this mode of thought easily lapses into a kind of pantheism in which these "moments" are simply parts of the divine process or being.

Response   It should be clear from the start that both these approaches undermine not only the idea of the soul but with it the belief in the life everlasting.

Turning to the first view, that the soul is nothing more nor less than certain aspects of the body in its functioning, we may note that it is a very old theory. The ancient Greek atomists thought of the soul as consisting of refined atoms. Augustine dealt with this view by stating in *On the Trinity* that the soul is not the body, nor the functioning of the body, nor anything other than itself. Calvin too gave a kind of classical utterance in *Institutes of the Christian Religion* to the distinction between the soul and the body.

There are several convincing reasons for regarding as misguided all efforts to reduce the soul to the body or its processes. Before stating them, however, we should note in passing that both the Bible and common sense require us to recognize the intimate interaction of the mind or soul and the body. From some standpoints we would rightly assert that man is a psychophysical organism, that in this life body and soul are inextricably interdependent. But it is one thing to speak of this mysterious and undeniable fact of interaction and it is quite another thing to say that because of this interaction they are one and the same reality. Consider, then, several reasons for holding that the soul cannot be reduced to the body and its processes.

First, what we mean by "ourselves" is different from what we mean by our "bodies." When I think of myself (the I who thinks, feels, decides) I do not have in mind my finger, or my brain or my nervous system. I have in mind only myself. So I can think of myself or ego without thinking of my brain or nervous system. Therefore, the two are distinct in meaning. Second, I entertain meanings, while my brain and nerves simply exist as things in process. The existence of the brain does not imply the experience of meanings. But the mind knows itself as an experiencer of meanings. Third, the mind or soul can know itself immediately only from within, whereas it knows the brain or nervous system only by inferences from without. I know myself to be myself from direct inner awareness. For I am present to myself and known from within by myself. Fourth, the mind or soul transcends itself by means of memory, imagination, and purpose; the brain and nervous system have no such power. Fifth, a mind or soul can communicate with other minds; a brain cannot do this. Sixth, a mind or soul can relate itself to God in worship; the brain is out of its element here.

None of these remarks does justice to the soul. They are sufficient, nevertheless, to show that we are dealing with a reality that cannot be reduced to the body and its functioning.

As to the second way of denying the soul, namely, by saying it is nothing more nor less than a succession of thoughts, feelings or decisions (which may be aspects of God's being) two comments are in order. The first is that I experience myself as far more than a succession of moments, decisions and the like. To be sure, there are the innumerable successions of conscious states. But there is also my abiding ego initiating and experiencing these things. For example, there was a time when I was a small boy growing up in a missionary home in Korea. I flew Korean kites, played games with the children there, and spoke their language. Since those days many things have happened to me. Endless successions of thoughts and impressions have come and gone. Thousands of decisions have been made. Yet, *I* have experienced them all. The abiding self or soul is far more than the particular successions of experiences and choices. There is a continuing line of self-identity here. So the efforts to reduce the soul to successive states of consciousness are also misguided. They run counter to the whole range of assumptions and experiences involved in promises, contracts, and written and unwritten agreements, that go into all interpersonal relations.

With this understanding, we can return to the Biblical teaching with the conviction that it has far more to offer than some might at first suppose.

Doubt The third doubt has to do with the difficulty of taking man so seriously in this mysterious universe. How can he be important in God's eyes? The Copernican revolution has taken place. The earth is not at the center of things. Man is utterly inconsequential in relation to the universe. He is a cipher, a nonentity, a thing "made after dinner from a cheese-paring." What is man in relation to the 100 billion stars in our galaxy? And what is his worth in relation to the 100 billion or so other galaxies that are comparable in size to ours? Besides man's insignificance in relation to the vast stretches of things in space, he is equally inconsequential in relation to time. He is a candle in the wind. His flickering light goes out quickly. Yet the universe is billions of years old and keeps going. Man looks back on an infinite past and forward toward an infinite future, and such a life as he has swiftly passes away. In terms of geological ages, what difference does it make to say that billions of human beings have been born, lived to maturity and died without leaving much of a trace of their existence?

Response Physical size and location have nothing to do with value. The smallness of man's body and its location on an obscure little planet is of no consequence in the cosmos of values. The physical universe is a means, not an end. Where is the glory of a planet or a star or a galaxy when it cannot know, or love, or enjoy, or act purposively? What is the special value of size without a mind to understand, to feel, to act? The ideal values include truth, beauty, love, justice, friendship and worship. Can we measure these in feet or miles or light years? The dignity of man is not measured in distances but in his capacity to participate in the realm of values. Therefore, his value pertains to his person or soul. The Biblical teaching is not that man is at the physical center of the universe. Rather, it is that man is central in God's plan to realize moral and spiritual values in community.

Similarly (with regard to time) values do not essentially pertain to the number of years of endurance. Otherwise a stone would have far more value than a man. Planets and galaxies would be the most valuable things in the known universe. Where is the glory of a galaxy, which has existed for billions of years but which never thinks a thought, never laughs nor cries, never enjoys nor creates beauty, never loves, never rises to deeds of justice, and never acts to realize a dream? Mere endurance does not take us into the dimension of ideal values. Man, though his life on earth is brief, is the unique bearer of moral and spiritual values in community. To be sure, a being of value must endure to have continuing meaning. Hence, the relevance of the New Testament teaching on the life everlasting. But that is another matter. The point here is that far more than endurance is indicated in order to enter the cosmos of values. Here again the clue to the preciousness and dignity of man is found in his ability to participate in the sphere of values. Ultimately, of course, his life has no enduring value unless God has chosen him for an everlasting life of creative adventure with Him in the realization of moral and spiritual values. This is the Biblical teaching.

There is an implication in all this that is of supreme importance as we look toward the immediate and long-range future of mankind. I refer to its relevance for the solidarity of the human race. In the realm of values racial differences recede into the background and the capacities and qualities of men come to the fore. Ideal values cannot be cooped up within a race, or a nation, or a culture. Nor can they be confined within a time-span, as if the earlier or the later could be the best. Modernity has no corner on values. For some things are neither new nor old but ageless because they come from God and are realized in men of all races and eras.

Against the background of these thoughts the Biblical heritage appears as a necessary corrective to the inadequacy of modern perspectives on the nature and destiny of man. What has been said here, however, is wholly inadequate without an honest recognition of man's failure to realize these values. So we turn next to the Biblical teaching on man as alienated from God.

8

MAN AS ALIENATED FROM GOD

The wisest people of all ages have observed that there is something wrong with man. Some have called it ignorance; others, passion; still others, pride and selfishness. A wide variety of names and images have been used to express the major problems of human nature. Plato likened man to a chariot drawn by two horses, one being refined and well ordered, the other, crude and unruly. Kant spoke of a "radical evil" in human nature. Pascal said of man that he is "incapable of truth and good." La Rochefoucauld called man's self-love "one long and mighty agitation." William Hazlitt spoke of envy as the universal passion. Schopenhauer, with his usual pessimism, wrote, ". . . it seems to me that the idea of dignity can be applied only in an ironical sense to a being whose will is so sinful, whose intellect is so limited, whose body is so weak and perishable as man's." One of the shrewdest observations on this theme is that human history is "the despair of philosophy." For whatever else man is, he is an unpredictable problem to himself.

THE MAIN ALTERNATIVE VIEWS

There are at least five ways of approaching sin that are in varying degrees contrary to the Biblical teaching. First, there is the idea that sin is hardly to be taken seriously at all. For example, it has been observed that in the writings of A. N. Whitehead sin is scarcely considered a major theme for reflection and comment. Of course, Whitehead makes all sorts of value judgments about the mistakes and foibles of men. But, like Goethe, he did not seem to have any sustained interest in the sin problem. William James has spoken of those healthy-minded persons who think on the more positive sides of life.

Second, there are those who recognize the fact of evil in history but who do not consider it sinful. For example, Hegel could speak of history "as the slaughter-bench at which the happiness of peoples, the wisdom of states, and the virtue of individuals have been victimized." Yet he could say also that whatever is, is right. He viewed man's selfishness, pride, and even his inhumanity as factors in the dialectical movement of the divine Reason. Hence, though there seem to be vast evils in history they are not really the expressions of sin or wrong living. These are only stages in the movement of the absolute Spirit toward His ends.

Third, and closely related to the second is the theory that so-called sin is the result of inner or outer forces beyond our control. There is no effort here to deny the fact of evil motives and deeds by calling them good in disguise. But there is the thought that man is not really responsible for the evils he causes. This view takes many shapes. We may suggest five.

1. Some have said that sin is really man's animal nature expressing itself; it merely awaits the necessary evolutionary developments that are to come. Similar in principle to this is

the idea that man's sin is really another instance of cultural lag. With the advancement of culture and refinement, it will tend to disappear. For sin is cultural immaturity.

2. Others have said that what is usually called sin is a disease. Crime, at least in its extreme forms, is a disease. It may have its primal origin in an error in the make-up of the genes. Alcoholism too is a disease.

3. Many observers emphasize the environmental factors and suggest that sin is really a way of living that comes from slums, poverty and mistreatment generally.

4. Others have come to stress traumatic or other unfortunate past events in a person's life. They suggest that the subconscious processes, which now do their deadly work, produce the anxieties, complexes, and twists of mind that lead inevitably to "sin."

5. Still others have thought of sin as a structural feature of human nature. Kant's "radical evil" suggests this. Among some Christian theologians the idea of original sin conveys this thought too. This has also been called the doctrine of total depravity. Man is a fallen creature. Sin inevitably comes out of the kind of being man now is. The vast quantities of theological discussions on original sin are a kind of monument (like the colossal ruins of an ancient Egyptian temple) to this way of thinking about man's sin. This theory that man is so constituted that his nature drives him to sin comes to popular utterance in the formula: "It's in the clay."

According to a fourth general approach, sin is translated into psychological language. Guilt becomes a complex. Sin turns into anxiety, or frustration, or resentment, or boredom, or a sense of being alone in the world.

A fifth view interprets sin entirely in ethical rather than religious terms. Here sin is immorality; it is the deliberate violation of the moral order or a wrong attitude or deed toward any human being. According to this view man is responsible for what he does and stands morally condemned for conduct that violates ethical principles or strikes against the well-being of people.

So we find in these theories everything from the easy conscience, which totally absolves man, to the hard-hitting conscience, which totally condemns him.

When we turn from these and similar ways of looking at man's misdoings to the Biblical teaching we move into a different world. The main difference lies in the central theme of the Biblical writers: Man's sin must be seen in relation to God who is the Ground of the moral order. We shall develop this theme under four topics: (1) the definition of sin; (2) the universality of sin; (3) the concreteness of sin; and (4) the bearing of sin on man's destiny.

1. Sin is identified by two things. First, it is wrongness with God. This may or may not mean an *awareness* of wrong living and of being unforgiven. Essentially it is the absence of an active faith in God. In the Biblical teaching the failure to put God first is the essence of sin. "You shall have no other gods before me." This means that rightness with God in this I-Thou relationship consists in the conscious recognition of God as the Lord of a man's life. This comes to explicit focus in the Old Testament in the covenant-relationship in which man's trueness to God is measured by his trueness to the Commandments. In the New Testament it comes to focus in man's trueness to Jesus Christ as Lord. Implied in this is the willingness to take seriously God's moral and spiritual aims for all men. This rightness and wrongness refers to the attitude and response of each individual but it is viewed also as a corporate response of the community of believers. Thus in the Old Testament the people of God join in acknowledging the claims of the one true God. And in the New Testament, though the faith is personal and individual, it is nurtured and shared within the community of faith.

There is a second measure of sin, namely, a man's wrongness toward himself, his neighbors, and his material possessions. This aspect of man's wrongness with God will be discussed in more detail after some remarks on the universality of sin.

2. Another major thought on sin concerns its universality. The Biblical writers are of one mind that man has misused his freedom by turning away from God. So he is a creature in alienation. This is the primary negative theme of the Bible as a whole, and it is stated with surpassing force by the prophets, Jesus and Paul. "The sin of Judah is written with a pen of iron; with a point of diamond it is engraved on the tablet of their heart . . ." (Jeremiah 17:1). Jesus said, "For out of the heart come evil thoughts, murder, adultery, fornication, theft, false witness, slander. These are what defile a man . . ." (Matthew 15:19–20). And Paul wrote, ". . . all have sinned and fall short of the glory of God" (Romans 3:23). Because of man's inveterate tendency to turn away from God and His aims, the Biblical writers maintained a constant warning against sin and its consequences. They spoke of the wrath and judgment of God. They taught and preached that God takes sin seriously.

The Bible withholds nothing when it comes to man's sinfulness. It whitewashes nobody, not even Peter and Paul. Over all human existence are written the words, "All we like sheep have gone astray; we have turned every one to his own way . . ." (Isaiah 53:6). Whatever else the Christian doctrine of original sin means, it encompasses this universal fact of the gravitational pull in all men away from God and His values. Jesus showed that the source of the difficulty is not merely in specific rules broken, or precepts ignored, or deeds done. The heart of the problem lies in man's wrong relationship with God. Man seeks his own way and so fails to move with God toward the realization of his destiny as a creature made for the Kingdom of God. Man's sin is his guilt for his part in the processes of alienation from God. Particular sins are merely evidences of that alienation. Therefore, in the eyes of the prophets and Jesus, the basic tragedy of human history is this universal wrongness with God. For man, when wrongly related to God, is an unauthentic mode of existence.

3. The concreteness of man's sin is seen by the Biblical writers in man's wrongness with God, which necessarily issues

in his wrongness toward himself, his neighbors, and his money and property. The priority of God is basic. But the fact of one's wrongness with God is verified by man's action in the arena of life. Here is where he has to deal with *himself,* his *fellowmen,* and the world of *material possessions* under his control. A brief word about each of these in that order is necessary.

A primary sign of man's alienation from God is seen in his attitude toward *himself.* He may be proud and boastful,. arrogant and rude, smug and self-satisfied. Or, he may have an irresponsible attitude toward the development and use of his talents and so allow himself to fall into an easy contentment with mediocrity. God abhors laziness the way nature abhors a vacuum. A man who does not see himself as a creature who, like a garden, must be cultivated, is alienated from God whether he is aware of it or not. God led Moses against the people of Israel when they murmured in the wilderness and longed for the fleshpots of Egypt and slavery. The wisdom literature is full of precepts along the line of the proper use of time and energy. Trueness to oneself is an implicit teaching concerning man's relations to God. "So teach us to number our days that we may get a heart of wisdom" (Psalms 90:12).

Jesus suggested this kind of responsible attitude toward oneself in His parable of the talents in which God expects the talents to be used and improved. Paul, too, was a living example of the Christian who ever strives to improve on what he has. Straining, striving, running, fighting the good fight, holding the vision, these are the things he felt as a Christian he must do.

In this regard, then, Calvin's idea of the *elect* as being chosen for responsible leadership in this world is Biblical. And Wesley's idea that time is precious, energy sacred (so that no Christian should be triflingly employed) was likewise nurtured on Biblical soil.

The strongest and clearest evidences of man's alienation from God are seen in his wrong relations with his *fellowmen.* For man's relationships with his fellowmen are organically connected with his rightness or wrongness with God. The point is that God is so intimately involved with and concerned for each of His children that a wrong relationship with any of them involves alienation from Himself.

At first this idea was more or less limited to the relationships within the community of Israel. But some of the later prophets began to get the vision of the one true God who alone was Lord of all the nations. In the New Testament, though the ministry of Jesus was confined largely to the people of Israel, there was the swift movement of the early church into the world. Paul saw the universal scope of the gospel of salvation through Jesus Christ. Jews and Gentiles, Greeks and barbarians, were all alike in their need of God's creative love in the community of faith. All this leads the Christian to understand that a man's relations to any other man, or group of men, whether black or white, rich or poor, educated or unlettered, are organically connected with his relationships to God. Jesus did more than any other person in the history of religion to clarify this thought and to put it into the simplest terms. He illustrated it in His parables and stated it in His precepts. His strongest remarks on it concerned what He said about forgiveness, reconciliation and judgment. God forgives us only when we forgive others. A prayer will be ineffectual if a man remembers at the altar that someone has something against him. Jesus said he must first be reconciled to his brother and then offer his gift at the altar. All this symbolizes the whole gamut of human relations which, depending on their nature, draw us to or separate us from God. For "as you did it to one of the least of these my brethren, you did it to me" (Matthew 25:40).

Theologically speaking this idea may be expressed in terms of the I-Thou-thou, or the person-to-Person-to-person relationship.

Closely related to human well-being is the use men make of their natural resources and *material possessions*. In the Biblical teaching there is a direct connection between man and God and the stewardship of money and property. Man is responsible to God for the use he makes of his physical environment. In other words, rightness or wrongness with God goes beyond human relationships to man's responsible use of the earth and its resources and, by implication, of the moon and the planets within his reach. Man is the only known creature who bears this responsibility before God. The Commandments about stealing and coveting imply respect for property rights. They imply also the call to the stewardship of property as a responsibility before God. For the earth is the Lord's and the fullness thereof.

The Bible teaches that man is in charge of the earth and is to subdue it to his ends. God has put all things under his feet. But man defies God whenever he uses the earth wastefully and spends his financial resources foolishly. Jesus was constantly using examples of good and bad stewardship to illustrate the work of the Kingdom. But in doing so He assumed the importance of a responsible use and development of material possessions.

It was no accident that science and technology arose and developed in a culture steeped in the Biblical teachings on man's responsibility to God for his use of the earth and what it produces. The whole scientific and technological revolution is in the line of the Biblical heritage in so far as it contains the emphasis on understanding the material bases of human life with a view to their responsible use. Stewardship requires understanding what is available and making the best use of it without needless waste. At this point, then, science and technology are deeply rooted in the Biblical heritage. But their misuse, which leads to waste and destruction, illustrates the extent of man's sinfulness in the use of these resources.

4. This brings us to another major teaching of the Bible about sin, namely, its bearing on man's destiny. Sin does not merely cut man off from God, it also affects his role and status in the Kingdom of God yet to come. It is organically connected with his destiny. Man's future ultimately rests with God. Therefore the quest for rightness with God has priority over all other human interests. In the Biblical revelation man is the kind of being who is called or chosen for a faith-relationship with God. For in this way, by God's initiative, the full ranges of God's benefits come to man in this life and the next.

This theme will be developed further when we consider the life everlasting. Nevertheless, it needs to be mentioned here so that the full seriousness of the sin-problem can be felt. There is no possibility of standing on Biblical soil in a mood of complacency and self-satisfaction. Always there is the creative tension growing out of alienation or the never-ending threat of it.

SOME MODERN DOUBTS AND RESPONSES TO THEM

It was inevitable for the pervasive atmosphere of doubt in the modern world to press in upon the Biblical teaching on sin. This is partly due to modern man's intense interest in the study of man as a problem; and it is due also to the naturalistic assumptions which, as we have seen, tend to shape the modern mind. In particular, there are four doubts about the Biblical teaching on man as sinner that bear careful attention here.

Doubt   The first concerns the psychology of sin. As soon as we doubt that God makes any difference we doubt that man can be related to God as sinner. So, instead of thinking of sin as a wrong relationship between man and God, we naturally tend to view it as a kind of psychological maladjustment. This is precisely what has happened in the modern mind.

Response   Psychological studies have made immense contributions to man's understanding of himself. Nevertheless, there is good reason to recognize the radical limitations of psychology in the sphere of morality and wrongdoing.

The basic question is this: Is there a God who made man to be a special kind of creature and who therefore has the right to expect an appropriate response? This takes us far beyond the ranges of psychology. If God is, and if He has such a claim upon man, then any effort to understand sin within the thought patterns of psychology is superficial in the extreme.

This is why we look beyond psychology to the Biblical teaching for a deeper understanding of the ways of handling the sin-problem. If sin can be understood wholly within the categories of psychology, the answers to it would tend to be found in psychologically oriented forms of counseling. These may be useful. But they are inadequate because they do not come to grips with the basic problem, namely, how a man becomes rightly oriented toward God. This is why, in keeping with the Biblical understanding of the nature of sin, the Biblical teaching includes the call to repentance and faith as the only means of overcoming it. For this is the way to enter into honest and right relationships with God.

Doubt   The second doubt arises in the minds of those who think of sin as a kind of social maladjustment. What has been called sin is not a wrong relationship toward God but toward men only.

Response   Many valuable contributions have been made by the societal studies of the present century. It would not be going too far to say that these studies are among the most crucial achievements of the modern mind. Though there are—and will always be—conflicting trends, they are so important for the future of mankind that our chief concern may well be whether or not they have come along in time to help save the human race from self-destruction.

Nevertheless, we are aware also of the inadequacies of these studies. They cannot as such identify the moral and theological meaning of man's wrongdoing. Here again everything depends on the reality and claims of God on men in the associational relationships. If God is being defied in these relationships, then men must reckon with Him as well as with their fellowmen. And of course this is what the Biblical writers have stated in no uncertain terms.

Besides this inadequate analysis of the nature of sin, social scientists tend to assume that the answers to man's basic moral problems are political, or economic, or cultural. So they tend to look wholly within society for its redemptive processes. There is much value in this. For few procedures are more important than those of identifying the concrete factors that influence men's lives. But any mere sociological approach is inadequate for two reasons. First, it does not sufficiently recognize the truth of the Biblical emphasis on man's initiative and his consequent moral responsibility for what he does. Second, it fails to recognize the activity of God in these very processes. Man needs to look beyond the claims and resources of human societies in order to do his most creative and redemptive work in societies. He needs to hear the voice of the living God who says, "For my thoughts are not your thoughts, neither are your ways my ways" (Isaiah 55:8).

Besides all this, the societal studies by their nature exclude from view the connection between man's sin and his destiny with God in the new community, beyond this present life. This is another serious deficiency in both the psychological and societal studies, but we need not discuss it further at this point.

Doubt   A third doubt sometimes goes with the first two. This is the doubt that there is any such thing as sin at all. Man is determined by forces beyond his control. Therefore, the Biblical teaching on sin is unrealistic. Is man really free to make choices and so turn away from God?

Response   We must begin by stating further what the problem is in its modern setting. The ancient doubt about man's freedom has returned to the scene armed with far more evidence than ever. What makes it modern is not the doubt itself but the massive array of data brought to bear on the problem of freedom as opposed to determinism. We must at least suggest something of these evidences. Biologists and chemists may give an impressive assortment of data to show that man acts the way he does because of physiological and chemical processes. They may expound on the thesis: "Man is what he eats." Or they may show how chemicals affect our sense experiences, or our emotions, or even our thinking. The mass of data here can appear overwhelming. It is but a step from all this to the thought that everything man does, from the brutal acts of tyrants to the magnificent deeds of saints, originates in body chemistry rather than in his responsible freedom. So we can easily understand the doubts about the power of choice arising from contemporary experience.

From another quarter, Sigmund Freud said that our conscious thinking and acting are caused by subconscious processes. He went so far as to say that "it is impossible to think of a number, or even a name, of one's own free will." Similarly, students of society and culture have suggested that man's "free" decisions are actually caused by larger environmental and cultural factors. So, in effect, man is free to do the necessary or nothing. Even among some theologians there is still the idea that man is so caught up in forces other than himself that he can no more turn to God by his own choice than a cork can change its course in a swift stream.

The basic response to all forms of determinism, whether physiological, chemical, psychological, sociological or theological, is to show that it is contrary to the evidences of relevant experience. We know, of course, that man's freedom of choice is limited by many factors. But this does not rule out the kind of freedom we are discussing here.

Briefly, there are five arguments drawn from experience which, when taken together, are decisive in favor of the belief that man has some real power of contrary choice. First, with rare exceptions, a man feels free in the moment of decision. So any theory of absolute determinism founders on this elemental and universal experience. Second, in nearly all community relationships, including legal ones, men assume that they and others are responsible in varying degrees for what they do. A man's signature, except when forced at gun point or in some other way, is a sure sign of his ability to make responsible choices. Third, without freedom there would be no truth or knowledge. This argument is as decisive as any. For if it does not hold, science and all other knowledge would be undermined. Why? Because everyone would have to believe as he did on any matter. If one scientist or theologian disagreed with another, it would be because he *had* to do so. In that case which one would be right? Where all beliefs are equally determined by external or internal factors, none can be accepted as true or false. So the freedom to reflect, to withhold judgment, to weigh evidence is a presupposition of science and all knowledge. Fourth, without freedom of choice man would be reduced to a puppet and lose his dignity and value. Fifth, progress in any sphere would be an illusion because all achievements would be the products of forces beyond man's control.

In the light of these arguments the Biblical teaching on sin can be taken seriously by those who must first analyze the problem for themselves. For it is evident that all forms of absolute determinism, though containing some truth, are basically false theories. The way remains wide open, then, for the recovery of the sense of a responsible relationship between man and God. This, of course, is where sin can become a possibility.

Doubt   A fourth doubt about the Biblical teaching arises in the minds of those who feel that while man has a measure of freedom there is no need to exaggerate his sinfulness. Is there not the danger of becoming morbid on the subject? In part this doubt arises from the fear of damage to human personality from an undue stress on sin. The prophets and others make too much of man's sin. Christians have also overemphasized man's supposed "original sin" or depravity and his worthlessness as a creature.

Response   It is possible to have morbid conceptions of wrongdoing. Guilt can become a complex rather than a creative negative factor in the religious life. The efforts to overcome the fear of guilt may lead to an unrealistic pietism or to a barren legalism. Sometimes people have tried to keep their lives so antiseptically right that they have become bogged down in trivialities. And it is beyond question true that the doctrine of "original sin" has often been overworked.

But as we look toward the twenty-first century this is not a major problem. The more pervasive problem lies in the direction of an easygoing attitude toward right and wrong in relation to God. This does two things. First, it keeps a man from the healthy attitude of recognizing that human nature does have built-in problems. Knowing this, he can strive more realistically for the best values. Second, it reduces the Christian understanding of God's redemptive concern and gracious assistance to nonsense. If gross selfishness and pride are not so bad, why bother with God's forgiving and creative love? If mediocrity is accepted as par for life, why look to the community of faith for worship and spiritual resources?

In this connection we can see the point of Augustine's criticism of Pelagius. The latter stressed the idea that the primary mission of Jesus was to be a much needed example to men; beyond that there was no deep mysterious sphere of divine redemption through Him. Augustine, on the other hand, emphasized man's need for forgiveness and empowering grace from God. There is good reason to believe that he exaggerated man's depravity and sinfulness. But there was enough realism in his thought to correct the sentimentality of modernity. As we reflect on the problems of war and peace, race relations, crime and man's continuing chronic selfishness and inhumanity, we see that the Biblical teaching on sin is as relevant as ever.

Consequently, the emphasis of the Biblical writers on man's need for God's help, which is made available through faith, may have appeal again. The church's mission, with its preaching and sacraments rightly understood, may be seen anew in its relevance to the men who now look toward the twenty-first century. For selfishness, pride, injustice, complacency, meanness and mediocrity are still among man's most formidable problems. Therefore, repentance and faith, preaching and the sacrament of the Lord's supper, worship and prayer, love and service are as relevant as ever as we look toward the twenty-first century. If these evils in human experience are not taken seriously, men tend to move toward mediocrity. And certainly it does not require the grace of God to be mediocre persons. It would be pleasant to dream that the basic conflicts and bunglings of human nature would be resolved by the coming of a new century. But both the Biblical writers and obvious experience join in the reminder that this is an illusion.

The prophets, Jesus, and the apostles insist that sin or wrongdoing is not only real but the primal tragedy of man as a creature made for a magnificent destiny with God. Their heavy emphasis on the sin-problem would be morbid only if there were no clear answer to it. But in the Christian religion sin can be faced in all its depth and ranges because God's answer to it is proclaimed. Therefore, on the positive side, the belief in God's redemptive and creative love is the central teaching of Christianity. To it we turn next.

Part IV

On the Redemptive-Creative Process

9

JESUS CHRIST AND THE
REDEMPTIVE-CREATIVE PROCESS

Whenever human problems are taken seriously men devote time and effort to the search for answers. For example, where poverty is accepted with indifference, as an inevitable condition of millions, who will search for answers? Where racial prejudice is viewed as natural, normal, and acceptable, who will strive for ways and means to rise above it? Where any social problem is viewed with a casual air, then the political, business and civic leaders will do nothing about it. In Christianity, God's redemptive-creative process is taken seriously because man is seen as a creature who desperately needs divine assistance.

THE MAIN ALTERNATIVE VIEWS

Reinhold Niebuhr expressed with clarity and vigor the main options regarding the redemptive process. He said that there have been three approaches.

First, man is a part of nature and the answer to his problems comes from rising above the natural realm of change by means of his changeless reason. Only in this way can man free himself from the recurring cycles and ceaseless changes of nature. The supreme representative of this mode of thought was Plato. While he and other spokesmen of Greek classicism said a good many other things, this was a basic feature of their understanding of the redemptive-creative process. Similar to this is any perspective that finds deliverance for men by seeking a vision of the eternal values, whether intellectual, esthetic, moral, or religious.

Second, says Niebuhr, there is the modern approach that thinks of the development of man's power and freedom as the answer to every problem "as the way of emancipation from every human evil." Some today would use Bonhoeffer's words, "man has come of age" to express this idea. There are numberless variations on this theme. The Marxist defines the redemptive process in terms of the revolutionary changes effected by the proletariat in the economic structure. Others see "salvation" by means of educational and cultural transformations of one sort or another. Still others, look to changes in political platforms and structures. Some have thought of these redemptive processes as totally human. Others have seen them as in part the divine activity working through long-range evolutionary processes toward better and better societies.

Third, there is the vastly different approach of the Bible.

THE BIBLICAL TEACHING

Instead of seeking refuge in an abstract eternal realm, the Biblical writers call for a faith-relationship with the living God. Instead of placing confidence in history as itself redemptive, they require men to look above themselves and beyond history to the God who involves Himself with men in history.

The Biblical teaching on what I have called the redemptive-creative process is that God takes the initiative in doing three things in behalf of men. First, He accepts and forgives them. Second, He empowers, inspires, and renews them in their desire to realize moral and spiritual values. Third, He conquers death for the purpose of inaugurating a new era of creative living.

The divine redemptive-creative process in each of these comes to focus in Jesus Christ. But the total process is understood to have begun at creation and to have developed amid the struggles and problems in the history of Israel. Abraham, Moses,

David, and the prophets symbolize the extensive periods of preparation in the movement from the old covenant to the new. Moreover, the redemptive-creative process, which came to focus in Jesus Christ, continues after His crucifixion and resurrection through the agency of the Holy Spirit in the community of faith. Seen in this light, the whole process is one in which God has taken the initiative to act with and for men to accomplish some of His aims for creating and sustaining the universe and man.

The essential Biblical message here is that God loves man, is concerned about him, and is unfailingly ready to release His resources for forgiveness and creative living. If man fails to respond in faith, he not only misses the sense of the presence of God (the greatest of all experiences) he also fails to receive those divine resources for creative living without which no man can reach the highest flights of service to his fellowmen.

In this chapter we shall consider the Biblical teaching under the first two of the three areas of the redemptive-creative activity mentioned above. The third will be treated in a later chapter on the life everlasting.

First, God takes the initiative in accepting and forgiving men. We have already seen that the Biblical writers take sin seriously. So much so that the tragedy of man's wrongness here before God is the major negative theme of the Bible. It is a presupposition of the Biblical revelation on man's situation that he needs to experience the sense of being forgiven and accepted by God.

But the seriousness of sin could never have been communicated among the people of Israel without the Ten Commandments and the covenant-relationship between those people and their God. Something of the covenant-relationship was begun through Abraham, Isaac and Jacob. But Moses was the main leader in this because he specified the Commandments whereby men could identify their trueness to or disobedience of God. In other words, the requirements of God needed to be made clear. The prophets, then, could keep calling the people back from their disobedience of the Commandments to repentance and to the divine acceptance again. All this represents one of the most remarkable developments in the history of religion.

So man's sense of the need for forgiveness is in exact proportion to his awareness of turning away from the requirements of God. Mediocre people, or those who have low moral standards, will feel no need for forgiveness. For this comes only where there is the vision of what men ought to be and of what is expected of them. The God of the Bible has great expectations of men. He created them for a lofty purpose. Hence, the sense of sin, the need for forgiveness and acceptance. For this reason the voice of the prophets calling men to repentance and to the renewal of their covenant was like fresh air over the land. And the assurance of God's eagerness to forgive and to accept was like refreshing rains falling down on parched land.

> Come now, let us reason together,
>   says the Lord:
> though your sins are like scarlet,
>   they shall be as white as snow;
> though they are red like crimson,
>   they shall become like wool (Isaiah 1:18).

God's initiative in forgiving and accepting men has expressed itself with the fullest possible clarity in Jesus Christ. He, like some of the prophets before Him, moved beyond the Ten Commandments as the primal instrument for awakening man's sense of wrongness with God. He led them to see that the inner spirit and attitude of a man is the true basis for identifying the breaking of God's covenant. Micah saw this when he called men to justice, kindness, and humility (6:8).

But in the Sermon on the Mount and in the parables and other sayings of Jesus we notice a remarkable shift from the *legalism* of the Old Testament to the *personalism* of the New. Here it is not merely what we do to our neighbor but how we feel toward him. Do we forgive in our hearts? Are we actually concerned for him in his need? Is it the sustained disposition of our souls to seek God's Kingdom and thus to love those whom God loves, namely, all men?

Here the ranges of sin were expanded, and man felt all the more keenly the deeper meaning of his disobedience. Consequently, there had to be a commensurate extension and clarification of the process whereby men could be forgiven. This was effected through the understanding in the New Testament that God chose to act through the life and death of Jesus Christ to forgive and restore men to His good favor. No longer were there to be the sacrifices and burnt offerings. Now there was to be the clear understanding that God had communicated His eagerness to forgive and accept through Jesus Christ. This was effected supremely in the suffering and crucifixion of Jesus. So wherever the cross is at the center of preaching, sacrament, and worship, there men are reminded again of what God has done in their behalf to communicate His readiness to forgive. The Biblical language used throughout Christendom to express all this is simply that Jesus Christ died for the sins of the whole world.

Some contemporary thinkers make a big point of the way Christianity, in looking back to the cross and to what God did in the past, gets bogged down in the past. But they forget the main point, namely, that Christians look back to the crucified Jesus because they find there the *promise* of forgiveness and new life for the present and future. The Christians never look back to Jesus Christ crucified and risen without seeing in Him this magnificent promise of hope and victory. This is why, in nearly all Christian churches, the cross is the sovereign symbol and is the structural basis of the Eucharist.

Secondly, the Biblical writers go far beyond God's initiative in forgiving and accepting men and speak of God's creative operations in man's life. It is one thing to be forgiven, it is another to be empowered and equipped for creative living.

A basic presupposition of the Bible is that man is called by God to enter upon a magnificent pilgrimage or adventure while he is on earth. There is in nearly all of the outstanding characters of the Bible a divine discontent with things as they are.

Abraham envisions the promised land. Moses, after being confronted by God, felt he had to lead his people out of their slavery toward that land. The prophets were men deeply dissatisfied with the way people were living. John the Baptist came preaching the necessity for repentance and change. Jesus came announcing the inauguration of a new era. "The kingdom of God is at hand." Paul, though fighting the good fight, was always looking for more of God's benefits. And, of course, even better things were to come to the faithful in the new age beyond death.

The Biblical writers teach that men are not only called to creative and adventurous living here and now but are assured of God's help in the process. This help is needed for two reasons. First, it is necessary because there are so many difficulties along the way. Life is like an obstacle course. Besides the gravitational pull toward selfishness, self-indulgence, and mediocrity, there are the constant battles against ill-health, fatigue, discouragement, poverty, and at times the indifference and even the inhumanity of others. The Bible is a book about men in discouraging and difficult circumstances who were given the power to see life through on a higher plane. The people of Israel had a fight on their hands from start to finish. The Biblical writers do not address themselves to men who want to avoid the strife and run from the moral issues of the human world. They saw clearly that it is hard enough to live courageously even with God's help; it is impossible without it.

Against this background the great sustaining passages of the Bible have their universal appeal. Men can walk without fear through the valley of the shadow of death because God is with them. The Lord is their refuge and strength, a very present help in trouble. Their help comes from the Lord, who made heaven and earth.

He gives power to the faint,
    and to him who has no might he increases strength.
Even youths shall faint and be weary,
    and young men shall fall exhausted;

but they who wait for the Lord shall renew their strength,
>   they shall mount up with wings like eagles,
they shall run and not be weary,
>   they shall walk and not faint (Isaiah 40:29–31).

Jesus forewarned His disciples of temptations and trials. And He left not only His words but His example as one who triumphed over the worst that could be done to any man. "In the world," He said, "you have tribulation; but be of good cheer, I have overcome the world" (John 16:33).

Paul was the master spokesman of the earliest followers of Jesus in talking about the divine resources for men in difficult circumstances. The love of God in Christ was so effective that nothing could separate the faithful from it, not tribulation, nor poverty, nor persecution, nor death, nor anything in all creation (Romans 8:35–39).

There is a second reason why men need the divine resources for creative living. This is because they cannot find within themselves and in the many resources of this world the fullest measure of inspiration for creativity. There are, of course, many resources for the most productive use of talents both in the individual and in civilized societies. But the Biblical writers are convinced that, over and beyond these, men require God's help for the most creative and adventurous living. The finite needs the support of the Infinite, the imperfect calls for the resources of the Perfect, and the transient requires the help of the Eternal.

The call to creative advance is especially clear in relation to the Kingdom of God. To this end men will receive divine help. Jesus said that those who hunger and thirst for righteousness will be satisfied. The prayer for God's will to be done on earth as in heaven presupposes the divine assistance toward that end. Jesus taught that man is to love God with all his heart, soul, mind and strength (Mark 12:30). This too implies the call to growth in all aspects of life that are related to God. Paul teaches that for those who trust God there is the "immeasurable greatness of his power" (Ephesians 1:19). He prayed that God would fill the faithful "with the knowledge of his will in all spiritual wisdom and understanding" (Colossians 1:9).

By implication the Biblical writers suggest that all talents belong to God and are to be used for His glory. God has a claim on every man. And it was God who gave to man the ". . . ability and intelligence to know how to do any work . . ." (Exodus 36:1). The main point here concerning God's help for creative living is this: Whenever men open themselves to the God of the Bible, they begin to sense the divine pull toward the best use of whatever abilities they have. They become aware that God wants them to take their minds as far as they can. They realize also that God will go with them and strengthen them in these endeavors.

The primary agent of this creative process on God's side is the Holy Spirit who is God in His nearness. We shall see in a later chapter that the distinctive mission of the Holy Spirit is to draw men toward Christ and His community. But it is also a part of the work of the Holy Spirit to encourage and strengthen all men in every worthy endeavor.

SOME MODERN DOUBTS AND RESPONSES TO THEM

We have observed at the outset that the modern mind doubts the reality of any divine redemptive process. And, of course, the thought that such a process would come to focus in Jesus Christ seems to be more mythological than real. Such historically significant words in the Christian vocabulary as "incarnation" and "atonement" belong among the mythological accretions of the centuries. The modern mind doubts also that Christians can specify the redemptive-creative work of God. Against the background of these general observations we may now turn to doubts in particular that disturb many sincere inquirers.

Doubt   There are doubts about Jesus Christ Himself. We are not certain that He lived; and, if He did, we are not sure of the records about Him. How then can there be a redemptive-creative process coming to focus in Him? Besides this, why look back? Why not think of the present and future as the sources of meaning and salvation?

Response   There are several interrelated doubts here. One has to do with the historical Jesus. Did He live? What do we really know about him? After considering these questions we shall turn to the scandal of saying that God's redemptive-creative process came to unique utterance through this one historical figure.

There are three indispensable factors in understanding Jesus Christ as He is presented in the New Testament, namely, historical events, the interpretation of those events, and the call to respond to God's appeal through Christ. If any one of these is omitted, something is missed and we fall into a one-sided or distorted view. So if we leave out or neglect the historical Jesus, we turn the gospels into myth or legend and lose the sense of history with which Christians have always been concerned. Our interest here is in the historical Jesus.

How do we know that Jesus lived and that the gospel materials portray Him as He actually was? The best answer to this that I know is that the gospel writers themselves show a keen interest in historical persons, settings and events. This becomes evident when we read their accounts with care. To be sure, they also had other interests in mind. They may have written to enrich worship services, or to combat false teachings, or to proclaim the gospel. But among these interests (and in support of them) was this concern to portray events as they actually occurred.

There are at least three strong reasons for believing that the four gospels give us essentially accurate accounts of Jesus. First, the interest in historical accuracy is presupposed in the heritage of the authors of Matthew, Mark, Luke, and John. The Hebrew religion was *historically* oriented. God acted in the events of Israel's history. God revealed Himself in and through historical persons and happenings. So there would have been a strange discontinuity with the religion of Israel if these writers had suddenly turned to a Christ who did not live or to one of whose earthly life we knew little or nothing. It is unreasonable to believe that these men, who were conditioned to think of God as acting in history, would turn to mythological constructs about a Nazarene as the center of God's revelation.

Second, the gospels themselves reflect a keen interest in historical persons and events. Jesus was born in a Roman province, nurtured in the Jewish faith, and crucified under Pontius Pilate, all of which were historical realities.

The gospel writers not only give a brief identification of the setting of Jesus' life in the Roman province, in the Jewish background; they also report specific historical-geographical settings. Bethlehem, Nazareth, Capernaum, Samaria, the Decapolis, little Bethany, Jerusalem, the Sea of Galilee, the River Jordan, the Mount of Olives and innumerable other geographical places are designated. Then there are the more particular sites, such as the temple, the pool of Bethesda, a specific synagogue here and there, Jacob's well, and the like. Of course our knowledge of these places comes not only from the gospels but also from archaeology, geography, and studies in Jewish and other literature.

Moreover, particular individuals are named or identified with whom Jesus had direct personal dealings. There was John who baptized Him, the twelve whom He selected, Mary, Martha and Lazarus whom He visited often, Jairus the president of one of the synagogues, Nicodemus who came to Him by night, Bartimeus, whose sight He restored. There were Caiaphas and Judas, Pilate and Barabbas, Simon of Cyrene, and Joseph of Arimathea. Then there were those many individuals who, though not named, are spoken of as real persons to whom Jesus responded realistically in life situations. A palsied man, a leper, a crippled person seeking help at the pool of Bethesda, a blind man, a woman suffering from hemorrhages, a Syrophoenician woman and her sick daughter, a rich ruler, these and others crowd in upon the historically realistic situations in the life of Jesus. There were also the Pharisees, the Saducees, and others, of whom we have considerable knowledge from sources outside the gospels.

The point is that the gospel writers so present their accounts of Jesus within the person-to-person settings of this earthly life that He cannot be properly understood apart from historical events. Jesus lived as a person among persons; He reacted to questions and situations realistically. He taught in parables drawn from the stuff of life. And He often expressed ideas made more graphic because of their opposition to some of the teachings of the priests and scribes of His day.

Jeremias, in his great book on the parables of Jesus suggests that the elaborate parables were used to justify (against the Pharisees and others) Jesus' mission and preaching to sinners, to the poor, to the needy, to outsiders. Their main object, he says, was "defence and vindication of the gospel." What impresses us here is the realism of the gospel writers in portraying Jesus in crucial interpersonal relations. This is why Jeremias insists that ". . . the conclusion is inevitable that in reading the parables we are dealing with a particularly trustworthy tradition, and are brought into immediate relation with Jesus."

Again, the accounts of the passion, crucifixion and resurrection of Jesus show graphically the interest of the gospel writers in historical events. When one admits that the crucifixion took place (as even the most skeptical are apt to do) he has already affirmed far more than meets the eye. For this requires an explanation in terms of the many events that preceded it. The explanation must have the kind of authentic ring we find implicit in the gospel accounts. The same can be said of the experiences of those who witnessed the empty tomb and the risen Lord.

A third reason for believing in the historical Jesus is that the Christian movement following His death and resurrection cannot be explained without Him.

We do not get the impression from the study of Christian history that we are dealing with men who followed a half-legendary figure who went about doing things in a storybook world. Could such an historic community of faith have come out of the *Iliad,* or the *Odyssey*? Yet even these epics had many roots in history. Do we not all recognize vast oceans between Socrates as an historical figure and the half-legendary characters of Homer? How much more is this the case with Jesus whose earthly life was of very special interest to His many followers. The very principle of apostolic succession (in which the Christian ministry goes back to Jesus through the apostles) shows the historical concerns of Christianity from beginning to end.

Before leaving this theme of the importance of the historical Jesus for Christianity, we need to respond to these questions: Why get bogged down in the past? Why not look to the present and future? Nothing could reflect a more superficial understanding of Christianity than to suppose that it is a religion that gets lost in the past. On the contrary, it has its appeal almost entirely because it connects God's acts in the past with His promise of forgiveness and new life both now and in the future. The Christian receives God's grace now and lives in hope with respect of the future because he has revealed in Christ his available resources for any future. This is why Christianity is necessarily the religion of hope.

Doubt   A second kind of doubt that naturally arises in the modern mind as it thinks about Jesus Christ and the supposed redemptive-creative process concerns the "scandal of particularity." This doubt can perhaps be best stated in the form of a question: Why should we suppose that God would single out a particular man, Jesus, as the one through whom to reveal Himself, to forgive sins, and to share His promise for the future?

Response   This question has been asked from the earliest days of Christianity. Paul wrote of preaching Christ crucified as "a stumbling-block to Jews and folly to Gentiles, but to those who are called, both Jews and Greeks, Christ the power of God and the wisdom of God" (1 Corinthians 1:23–24).

Whether ancient or modern, it is a real problem. Many people find it hard to believe that the God of the universe would select a particular people and a single individual as distinctive media for revealing Himself to mankind. I see no way of completely doing away with the "scandal of particularity" here. But I do not share with those theologians who suggest that this involves either a paradox or a contradiction. Some of them go so far as to say that we are to believe in God's revelation despite the contradiction. Others even say we are to believe *because of* the paradox or the contradiction. This seems to me clearly unsound. No beliefs that contradict each other can be accepted. I suggest here that everything depends on God's way of revealing Himself and of acting in behalf of men. If God chose to do this through a man who was specially open and responsive to Him, there is no scandal about this. If we do not find the event repeated, and therefore verifiable as are recurring events, this does not make for any logical difficulty. For there are many events that never happened again, but which nevertheless occurred.

There are at least two considerations that may help to show the plausibility of the Biblical teaching. First, we are not dealing with an individual, Jesus, who came upon the scene like a bolt out of the blue. There is the vast *epic of revelation,* beginning with Abraham and moving through Moses, David, and the prophets toward fulfillment in Jesus Christ. There is the long history of the people of Israel, with their varied experiences of triumph and disaster, and the recurring responses to God. In fact, though the details are not filled in, there is the even more comprehensive movement from creation to the love of God made known in Jesus Christ.

So everything goes back to the one true God who used the only means that could get across to men His love, namely, human beings in historical situations. But these men had to follow each other in some kind of continuity. Otherwise there would have been only broken arcs or isolated fragments of truth. Scattered pieces of colored glass do not make a rose window. Isolated individuals, however saintly, could not disclose the reality of God in history. It relieves the tension some to realize that God involved Himself in a long process, wherein prophets, priests, and wise men followed upon each other in a vast progression that reached its summit point in Jesus Christ.

The second consideration that helps us to see the plausibility of the Biblical teaching here is this. *Theoretically,* the "scandal of particularity" is inescapable in the sense that no one could have predicted God would have acted in this way. Why should God, the Ground of all things, act in this way and not in some other kind of event whether unique or not? But *practically* we do in fact find that through Jesus Christ (as in no one else) men have sensed the presence of God and found their lives renewed by Him. As Paul said, Christ crucified is the power of God and the wisdom of God made available to men. It is very difficult to know what to do with a fact other than to accept it and, where indicated, to act on it.

Doubt   A third doubt about the divine redemptive-creative process concerns what seems like an unreasonable emphasis on the sin-and-forgiveness syndrome as the main obstacle to salvation. Paul stressed this. Luther made it the central theme of his theology under the formula: "Justification by faith alone." In the Lutheran heritage everything else seems to have been based on this one principle pertaining to sin-and-forgiveness. This has been true in large measure throughout all Christendom. The cross or crucifix and the sacrament of Holy Communion are central. Here doubts arise from within Christianity itself as to whether or not this emphasis is contrary to the full teaching of the Bible. Doubts arise also concerning the relevance of a Christianity, the focus of which is on the one issue of sin-and-forgiveness. Does Christianity speak to the total needs of men beyond this?

Response   Such doubts too are wholesome. They assume that there is an enduring place for some emphasis on sin-and-forgiveness. But they question the degree of stress put on this in the Bible and in the church. Forgiveness is important in the Bible and in particular in the teaching of Jesus. But can this be the center around which all else revolves? Paul wrote that one of the teachings "of first importance" he received after he became a Christian was that ". . . Christ died for our sins in accordance with the scriptures . . ." (1 Corinthians 15:3). But, again, is this the basis on which all his other teachings rest? A study of Christian history, of its preaching, prayers, sacraments, liturgy, and worship, reveals that the forgiveness of sin is a central theme of the Christian religion. But is it the be-all and end-all?

It is not true to the Biblical teaching as a whole to stress sin-and-forgiveness to the neglect of God's creative acts in human life. The good news of God's forgiving love will always be an essential feature of Christian teaching and preaching. Men can be forgiven no matter what they have done. But we are to think of this as a part of the larger work of calling men to move with God toward a meaningful future. We are not only justified (forgiven) by faith. We are made open and receptive to God's creative activity in transforming, renewing, and redirecting the lives of men. More than this, we act on the *promise* of God that He will go with us into the future. Consequently, there is good reason for the modern mind to question the one-sided stress on sin-and-forgiveness to the neglect of the total action of the grace of God.

Here is where the theology of Wesley and of many thinkers in the Catholic heritage is needed to balance the theology of Luther. Forgiveness is only the start of the life redirected and renewed for creative service. To use traditional language, forgiveness is the beginning of sanctification. The cross and the sacrament of Holy Communion stand for two things: forgiveness and the call to self-giving courageous service. Resources for creative living are thus released to man through Jesus Christ. This redemptive-creative process may have sudden beginnings as in flashes of illumination or moments of decision. But generally it becomes the silent unheralded process of faith whereby men are progressively delivered from the stultifying hold of pathos and inner conflict and released for the life of hope.

We may merely summarize by saying that the Biblical teaching on sin-and-forgiveness needs to be understood as a part of the larger activity of God in man's behalf. Therefore, while the Protestant stress on justification by faith alone stands, it cannot be wrenched from the total movement of the Christian life and still appeal to the modern mind. The Reformation has had its day. The new Reformation which accents the total redemptive-creative action of God must come to the fore. The work of God as redemptive-creative assists men both to begin and continue their adventures with God in the creative use of their talents. No one ever enters into the full promise of this on earth. But there is enough power felt, even within man's distracted and disturbed existence, to live in the hope of receiving more grace for the creative advances with God into the future.

Because we shall be considering in more detail the creative activity of God in men in some of the chapters that follow, we need not pursue it further here.

10

THE HOLY SPIRIT AND THE
RESOURCES FOR LIVING

Some describe the present era as marked by the sense of the absence of God. They say that modern men cannot find assignable meaning in the idea of God's presence because they have no experience of it. Christianity, on the other hand, has said that God graciously makes Himself and His resources available to men whenever they respond to Him with honesty and faith. The awareness of the immediate presence and influence of God is the essence of vital religion. This aspect of Christianity has been developed primarily under the teaching on the Holy Spirit.

THE MAIN ALTERNATIVE VIEWS

The major views on the Holy Spirit range all the way from those which deny the operation of the Spirit altogether to those which regard Him as actively at work in the life of every Christian. We shall turn now to a brief statement of some of these options.

First, there is the view that it is meaningless to speak of the divine presence in any form. Such language has no assignable reference to experience, particularly to sense experience.

Second, there is the theory that begins with the naturalistic presuppositions of the modern mind and therefore assumes that there are no spiritual or nonmaterial energies. All talk about the Holy Spirit, then, is another example of man's inexhaustible capacity to become the victim of illusions.

Third, among Christians there are many views that express aspects of the Biblical teaching. Some think of the Holy Spirit primarily as moving into the lives of men in the form of inner suggestions, impressions, and hunches. Here the stress is on divine guidance. Others think of His work chiefly as outer signs and unusual behavior.

Fourth, there are within the church many who view the work of the Holy Spirit more comprehensively. Here again there are various approaches. Some tend to identify the work of the Holy Spirit with man's highest ideals and aspirations. Man seeks ideal values such as goodness, beauty and truth. This deep inner impulse is thought of as the work of God in the life of man. In keeping with this way of thinking some view the Holy Spirit as all the good factors at work in interpersonal relations. This may be called the immanental view because God's presence is actually identified with man as he lives in community. Perhaps the most comprehensive statement of an immanental view was made by Hegel who identified the Spirit with all the operations of God in the progressive realizations of culture and civilization.

Others who think comprehensively view the work of the Spirit in relation to mystical experiences. They suggest that the Holy Spirit is the unseen power working in men to merge their spirits into the divine Spirit. Or, His work is to lead men step by step up the ladder until they receive the vision of God. The goal of the Spirit's work is either absorption into the divine Being or the beatific vision of God. Perhaps the highest expression of a mystical view is found in the writings of certain philosophical and theological minds. They think of the Holy Spirit primarily as the divine presence in human experience. Men sense God's presence and this is the work of the Spirit.

These various approaches to the Holy Spirit (which merely hint at the innumerable options on this theme) suggest that perhaps in the Bible itself there are different ways of understanding the Spirit's work. This we must now consider.

THE BIBLICAL TEACHING

As is so often the case, the Biblical teaching here cannot easily be brought into a single theme. Nevertheless, an attempt will be made to show that the developing teaching of the Bible brings together its various approaches and emphases into an essentially unified view. This view, with some exceptions, is only broadly and vaguely present in the Old Testament. The Spirit of God, or God in His nearness, was manifest on a certain level in the creation of the universe and man. He was present in the processes of sustaining the universe. He was present also in some sense in every individual within the community of Israel. He manifested Himself in the moral and spiritual force of the prophets. There was also the promised outpouring of the Spirit on all men (Joel 2:28–29). All of this is a part of the large background and atmosphere that prepared the way for the New Testament teaching on the Holy Spirit. Against that background the writers of the New Testament brought a new emphasis on the Holy Spirit that grew out of the experiences of the earliest Christians.

A living faith at last comes down to this: God enters into and vitally affects the lives of men. God had been present with the outstanding men of the Old Testament. In the New Testament what we find is a new release of God's presence and energy. This fact is clearly asserted by the various writers. It is even identified as the fulfillment of Joel's prophecy (Acts 2:17–21). This is one of the reasons for speaking of these distinctively Christian canonical writings as the *New* Testament. The Christian teaching on the Holy Spirit emerged out of this new release of divine energy and influence. In fact, it *had* to emerge for these new realities in religious experience. The doctrine of the Holy Spirit was necessary to explain what those early Christians knew and felt.

This brings us to the developing teaching of the New Testament on the Holy Spirit. What are its distinctive characteristics and its indispensable features? There are at least four thoughts which in their interrelatedness constitute the New Testament teaching on the Holy Spirit.

1. The first, though not distinctive to the New Testament, is indispensable to it. This is the idea that God and man are so much akin to each other by God's arrangement that the Spirit is present on some level in every man. This is to say again that whatever else God is He has revealed Himself in the Bible as the One who involves Himself intimately with men in their personal and interpersonal relationships. This in turn is made possible by man's essential kinship with God. In this way the whole idea of the divine presence has an initial plausibility.

2. A thought that goes into the New Testament understanding of the Holy Spirit is that His work is inseparable from the mission of Jesus Christ. Here we do not find a theory of the divine presence in general. Rather we find a view of God working in the lives of men in community under the sway of Jesus Christ. A distinctive teaching in the New Testament on the Holy Spirit is that He acts to continue the work begun by Jesus Christ.

Three sources in the New Testament come together in support of this major theme. First, there are the preparatory words of Jesus as reported in the Fourth Gospel (John 14:16, 26; 15:26; 16:5–15). Second, there are the events of Pentecost and of those that followed upon it as described in the Book of Acts. Third, there are the judicious and inspired utterances on the Holy Spirit by the apostle Paul.

All of these, where carefully studied are seen to come together on this one theme that the Holy Spirit brings home to men God's gracious work through Jesus Christ. Jesus said of the Spirit, "He will glorify me, for he will take what is mine and declare it to you" (John 16:14). At Pentecost there was a sound like the rushing of a mighty wind, and tongues as of fire appeared to rest on each one present, some of whom spoke in foreign languages (Acts 2:2–4). This last is not to be confused with speaking in unintelligible sounds, which is to be discussed later. It is easy to miss here the one thing that stands out above everything else in that first Christian Pentecost. This is the interpretation that Peter put upon it when he preached on Jesus of Nazareth. He said, among other things, ". . . God has made him both Lord and Christ, this Jesus whom you crucified" (Acts 2:36). What happened basically was that for the first time in any settled way the disciples and others realized in their hearts and minds that God had acted graciously and mightily in man's behalf through Jesus Christ. This divine action was for the first time grasped as God's way of promising new life in His Kingdom to those who respond.

Paul emphasized this theme too when he wrote, "Therefore I want you to understand that no one speaking by the Spirit of God ever says 'Jesus be cursed!' and no one can say 'Jesus is Lord' except by the Holy Spirit" (1 Corinthians 12:3). The divine presence is always understood by Paul as expressing the goodness and promise of God revealed in Jesus Christ. So Paul wrote, ". . . the Lord is the Spirit, and where the Spirit of the Lord is, there is freedom" (2 Corinthians 3:17).

3. This brings us to a thought that is a part of the New Testament teaching. This is the idea that the Holy Spirit is active in every important stage of man's religious experience. From beginning to end, the Holy Spirit is dynamically operative to lead men into ever-developing experiences of communion and work with God. It is easy to miss the main thrust of the New Testament writers by overemphasizing certain verses or chapters. One-sided approaches, which misread the Biblical teaching, can be avoided by holding before the mind the idea that it is the mission of the Holy Spirit to deal with men at all stages of their life with God for the purpose of reshaping them after the image of Christ. No atomistic view will stand careful scrutiny, nor will any idea of the Spirit as primarily passive. As

God in His nearness, He is a dynamic agent working to draw men to God and to help them grow in their life with God. Specifically, a part of the Biblical teaching in its developing movement seems to be that the Holy Spirit works at three levels of man's life in relation to God. These have been referred to in traditional language by the terms prevenient grace, regeneration, and sanctification. Without binding ourselves to those terms, we may nevertheless see the point of the Biblical teaching for the stages in man's Christian experience.

The Holy Spirit begins His work in men even before they make any conscious response to God. This "prevenient grace" is the grace that goes before grace. That is, in every man there is a God-given light. This is a basic presupposition of Christianity as a vital religion. It is the first stage in the process of becoming a Christian. The primary reality here is that men have a kind of intuitive awareness of God. They perceive from what they know about the world and about their own finite existence that God is. Paul directs himself to this when he writes, "For what can be known about God is plain to them, because God has shown it to them. Ever since the creation of the world his invisible nature, namely, his eternal power and deity, has been clearly perceived in the things that have been made . . ." (Romans 1:19–20). Paul addresses himself to another aspect of this God-given inner light as conscience when he writes of the Gentiles, "They show that what the law requires is written on their hearts . . ." (Romans 2:15).

All of this is to say that the Spirit of God is, from the very start, nearer to us than breathing, closer than hands and feet, even before we cross the threshold of grace. Every man has within him, then, the assistance of the Holy Spirit from the start. This enables him, along with his own response, to turn to God for new life and hope. This *primal presence of God* in all men is the sign and token of the further things God has in store for them. It prepares the way for those limitless levels of divine assistance that the New Testament speaks of as the grace of God.

The second stage in the process of becoming a Christian is

that of the rebirth of the soul by faith. The work of the Holy Spirit begins the actual process of salvation when a man consciously opens his life toward God by repentance, which is basic honesty, and faith, which is trust. This is sometimes called conversion, sometimes regeneration, and sometimes the new birth. It might even be called the new being. It is a part of the teaching of the New Testament that this new beginning with God is somehow made possible with the aid of the Spirit. The Spirit works coordinately with man's commitment and faith to make possible this new life in Christ. As Paul puts it, "For the law of the Spirit of life in Christ Jesus has set me free from the law of sin and death" (Romans 8:2).

The teaching of the New Testament here is that the Holy Spirit *recreates* human beings and thus sets them on their course toward an everlasting destiny. This is the gateway to the continuing adventure through life with God. It is the beginning of the conscious sense of the presence of God and of the purposive movement of life toward realizing God's aims. It is the start of what Paul calls life through the Spirit who dwells in those who have faith (Romans 8:11). Perhaps more than anything else it is the beginning of the life of hope for the future (here and hereafter) based on God's promise communicated through Christ.

This brings us to the third stage in the never-ending process of becoming a Christian, namely, the progressive adventure with God in creative and unselfish service. As the terms "new birth" and "regeneration" suggest, the first stage of the Christian life is the beginning of a developing process in man's relationships with God. The New Testament teaching is that God goes with men into their continuing struggles and efforts to grow spiritually. This teaching needs to be understood in the light of what has already been said about the revealed purpose of God for man's life on earth. The teaching on the Holy Spirit here is organically connected with that divine objective for human existence. Consequently, the Holy Spirit ever strives and moves within men to help them grow into the full stature of authentic Christians. The Spirit seeks particularly to equip

146

the soul of man for creative adventures in the life of love for others.

In the New Testament that teaching does not suggest that once a man receives the power of the Holy Spirit everything is smooth and easy. Far from it. Jesus Himself knew temptation and experienced the severest types of agony. Paul and the other apostles knew by direct experience the pangs of human existence. They encountered ruthless opposition in their efforts to communicate the good news. Nevertheless, they were aware of the unseen presence of the Spirit that makes for righteousness.

The Christian doctrine of sanctification, affirmed among some Catholics and Protestants, is not a theological oddity tacked onto the teaching of the New Testament. Rightly understood, it is an organic part of its developing teaching. God is concerned to create good men, men of courage, of compassionate concern for human well-being, men with a keen sense of justice, men who strive for peace, and men who have the love of Christ in their hearts. Therefore, He makes Himself available to aid men in this developing process. The Holy Spirit, then, progressively recreates the human spirit until it becomes increasingly effective in spreading the good news to others.

4. A thought that goes into the total teaching on the Holy Spirit is that His creative power is available only when men respond in honesty and faith. The Spirit does not force His way. He moves with men in their first impulse toward openness. Stage by stage, step by step, He awaits man's response even while aiding it.

The basic Biblical teaching here is that there is no cheap grace. Certain conditions are to be met. This major practical theme of the Bible is perhaps best expressed in the form of "if . . . then" propositions. If men fulfill the conditions, then God will give them the power to be authentic persons. If they let the Spirit who makes for righteousness preside over their thoughts and desires, then they will be able to manage their own lives more effectively and, at the same time, share the good news with others. If men are open to the mind of Christ so that His goodness becomes their master impulse, then they can move into the world as the makers of peace. But if not (since the Bible does not deal in magic) there is no basis for hoping that either individuals or nations will avoid the disasters of history or the plagues of mediocrity.

What conditions are to be met? The New Testament presents various conditions which we may reduce to seven. The first is to begin by identifying oneself with a community of faith. There is no isolated Christianity. The new beginning, the new sense of direction, whether gradual or sudden, takes place in community. The New Testament teaches also that as Christians are members one of another, they receive nurture and grow spiritually in the community of faith. The Holy Spirit works through those who share in the faith. Second, there must be the desire for a new mode of existence growing out of a deep discontent with life as it is. Third, there must be basic honesty before God, which is the same thing as repentance. Honesty before God is a devastating experience. A fourth condition is faith, or trust in God's power to forgive, to renew and to redirect a man as long as he lives. This faith is the absolute trust in God for the past, present, and future. A fifth condition is the cultivation of the life of prayer and the habits of Christian living in the community of faith. Sixth, there must be love that necessarily expresses itself in active involvement with men in need, in sacrificial sharing, and in service. Finally, there must be the hope nurtured by faith that the God who has revealed His love in Christ will go with men through this world and into the next for the realization of ever greater things in the Kingdom of Heaven.

SOME MODERN DOUBTS AND RESPONSES TO THEM

Many honest doubts arise in the modern mind concerning the Biblical teaching on the Holy Spirit. Of these we may select three for special consideration.

Doubt　　　First, there is the doubt arising from the sense of estrangement and alienation. God seems conspicuous by His absence. Impersonal processes and irrevocable laws seem more real than any supposed divine presence. There is always the apparent indifference of nature to human values. Along with this sense of cosmic isolation there is the sense of the pathos and tragedy of life. Man's pain, deformity, mediocrity and meanness add to the dimensions of this profound mood.

Response   This doubt is inevitable. It arises in its modern forms out of the expanded and rapidly increasing knowledge of nature and of man. Though not new, it has reached ranges and proportions that affect the morale of numberless well-trained individuals, as well as of whole civilizations. It arises out of contemporary experience. Modern man feels cut off from any ultimate Ground of meaning. When he turns from nature to human nature and to history he finds little basis for sustained hope. He feels with Pascal that man is "incapable of truth and of good." He knows what Schopenhauer meant when he said that man dreams of immortality and finds it difficult to know how to spend an afternoon. What is history but the "despair of philosophy"? Who can make sense out of it? The first response, then, is to recognize the reality and importance of this doubt and to know that there are no simple answers to it. In fact, Christians themselves often experience passing moods when these questions seem overwhelming. Other responses are indicated.

This doubt can receive sustained nurture only under two conditions. First, it is nurtured by world-views according to which impersonal reality and process are ultimate. Here I see no escape, no hope. If there is no ultimate Mind or Self, as Hocking calls it, then there is not the slightest reason to believe in the presence and creative influence of the Holy Spirit. Man is alone in the universe in all his moral and spiritual endeavors. A second condition under which this doubt is nurtured develops when men ignore the continuing reports of those who sense the presence of God. Some men are so habituated to physical things and processes, or to psychological and societal factors, or to purely theoretical realms of thought that they

149

tend to rule out without a reasonable hearing the reports of millions of men who have sensed the presence of God.

The conclusion would seem to be that this modern doubt about the Holy Spirit thrives on two deep-seated prejudices that have captured the modern mind, namely, the prejudice against the possibility of constructing a world-view in which Mind is ultimate, and the prejudice against giving a full hearing to the evidences from religious experience.

Doubt   This leads to a second major doubt, namely, concerning the validity of the Christian experience of the divine presence. There are reasons why it is hard to take seriously those who report the sense of God's presence. Their reports conflict with each other. Consequently, men who are carried away with the belief in the presence of the Holy Spirit have often separated themselves and their followers from others. The result has been the curious development of over two hundred and fifty denominations and splintered religious groups. In many of these there are special claims about the presence and power of the Holy Spirit. Often when men claim that the Holy Spirit affects their lives the results are for the worse. The "spirit" makes the wrong kinds of differences in men.

The Holy Spirit leads some to speak in unknown tongues. He leads others to feel guided to think and act in certain unusual ways. Here there is no limit to what men may report. Every conceivable prejudice and breakdown of intelligence has been supported by the claim that the Holy Spirit has revealed it. In the ethical realm religious history is full of instances when men, in the name of God, championed injustice and inhumanity. War, slavery, racial prejudice, ignorance, poverty, economic injustice, torture, indifference and mental quirks— all these have been rationalized by reference to the will of God. How then can we put confidence in all this?

Response   This kind of question is wholesome because it requires us to make a distinction between authentic and unauthentic Christianity. Such a distinction is made in all fields.

There is the authentic and the unauthentic in science, medicine, art, literature, music, romance, education, politics, business, and in every other important human interest.

The validity of Christian experience rests at last on the lives of the saints. Granting a world-view in which God is, their lives are the irrefutable evidences of the authenticity and validity of Christianity. Similarly, the saints in all religions disclose that there is something authentic in them all. Outstanding men have outstanding experiences. Those who experiment and adventure more persistently and resourcefully than others have much more to say than others.

The question then arises as to how we may distinguish between the authentic and unauthentic in religion. Christians at their best tend to unite in saying that the Bible is the primal source here. They agree also that the Bible must be interpreted in the light of Jesus Christ. The guiding principle, which enables us to separate authentic from unauthentic Christianity, is the *vast developing teaching of the Bible,* which moves toward fulfillment in Jesus Christ. He, then, becomes the measure: His teaching, His example, and the spiritual resources He has released. The authentic in Christianity must be measured in the light of the broad progressive movement of the Biblical revelation on the one hand, and of the quality of one's deeds on the other.

This is why all talk about the power and presence of the Holy Spirit must, in its content, be Christ-centered. We have seen that this is a central and unique feature of the New Testament teaching on the Spirit. He glorifies Jesus Christ. He brings home to men the spirit of Christ. He helps them to bear the kind of fruit that comes out of the spirit of Christ. This governing principle has saved the Church from the disaster of being overwhelmed by "spiritism." By "spiritism" I mean the belief in unseen powers that are said to break into men's lives and cause them to act and think in certain ways. Religion can be dangerous or beneficent, creative or destructive. In religion we are dealing with power, and misdirected power is dangerous. This is especially true where there is an emphasis on the working of the Spirit.

Christianity itself has often suffered from the influence of those who felt themselves to be under the sway of the Spirit. Speaking in unknown tongues may be an example of it. Entertaining all sorts of prejudices, racial and otherwise, may be another instance. Following impressions and hunches is another. Sometimes unusual manifestations come out of authentic movements of the Spirit. Christians remember that Jesus never spoke in tongues, nor did he teach men to do so. Paul spoke in tongues but cautioned men about this when he wrote, ". . . I would rather speak five words with my mind, in order to instruct others, then ten thousand words in a tongue" (1 Corinthians 14:19). Here the danger arises from the view that the Holy Spirit is arbitrary, unpredictable, without aim or order. This is not the Christian teaching.

The Holy Spirit always creates and nurtures the spirit of Christ in men. He always nurtures the hope for the future based on God's promise in Christ. The Spirit is not arbitrary, because He has a specific aim or mission, namely, that of making real in the lives of men the presence of the God who revealed His love in Jesus Christ. It is this fact that spares authentic Christianity of all the one-sided, curious, esoteric, and even ridiculous notions and practices concerning the power of the Spirit. This is why, in the New Testament itself, men are asked to "prove all things," to "believe not every spirit" and to "test the spirits to see whether they are of God; for many false prophets have gone out into the world." One of the works of the Holy Spirit, then, is to nurture in men that practical wisdom and insight the love of Christ implies.

Doubt   A third doubt about the work of the Holy Spirit arises when men try to identify assignable differences made in the lives of men by the Holy Spirit. The doubt here arises not from the wrong differences made by the Spirit but from the absence of any assignable differences at all. The saints are not like the rest of us, so they do not count here. The other Christians are no different from anyone else. Like all men, they are simply expressing desires that can be explained entirely within the psychological realm; or they express modes of behavior that are explained by social and environmental influences. Aside from these human and environmental factors there are no assignable divine resources at work in men.

Response   The primary value of this type of honest doubt is that it makes Christians consider what, if any, are the real differences made by the Holy Spirit. The only way to talk sense about the Spirit is to identify what He does. If He makes no difference, there is no reason to affirm His work.

In the light of what has been said above it is clear that we must think of the primary work of the Holy Spirit as the unseen presence of God affecting the whole range of man's higher life. This frees him from the piecemeal or atomistic interpretations of the work of the Spirit. The comprehensive teaching of the New Testament is not that the Spirit moves in some one area of life but in the full ranges of man's moral and spiritual existence. The fruit of the Spirit, wrote Paul, is "love, joy, peace, patience, kindness, goodness, faithfulness, gentleness, self-control . . ." (Galatians 5:22–23). In other words, the work of the Spirit is to change and renew the whole person.

In particular the Holy Spirit does four things that men need. First, He assists them to experience a growing awareness of the presence of God. This is a *unique experience* reported by men of all levels of life and thought—from philosophical minds to men of little learning, from saints and theologians like Augustine and Thomas Aquinas to everyday Christians in thousands of churches. There is no uninterrupted sense of being with God. Those who have been receptive to the Spirit of God, however, have known the recurring awareness of His presence. Phillips Brooks seems almost to be speaking out of contemporary experience as men look toward the twenty-first century when he writes that our religious belief is not the far-off search for a distant God, but the turning, the looking, the trusting, the holding fast to a God who has been always present, who is present now. The awareness of the immediate presence and influence of God is the essence of vital religion. When this is absent religion becomes unreal; it is reduced to forms and ceremonies, duties and restrictions, dogmas and theories. The sense of the divine presence leads men into a new dimension of existence. For there is an infinite spiritual distance between those who are bogged down in the sense of isolation in an impersonal universe and those who experience God's nearness.

This experience binds men of all religions together. In Christianity, however, it seems to have become more explicit in more people because the God who enters into communion with men is the One revealed in Jesus Christ. Here his concrete goodness is clearly understood. This moves the hearts of men deeply, fills them with gratitude and joy, and gives them the mysterious confidence that comes from knowing that they belong to God. Paul referred to this when he wrote, "For you did not receive the spirit of slavery to fall back into fear, but you have received the spirit of sonship. When we cry, 'Abba! Father!' it is the Spirit himself bearing witness with our spirit that we are the children of God" (Romans 8:15–16).

This, with all that it implies for the renewal and joy of creative living, is the greatest contribution of the Christian religion to mankind. It is a unique and growing experience. It transforms every other relationship. It changes the whole tone and quality of life. For this reason it sounds curious that men anywhere would be willing to linger for years in a sphere of essential meaninglessness when there is the clear option of experiencing the presence of God.

Second, the Holy Spirit binds men to each other in mutual respect and love. This process begins in the Christian as he identifies himself with the community of faith under the Lordship of Jesus Christ. The mysterious working of the Holy Spirit that binds men to God also binds them to each other in the fellowship of a shared faith. It was no accident that the Holy Spirit formed the earliest Christians into a community of faith at the first Pentecost. It is no accident either that the same

Spirit who formed the church in the beginning should be the continuing source of its life and mission.

Christians share in the sense of God's presence, which has become available to them through Christ. The Holy Spirit, who binds them together in community, illuminates their understanding of the Bible, of Jesus Christ as Redeemer and Lord, and of the deepest needs of men. The Spirit moves within the community of faith through its ministers and teachers to assist in the never-ending processes of understanding and communicating God's living Word. He enables men to sense the real meaning of preaching, of the sacraments, of the liturgy, and of the prayers and hymns of the church. He delivers them from supercilious criticisms and helps them to lay hold upon the deeper realities of the Christian faith and life. The Holy Spirit alone provides the sustained motivating influence of the ecumenical quest of the churches. He ever strives with Christians to keep the church involved in its relevant mission in the world.

The power of the Holy Spirit leads men also to identify themselves, as Jesus did, with those outside the faith. The Spirit awakens the sense of a common humanity in need of God. He moves men to understand, to accept, and to appreciate each human being for what he is and for what he can become. Just as nature abhors a vacuum, so the Holy Spirit abhors the attitudes and deeds that put man against man. The concern of Christians, however, goes beyond a mere human interest because the Spirit moves them to communicate the joy of the presence of God along with their other deeds of service.

A third specific effect of the Holy Spirit is to provide a sustained dynamic for unselfish service to mankind. It has always been natural and easy for the sense of God's presence to be regarded as an end-in-itself. Why bother with more? Consequently, many Christians have been so content to walk with God that they forgot about their fellowmen. This is contrary to God's purpose and will always end in the sense of God's absence. Similarly, many have found satisfaction in the community of faith without any genuine concern for others. This too cannot stand.

Here we encounter the basic Biblical truth that everything binding us to God binds us to men and whatever separates us from men separates us from God. Therefore, the Holy Spirit necessarily moves Christians toward compassionate concern for men in need and toward resourceful action in meeting human needs. The Spirit uses the example and summons of Christ toward this end. It is impossible to be under the sway of the Spirit without having a sustained desire to make this a better world where all men can thrive in every important interest of their lives.

A fourth work of the Holy Spirit is to enable Christians to read the promises of God in the past and therefore to live in hope. Those promises are mediated primarily through the life, death and resurrection of Jesus. With the help of the Spirit, they look to the past to read there the bold promises of God for any conceivable future. This is the ultimate resource for Christian activism and responsible living here and now.

The presence and resources of the Spirit become available not by accident but by the cultivation of the divine presence. The primary means to this end is prayer, which we shall consider next.

11

PRAYER AND CREATIVE LIVING

The two most important truths about prayer in general are: first, it is the heart of religion and, second, it is a primary source of morale and creative living. These require at least brief comments before we consider the alternative views on prayer.

To understand prayer is to understand the unique dimension of religion. For religion has to do with a living relationship between God and man. No other major human interest has this as its aim. Without this, every activity, whether ceremonial, liturgical, theological, moral, or churchly, is outside the sphere of the religious. The divine-human relationship in living encounter is the specifically religious dimension. For this reason prayer is at the heart of religion. Schleiermacher wrote, "To pray and to be a religious person are one and the same thing." Heiler, in his remarkable book entitled *Prayer,* expressed the same thesis when he wrote, "Religious people, students of religion, theologians of all creeds and tendencies, agree in thinking that prayer is the central phenomenon of religion. . . ."

Prayer has also been for millions of people a primary source of morale in difficult circumstances and of creative living amid the gravitational pulls toward mediocrity. Whether or not prayer can continue to be an authentic practice for modern men is a question involving the entire future not only of Christianity but of religion in any form. Therefore there is no more crucial issue for Christianity and the Biblical heritage generally than that concerning the validity of prayer. The essential issue here concerns simply whether a human being who prays is oriented toward reality or is merely living in a realm of imagination. If the latter, there is no place for prayer as an authentic practice. Prayer becomes phoney as soon as it moves out of the dimension of realistic encounter. The form would be retained without its substance. If there is any theme on which our best thinking is needed, it is on the validity of prayer. As we have seen, we put ourselves in a position to compare and judge our ideas by reflecting on the alternative views. So, again, to prepare ourselves for the Biblical teaching we need to have before us some of the major options on prayer.

THE MAIN ALTERNATIVE VIEWS

The theories on prayer may be divided into those that deny and those that affirm its validity. Each of these in turn takes different forms which need to be distinguished from each other.

First, we shall state briefly some of the views of those who deny the validity of prayer altogether. Many do so on psychological grounds. They say everything that takes place in prayer can be described and explained psychologically. Others deny the validity of prayer by emphasizing its crude beginnings in primitive societies. Just as our idea of God is the product of history so is the practice of prayer. Still others say that prayer does not deal in reality because the only known forces outside of the human world are physical. Those who pray imagine wrongly that there is a nonphysical Mind or Spirit who can exert real influence upon men and events through prayer.

All three of these denials from psychology, cultural evolution and natural science, may come together in an example used by Vilfredo Pareto, the well-known Italian sociologist of some decades ago. In his *Mind and Society* (1935) he distinguishes between rational and irrational human behavior. He illustrates this at one point by saying that if men are in peril at sea they may pray or row. The former is irrational activity; the latter, rational. Why? Plainly because, in his view, there is no God whose energies can make any difference within either men or nature.

The second types of theory on prayer have been developed by those who believe in its validity but differ as to its nature. Broadly speaking, there are three theories as to the nature of prayer. These may be identified by the terms, *pragmatic, mystical,* and *prophetic.* Heiler has rendered outstanding service in writing on the last two of these.

According to those who think of prayer as *pragmatic* there need not be any conscious effort to commune with God or to invoke His blessing. No time needs to be set apart for prayer because prayer is living and doing. Conversing with others is prayer. Doing good deeds is prayer. Planning programs for Christian action is prayer. Study is prayer. In fact, everything a sincere Christian does is prayer. Theologically, this view leans heavily toward nontheistic humanism. The human is divine. Interpersonal relations are divine. So, since there is no God who can make any difference from beyond ourselves, whatever there is to prayer must be identified with man's activity. Nevertheless, it would be possible to believe in the reality of God and still think of prayer as the carrying out of duties. This was

Kant's view. The practical result of this approach is to become radically involved in the affairs of this world but without much sense of conscious communion with God in the process.

Those who believe in what Heiler calls *mystical* prayer tend to minimize any person-to-person communion or encounter with God and to emphasize the sense of mystical union with God. Prayer has one or both of two objectives: absorption into the divine Being or the beatific vision of God. The method is by way of ascent, step by step, up the ladder of prayer toward God. Theologically, this perspective on prayer tends toward pantheism. The finite is merged into the Infinite. There is the experience of unspeakable joy and peace. In mystical prayer this note of the ineffable or incommunicable is often sounded. The beatific vision is too magnificent for utterance. In relation to practical affairs there is in this type of prayer a tendency to regard this world and its interests as unreal, distracting, and trivial. So the practical result is that mystical prayer tends toward withdrawal from vigorous and resourceful involvement in the affairs of this world.

The third view is *prophetic* prayer. This is the theory that prayer is communion with God. To experience this men must spend time apart from their activities and engage in meditation, silence, and verbal utterance in the presence of God. Just as in friendship there are times when we act together and times when we commune through conversation or silence, so is it with us and God. Often in prophetic prayer men struggle and agonize with God over the desperate issues of life. This is particularly true in intercession, which is one of the most important aspects of prophetic prayer. This brings us to the Biblical perspective on prayer.

THE BIBLICAL TEACHING

The Bible is unrivaled in all religious literature in the quality and continuity of its teaching on prophetic prayer. It teaches about such prayer in two ways, namely, by example and precept. Through the prayer-life of the prophets and others, and especially through that of Jesus Christ, the essential nature of

159

prophetic prayer is communicated. In addition to the Biblical portraits of men of prayer there are explicit teachings and admonitions that help to complete what the Bible conveys on this theme. From these two sources, then, we may bring together five characteristics of prophetic prayer expressed or implied in the Scriptures. There are others that might be mentioned, but the five to be discussed are the most basic.

First, prayer is Person-to-person communion with God. From the start this takes prayer out of the realm of cheap begging. The men of the Bible who understand and practice prayer think of themselves as being involved in a living communing relationship with God. It is a *God*-man relationship. It is a unique kind of Person-to-person encounter. For it is communion between the infinite Person and a finite person.

This implies an awareness, on the part of those who pray, of their dependence on God. God alone is the Creator and Sustainer of life. The prophets and apostles are also aware that God is the ultimate Source of goodness. He is perfect in love, justice, wisdom and mercy. Here again this unique kind of Person-to-person encounter becomes visible. The men of the Bible feel themselves to be in urgent need of what God has to share with them. For He is the one who alone can forgive, lift up, redeem, and empower for creative living in the world. He alone is holy. So prayer is communion with God in the full awareness of the Person with whom man is in fellowship.

In all of this the Biblical teaching stands in contrast to both the pragmatic and the mystical approaches to prayer. In the West the tendency has been to reduce prayer to conduct. In the East the tendency has been to stress meditation with the aim toward mystical absorption into the divine Being. Within Christianity itself both of these tendencies can be found. There are Christian men of action and there are outstanding Christian mystics. Nevertheless, the basic teaching of the Bible is toward the Person-to-person communion of prophetic prayer. In this kind of prayer-life a man keeps his identity and experiences a harmony of his will with God's will. In this emphasis the Bible stands above and goes beyond all other sacred books.

There are a few examples of this level of prayer in the literature of other religions. But these instances are rare and widely scattered. Consequently, the Bible is unique in its exalted and cumulative expression of this kind of Person-to-person prayer. Jesus Himself represents prophetic prayer at its best. This was made possible, in part at least, by His remarkable emphasis on God as Father.

Closely related to this is a second teaching of the Bible on prayer, namely, that prayer is communion with God for the purpose of doing God's will. To be sure, the men of the Bible are aware of the sheer joy of experiencing the presence of God. Fellowship with God, like our human friendships, is an end in itself. But it is far more than that. It is the divinely appointed means for receiving the strength to realize moral and spiritual values in community in this world. This is the pragmatic function of prayer.

When Jesus confronted major practical problems, He prayed. And when He knew He had to face persecution and the cross, He went into the Garden of Gethsemane. There Jesus prayed, "Father, if thou art willing, remove this cup from me; nevertheless not my will, but thine, be done" (Luke 22:42). Heiler has called this the highest moment in the history of prayer. It was not a moment of action or of mystical ecstasy or absorption into the divine Being. Rather, it was a moment of agonizing encounter with the Father who was radically involved with Jesus in the crisis situation. In pragmatic prayer the tendency is to get involved without adequate inner resources, which come from communion with God. In mystical prayer the tendency is to withdraw from the world, to abandon desire, and thus to be rendered passive. In Gethsemane Jesus experienced a moment when His will and God's will came together in a magnificent harmony for the purpose of creative participation in the redemptive work of the Kingdom of God. It was preparation for suffering in order to accomplish a supremely important work.

A third teaching of the Bible on prayer grows out of the first two. It is that communion with God awakens concern for men.

Prayer turns away from self toward others. The prophets were eager to affect the lives of others for God. Jesus prayed for others and asked His disciples to "pray . . . the Lord of the harvest to send out laborers into his harvest" (Matthew 9:38). He prayed for all those who were to be His followers in the generations to come (John 17:9, 20). He prayed that they might be one (John 17:21). This intimate connection between communion with God and the love of man is seen in two ways. It is seen first in the Master's teaching on forgiveness. He who is unwilling to forgive the man who has offended him need not imagine that his prayer for forgiveness from God will be accepted and answered favorably. So rightness with man and rightness with God are organically related.

This interconnection is seen further in the call to intercessory prayer. Intercession was a central feature of Christian prayer. Paul, the great missionary and pastor, made intercessory prayer a basic part of his strategy. He prayed constantly for the people in the churches he established (2 Corinthians 13:7–9; Ephesians 1:15–17; Philippians 1:3–5; 1 Thessalonians 1:2–3). He also urged Christians to pray for each other and for him (Romans 15:30–32; 2 Corinthians 1:11; 1 Thessalonians 5:25). The God who loves all human beings shares His concern with those who commune with Him in prayer. In this way they too are constrained to pray for and serve others.

Fourth, prophetic prayer always includes gratitude and praise. Prayer arises not only from the desire for forgiveness and rightness with God. It arises also from gratitude. This must express itself to the God who gives life and numberless benefits. The Father loves men and freely shares His benefits with them. So whenever anyone prays in the full awareness of God's self-giving love, he cannot help expressing thanksgiving. Communion with God is never adequate without thanksgiving. The psalmists knew this, so they had to express themselves in praise and thanksgiving. With some exceptions the last fifty of the psalms represent the most consistent and exalted effort in all literature to express gratitude and praise to God. Paul was a master teacher on this theme too. He taught Christians to rejoice always and to give thanks in all circumstances (1 Thessalonians 5:16–18). He wrote, "Have no anxiety about anything, but in everything by prayer and supplication with thanksgiving let your requests be made known to God" (Philippians 4:6).

Finally, the Bible teaches us that in prophetic prayer we expect the kinds of answers that are in harmony with the nature of prayer as communion with the God who seeks to realize His Kingdom. That is, prayer is answered only within the general bounds of the purpose of God. For this reason there is no authentic prayer that is not at the same time an expression of the greatest of all prayers:

> Thy kingdom come,
> Thy will be done,
> On earth as it is in heaven (Matthew 6:10).

Jesus demonstrated in His own life that the most important answer to prayer is a man redeemed and transformed until his dominant desire is to do the will of God. Somewhere in here lies the explanation of the practice among Christians of praying in the name of Jesus. This preserves the sincerity of the desire to do God's will, which was the supreme aim of Jesus; at the same time, it helps the Christian to understand God's will in terms of the Master's concern for the well-being of men.

SOME MODERN DOUBTS AND RESPONSES TO THEM

Modern doubts about all this arise from at least five sources. 1. Some doubt because of their belief in a law-abiding universe. 2. Many doubt because of psychological analyses. 3. Others doubt because of ethical problems involved in prayer. 4. Others doubt because of practical difficulties. 5. Still others doubt because of serious personal problems. Each of these needs to be thought about with care.

Doubt   First, there are doubts that come from modern man's understanding of a law-abiding universe. The assumption here is that all of the basic energies of the universe express

163

themselves in and through natural or even *physical* processes. More than that, they do so with patterns of regularity that are not to be changed by prayer. So a serious consideration of natural processes leads to a dim view of the efficacy of prayer. This would be particularly true in relation to prayer for people with terminal illnesses. It would be true also of all prayers for changes in the weather and in natural processes of any kind. The recognition of a law-abiding universe makes it hard to pray for a safe journey or, in some cases, for daily bread. Sometimes the doubts in this connection concern the greatness of the universe and the insignificance of man. The law-abiding processes of nature supersede the petty concerns of men. At best, in so vast a scheme of things, man's life is a mere trifle.

Response Regarding prayer in a universe of law several comments are in order. At the outset we need to recognize something hollow and unreal about any prayer that implies God takes lightly the laws of nature He has established. These steadfast ordinances of the universe make it possible for man to live and do his work. God sustains this kind of universe, and He is not in the business of counteracting His own order. So, any easygoing hope that God will disrupt the natural order of things because of our desires is a delusion.

On the other hand, we need to see that far more is done through orderly physical processes than at first appears. Meaning is communicated between two people by the sounds of their voices, by their intricate equipment for hearing, and by their brains. If men can commune with each other through the orderly processes of the physical realm, why may they not communicate with God through the medium of a law-abiding universe that God sustains. In fact, we have already suggested that God uses nature as one of His media of communication and involvement with men.

Moreover, we need to see that there may be unseen energies that do not flow into our lives merely through the physical processes of nature. In the physical universe there are certain types of energy: gravity, chemical processes, electricity, nuclear energy, and others. Why should we suppose that the only kinds of energy are these? Even so-called physical energy in its varied forms is a mystery. What is it? What about extrasensory perception, telepathy and the like? Those who pray believe that there are spiritual resources from God as real and practically important as any kind of physical energy. If God is, and if His energy pervades the universe, why should we insist that all of His energies must be expressed through physical things and processes? He is incalculably more than the universe He made.

There is one area of human experience that seems to show conclusively that there is such a thing as nonphysical or spiritual energy. And this kind of energy is of first importance. I refer to the curious fact that the mind of man has its own unique energy. Let me illustrate this. I saw a friend across the street, lifted my arm and waved my hand. Something physical happened when I did that. Many parts of my body moved. But could anyone give an adequate explanation of what happened by talking about muscles, bones, chemical processes and the like? Of course not. Why? Because the decisive causal agent is left out. My recognition of a friend, my desire to greet him, my policy to communicate my feelings with him—these are the real explanation of the consequent movement of the arm and hand. This type of nonphysical energy could be applied extensively. But if one sees the force of the illustration just used, he will understand all those other everyday occasions in which the same phenomenon may be observed.

While it is true that in this present world all our thoughts, desires, feelings and aims are *dependent* on the body and its physical environment, they are *not the same* as the body and its environment. A thought or purpose is not tangible.

In the human mind itself we have a concrete instance of a kind of energy that is nonphysical and spiritual. In the light of this it would seem quite arbitrary to suppose that there are no real dimensions of spiritual power from God. This is all the more evident when we consider the claims and lives of men who have gone far in the practice of prayer. We may conclude by saying that thoughts and purposes, which are spiritual or nonphysical, affect the body and other physical things. Mind controls and redirects nature without changing natural laws. Similarly, without altering the laws of nature, which express God's will, God could still release into human life His spiritual energies. Indeed, it may well be a law of reality that God's spiritual energies cause, control and affect the so-called physical energies of the universe. This opens up the whole realm of reality of which men of faith have spoken for thousands of years. Science is not the only road to truth because there are dimensions of reality beyond its reach. This is why science and religion should be seen as complimentary approaches to truth.

Much more needs to be said here but this is enough to clear the way for an openness to the divine resources through prayer of which the prophets, Jesus, the apostles and all those who have followed in their line have spoken.

Doubt   Second, there are the doubts that arise from psychological sources. Perhaps prayer is autosuggestion or self-hypnosis. Here the idea that man projects his wishes onto reality makes its appearance again. Is not prayer wishful thinking? Are there not perfectly satisfactory explanations of prayer in terms of psychology? If so, why bring God in or imagine that He makes any difference?

Response   The first comment on the doubts arising from psychological considerations is that many of them are honest. They are not to be regarded as merely cynical or destructive in intent. Anyone who appreciates the extensive achievements in psychological studies will find these doubts emerging and calling for some sort of credible response. So before we can be open today to the teachings of the Bible on prayer we need to reflect on such doubts.

In many instances prayer is wishful thinking. Men often want something so much that they identify their desires with the will of God. They often imagine what is not the case. Lucretius said that fear produced the gods. If one looks at the history of religion in its mediocre expressions (even in Christianity) one

166

is apt to suppose that prayer is little more than wishful thinking. But of course no honest man judges anything by its mediocre manifestations. We estimate the authenticity of science not by dabblers but by the Pasteurs, Darwins, and the Einsteins. So must it be in regard to prayer.

When we study the lives of the prophets, apostles, saints, and especially Jesus, we do not get the feeling that for them prayer is wishful thinking or autosuggestion and the like. This fact must be seen and appreciated for what it is. In the end, whether or not these men are engaged in a grand hoax when they pray and invite others to do so rests not on psychology but on the existence of God. The mere fact that a man's prayer-life can be described psychologically does not imply that there is no divine-human encounter in prayer. Men believe there is a world of houses, yards, streets, sidewalks, cars, and other people. This belief and the actions based on it may be studied by the psychologist. But the psychologist cannot say, on the basis of his discipline, whether or not those things are real. Yet everything that we do depends on the reality-question. So is it with prayer. Everything depends on the reality of God. If God is, prayer at its best makes sense. And in that case it cannot be reduced to wishful thinking and illusion.

It is important to remember also that God may use psychological processes, suggestions, thoughts and desires to affect our lives in prayer. For here, if anywhere, God is at work in His nearness, closer than hands and feet. God may use a man's conscience, or his imagination, or his compassion, or any other mental process in communicating His presence and power.

Again, in response to the idea that prayer is wishful thinking, one comment is in order: prayer at its best has never been a call to comfort and ease. Rather, it has been the supreme resource for doing what men did not want to do.

Doubt   Third, there are doubts about prayer from ethical considerations. Man should solve his own problems instead of looking to God for answers. So why pray? Besides this there is something unreal as well as unethical about praying for others.

God, if He exists, already knows their needs. If He loves them, He will do everything He can for them without our prayers. So why engage in intercessory prayer?

Response   These are among the most common objections to prayer that I know. They are both honest and penetrating. Does prayer really involve such a reliance on God as to weaken man's determination to work on solving his own problems? The greatest men of prayer have not shirked their duties. Nor have they been inclined to ask God to do for them what they needed to do by their own enterprise and initiative. This doubt has more point theoretically than in practice. It would seem that looking to God would reduce a man's efforts to work out his own life. But, paradoxically, this is not what happens when prayer is at its best.

Again, anyone who really wants to accomplish something needs all the help he can get. If he needs wise counsel, he seeks it. If he needs encouragement, he goes to someone who can give it. If a man needs help and looks to God for it, there is nothing about this which in principle differs from his eagerness to seek assistance from other men. The only real question is: Is prayer efficacious to this end? And this depends on the reality of God and the availability in fact of His resources. A man who fails to use all available resources for achieving his ends (including God's help) is missing the mark. *No man has exhausted the possibilities for creative living who has not made a sustained, honest and resourceful effort to pray.*

Another point needs to be made here. There are some basic problems that man cannot solve. He is finite and radically limited in what he can do. These problems have to do with life, death, and destiny. We do not want to get into the ridiculous position of playing God. Man's life is a gift from God. He did not make himself. He is ever dependent on forces other than himself. What more appropriate attitude is there than, in prayer, to give thanks to God for life and friends and a world in which to work, to enjoy and to share? Similarly, what more reasonable activity can there be than to look to the God who made us to help us through life and death? Who can by thought and enterprise do more than postpone the sure fact of death? Without God this becomes an overwhelming problem except for those who do not care for a continuing opportunity for creative adventure, that is, except for those who have lost morale. What good does it do to seek any worthy goals if life ends up at zero? There are some temporary gains. But for man, who has imagination, these cannot satisfy him. He requires an enduring meaning. Here prayer, far from robbing him of his incentives, provides a basis for the hope for the future with God. This in turn is one of the strongest motivating forces for creative living here and now.

Another deep-seated problem that man has been unable to solve has to do with sin and failure. It is easy for sophisticated despisers of religion to imagine that all man needs is education and cultural improvement. But this obscures what the Biblical writers, the novelists, the dramatists and the men of common sense of all eras have known, namely, that man has within him strong impulses contrary to his own best interests. His pride, self-centeredness, hostility, self-indulgence, stupidity and mediocrity in general tend to destroy him. Therefore, he needs the grace of God which is available through prayer. This much is sure: It does not require prayer to be a mediocre person.

Concerning intercessory prayer there is no ethical problem if we hold that God merely *persuades* others through prayers in their behalf. As to the charge that intercessory prayer is unnecessary because God already wants to do all He can, the best response I know is that this ignores the *policy* of God to work through people. Just as He uses our hands and feet, so too He uses our prayers as instruments for attaining His goals. Consequently, even though God knows the needs of all His children and is ever eager to help them, He wants our prayers for each other because there are some things He wants to accomplish only by that means. And if we judge by the effects of such prayer in binding people to each other, as well as in other results, we may observe a kind of experiential confirmation of the essential validity and value of intercessory prayer.

Jesus seems to have laid hold upon a profound God-appointed strategy for human redemption in the principle of intercession. Paul found it to be real. Millions of Christians have experienced an order of reality here that cannot be ignored without a casual disregard of fact. There are artificial forms of intercessory prayer, but there are solid reasons for believing that whenever men of good will join in a compact to pray for each other and for the world's need for peace, food, and health, God moves in the situation through such men and through such sustained prayers to bless all mankind.

Doubt　　　　Fourth, modern doubts arise also from practical difficulties. We hear often of unusual answers to prayer. Someone has been healed of an incurable disease through prayer. Or, a life on a battlefield has been spared because of prayer. Or, a business venture has been successful. Or, some perplexing problem has been resolved by means of prayer. Doubts arise whenever we take a close look at the facts. One person seems to have been healed, but what about others whose terminal illness moved on toward death despite all the prayers? So is it in all these other areas. Does God play favorites? A careful look at *all* the facts, or at a sufficiently large number of cases, will lead any thoughtful person to raise serious doubts about the efficacy of prayer in such instances.

Response　　　　The basic response to all this is that we must change our understanding of what prayer is. The assumption underlying these doubts is that prayer is a method of getting our own way. Man wants physical health, money, status, security. So he prays for these things. When he gets them, he talks of God's answers to prayer.

But this misses what is at the heart of the Biblical teaching on prophetic prayer. As we have seen, *the greatest answer to prayer is a man transformed and set on his course to do God's will.* This kind of result comes not from any glib talk about "answers" to prayer. It comes from agonizing with God over the struggles within and without that threaten a man's whole existence. Out of such prayer there may come something of the power to say, "Not my will, but thine, be done." God can heal the body of any disease. He does so with the aid of physicians and the healing processes of the body. He does so at times in ways that seem miraculous. Here we do not understand the ways of God. But the point is that we miss the heart of prayer, as understood by the prophets, Jesus and Paul, if we fail to focus attention on prayer as opening the soul to God for creative participation with Him and with our fellowmen in the work of the Kingdom.

Besides this, prayer is an end in itself in that it is the enjoyment of friendship with God. In this aspect, the only answer to prayer is the communion itself. Men talk of unusual answers to prayer. But they often overlook the "answer" in the sense of the presence of God.

Doubt A fifth source of doubt about prayer is not particularly modern but is nevertheless found in contemporary experience. I refer to the doubts arising from serious personal problems. These may have to do with temperament or disposition. They may concern our moods, or anxieties, or hostilities, or loss of the morale that is the will to live and to improve ourselves and the world.

Response Doubts from these sources have no intellectual force. This does not make them any the less important. Nevertheless, I do not need to go into lengthy responses to them because they have to do more with salvation and personality adjustment than anything else.

This is to be said, however. No man can see the validity and value of *any* laudable practice, whether in science, art, business, education, or prayer, when he has a bad spirit. In no area does knowledge become available without the desire to understand, to consider, to be open to truth. The chronic complainer cannot easily understand anything, let alone the presence and power of

God. The same attitude is required for understanding and appreciating prayer as is demanded for understanding and appreciating science.

12

THE LIFE EVERLASTING

The belief in the life after death has always been an essential feature of the Christian religion. If this teaching were removed from Christianity, its sense of the ultimate meaning and destiny of man would be lost. Without it there might remain the call to faith, reconciliation, love and good will. But this would not be adequately supported because it is difficult for men to have faith in God when death gets the last word. It is hard, if not impossible, to hold fast to the value of each human being when we believe that everyone will come out at zero.

Doubts about personal immortality are inevitable in the modern world. Men doubt its reality. They doubt also its relevance. As we press toward the twenty-first century we find ourselves in a secularistic atmosphere of persistent questioning about the life after death. It is particularly important here to identify the major options, to clarify the Biblical teaching, and to consider with care some of the honest doubts.

THE MAIN ALTERNATIVE VIEWS

There are at least six major options here which may be stated briefly.

First, there is the denial of any continued existence of the soul beyond death. When the body dies that ends everything for that individual. He is simply dead, buried or cremated, and removed from the realm of existence. The individual comes out at zero. This implies that all human life is ultimately meaningless.

Second, there is the belief in the immortality of influence. This is like the first in that the individual does not continue after death. He ends up at nothing. Nevertheless, his influence goes on. His good deeds continue to affect the successive generations of men. Consequently, there are incalculable cumulative benefits for mankind that follow upon a life well lived. These continue indefinitely into the future. According to this view, then, the life of every person has enduring meaning as long as there are men whose lives he has influenced.

A third theory related to the life everlasting goes deeper than the second even though it moves in the same direction. This is the theory that the individual comes to an end but not without contributing something to the ever continuing life of God. The influence of a man on his fellowmen may continue beyond death. But far more important is his unique legacy to God Himself. By living he has added something to God's experience of satisfaction as A. N. Whitehead has suggested. So the finite individual ends up in oblivion but the results of his having lived will be forever registered and experienced in God. This view implies that there is an ultimate meaning for life but not for human beings in their own selfhood or self-identity.

A fourth view, moving in quite another direction, is that each soul continues beyond death by a process of transmigration or reincarnation. That is, at death each soul moves into a new and different body. Often in this view there are ethical implications. For example, a bad person will live on as one of the lower animals. By a process of transmigration he may become a snake, or a dog, or a bird. This may continue indefinitely, or it might be a stage for a higher or lower reincarnation. In any event, as often understood in India and other parts of the world, the soul must undergo the consequences of sins previously committed by being embodied in an inferior form of existence. This teaching is usually accompanied by fatalism because the past unalterably determines the present and future and there is no grace of God to break the chain. It differs from the first three options mentioned above in that it affirms the continued existence of the individual soul after death.

The idea of transmigration or reincarnation has often been crude and fatalistic. But now and then it has reached a higher expression, as in some of the dialogues of Plato and in the writings of Plotinus. Plato taught that those who are bound by their sense experiences are unable to rise out of their status in this physical realm. Depending on their quality, they may become asses, or wolves, or bees and ants, or even men. So when the time for reincarnation arrives they take a suitable form of embodiment, whether animal or human. But those few who are not sense-bound and who have devoted themselves to philosophy will be freed from bondage to the physical body. They will have an immortality that belongs to those worthy of a purer and higher form of existence.

A fifth theory is that the soul is immortal by its very nature. Plato believed also that the soul in its intellectual nature was indestructible. That is, since it is capable of understanding and participating in the realm of the unchanging ideas it is bound to be immortal. Mathematics gave the clue to the eternal. For mathematical relations never change. The simple formula, $2 + 2 = 4$, never changes. So is it with all purely formal mathematical relations. Since the mind of man can participate in this realm, it must be immortal. Man does not overcome death by God's action, as the New Testament teaches, but by his very nature as an intelligent being.

The sixth view is that of the New Testament. To it we now turn for a more comprehensive statement.

THE BIBLICAL TEACHING

The teaching of the Bible concerning life after death must be understood in relation to the teachings on creation and on God's redemptive-creative action in relation to man. The end must be in keeping with the beginning. The outcome of the whole process must be commensurate with God's purpose for inaugurating man's life in this present universe.

We have seen that God created man to realize moral and spiritual values. He made men to become cooperative agents who by their response realize these values in community. But if men have no enduring status, then the whole project is placed in jeopardy. The purpose of God in creating men is made null and void. Besides this, the redemptive-creative initiative of God through Jesus Christ would lose its point also. For a mere temporary redemptive-creative process could not justify the affirmation of the New Testament that God has acted mightily and with finality in Christ in behalf of men. In the end, if death has the last word regarding the individual, then the whole sweep of the Biblical revelation on creation and redemption becomes a succession of divine exercises in futility. They would become the trifling acts of a capricious deity.

For this reason in the Biblical teaching the idea of creation moves toward the idea of God's plan for the life of the soul beyond death. The redemptive-creative process released supremely in Jesus Christ aims also toward its fuller realization in the life to come. Against this background we may see clearly the progression of the Biblical teaching. In God's action toward men the outcome is commensurate with the beginning, the end with the intervening processes.

For all of its strangeness to modern ears, this is the major factor in the Biblical teaching on the *Parousia,* or the return of Christ. Here is communicated the promise, however the event be specifically viewed, that God will not end His activity in our behalf with the cross, the empty tomb, and Pentecost. He goes on until Jesus Christ stands in His full glory as Lord of all creation (Philippians 2:11). This is to suggest that God, in His own way and time, will see to it that the same love which was embodied and consequently revealed in Jesus Christ will be clearly seen by men to be back of the universe and of the whole realm of finite existence. Creation, redemption, and consummation belong together in the living unity of the Biblical teaching. This is not to suggest that there will ever come a stopping point (as at the end of a play) in God's creative and redemptive work. It is rather to state that the purpose of God seems to call for activity by vast epochs. The developments in one epoch lead to those in another.

The Biblical teaching, then, leads us to entertain the sublime thought that by the grace of God men are enabled to pass from death to eternal life even now. This means a new beginning within a new dimension of existence. The prenatal state of a human being is preparation for a new dimension of existence on the level of freedom. So man's earthly life within the womb of the present order prepares the way for a new epoch of creative adventure with God beyond this realm. God is not in the business of creating finite souls without a future to receive His benefits. All of this constitutes the essential movement of the Biblical teaching on the life after death. Always there is the thrust toward meaning in the future.

The Biblical teaching has specific points of focus, however, which require special elaboration. To identify these we may begin with a few brief comments on the Old Testament and then move to a consideration of the New Testament. There are a few significant passages in the Old Testament that suggest the victory over death. "Enoch walked with God; and he was not, for God took him" (Genesis 5:24; see also Hebrews 11:5). Job asked the question, "If a man die, shall he live again?" (14:14). We may well believe he answered his own question in the affirmative (19:25–27). Now and then the psalmists spoke of victory over the grave (49:15, 56:13, 73:24–26, 88:10–12). In Proverbs we read of the righteousness that conquers death (10:2, 11:4). Other writers refer to a kind of life beyond death (Isaiah 26:19, Daniel 12). After finding such scattered passages, however, the search ends. There are hints that call for elaboration, as with seeds waiting to develop into full stalks and grain.

The New Testament speaks of the life everlasting with a degree of emphasis and with a moral quality unrivaled in all religious literature. The teaching there may be summarized under three major themes.

First, man can live beyond death only by God's action in his behalf. He is not by nature immortal, nor does he have any resources of his own that can guarantee anything regarding the conquest of death. Just as he could not create himself, so he cannot continue his own existence beyond death. Therefore, everything here depends on God's administrative policy. It is the teaching of the New Testament that God's plan for everyone is to conquer death so that all men may enter the Kingdom prepared for them. If anyone does not enter the Kingdom, this is the consequence of his failure to respond to the light God has given him. But God is merciful as well as just.

Second, the New Testament teaches that God's promise to triumph over death has been communicated clearly and finally in the resurrection of Jesus Christ. The four gospels tell of the risen Lord in such a way as to leave no reasonable doubt as to its significance for the earliest Christians. The cumulative impact of the events cited there cannot fail to impress the reader with their importance to those who wrote the gospels. The risen Lord appeared to Mary Magdalene and to Mary the mother of James (Matthew 28:1–10, Luke 24:1–11). He appeared to two followers, one of whom was named Cleopas, as they walked on the road to Emmaus (Luke 24:13–35). Then He appeared to the eleven disciples (Matthew 28:16–20, Mark 16:14, Luke 24:36–50). In the Fourth Gospel we read that He revealed Himself to the disciples on three different occasions (20:19–23, 20:26–29, 21:1–14).

According to the Book of Acts the risen Lord appeared to His followers over a period of forty days and spoke to them of the Kingdom of God (1:3). If we are to judge from the only reports we have, the conclusion is clear that the apostles and those with them took with utmost seriousness the direct encounters with the risen Lord (Acts 1:21–22, 2:32, 3:15). They were in the unique position of being the only actual witnesses to the resurrection of Jesus.

Paul identified himself with those witnesses because of his own encounter with the risen Lord on the road to Damascus. He viewed the resurrection as the crowning event without which all the rest was a rope of sand. It is not going too far to say that if this fact were removed he would not have been able to accept the Christian religion. He makes it a point to report on the appearances of Christ to the apostles and others (1 Corinthians 15:3–7). His reason for doing so was to convince them of the solid basis for the Christian anticipation of victory over death. He wrote, "If Christ has not been raised, your faith is futile and you are still in your sins" (1 Corinthians 15:17; see also Romans 8:34). The Christian lives in the sure conviction that in Jesus Christ God has revealed the secret mystery of His will to conquer death. The resurrection of Jesus was God's *promise* for man's future in His Kingdom.

The importance of this for Christians is nowhere more obvious than in the selection of the first day of the week as the special day of worship. This was a deliberate new move to suggest, in contrast to those in their own heritage who worshiped on the seventh day, that a new era had begun with the resurrection. Similarly, this same sense of significance is seen in the celebration of Easter as the greatest event in the Christian calendar.

The teaching of the New Testament, in its essential movement, is that God chose to reveal through the man, Jesus of Nazareth, His plan to conquer sin and death. This revelation could not have been communicated to men without the whole Christ-event, that is, without His life, death, resurrection, and post-resurrection appearances, and continuing presence through the Holy Spirit. These were brought together in the minds of the earliest Christians until they formed the clear disclosure of God's promise to conquer death and move with men into the glorious future of the Kingdom.

This brings us to the third major emphasis in the teaching of the New Testament on the life everlasting, namely, the fact that men are called to enter into it now. The promise comes to men as a call to respond now. The point is that the writers of the New Testament are interested in far more than the *fact* of this revelation. Otherwise they would have gone off into theological discourses and intellectual discussions of the meaning of the revelation. Similarly, they were interested in more than the resurrection as an event. It was an event that filled them with gratitude and made them want to share the good news of God's magnificent promise. They wanted to share the good news so others too might respond to God in faith and hope.

In the New Testament, then, this revelation becomes a *call* to pass out of the sphere of meaninglessness and futility into the new realm of hope.

This is done not by a vague confidence in God but by looking to Jesus Christ as Lord and as the One through whom God has graciously made known His love and promise of victory over sin and death. Consequently, the proclamation of the gospel in the New Testament carries with it the assumption that if men have faith in God's action through Christ, they will in fact enter *now* into the new life of forgiveness, meaning and hope.

According to Paul, Christ came to lead men into the resurrection-life on earth. Eternal life is the free gift of God *now* (Romans 6:23) as well as in the world to come (Romans 2:6–8). Men are now set free from the law of sin and death (Romans 8:2). For anyone in Christ is "a new creation" (2 Corinthians 5:17; see also Galatians 3:27, 6:15; Ephesians 2:10, 4:22–24). Christians are no longer to live "in the futility of their minds" (Ephesians 4:17, Colossians 3:12–17). They are to "walk in newness of life" (Romans 6:4). They have been "created in Christ Jesus for good works" (Ephesians 2:10). They are sons of God by faith (Galatians 3:26), and they show this by "faith working through love" (Galatians 5:6).

The teaching of the New Testament on the life everlasting may be summarized in a single paragraph. Man is made for two worlds, this one and the next. He cannot answer his own deepest needs respecting his destiny. The same power that equips him for the most meaningful living in the here and now prepares him for the life to come. God, in His infinite love and wisdom, wanted men to know His purpose, to rejoice in His promise, and to receive His help. The total Christ-event is His central medium for doing this. Christ comes to men with the good news of the victory over sin, futility and death. At the same time He comes with the call to respond, to enter into the new life now. This call, though encompassing the hope of the Kingdom, includes especially the call to enter into responsible living in this present world. In the New Testament the here and the hereafter are organically interrelated.

In chapter 1 it was observed that there are at least seven major teachings of the Bible subject to radical doubt in the modern world. One of these is the belief in the life everlasting. None of the doubts about this belief is new. But some of them bear the marks of the present scientific era. Doubts occur on several levels. In particular, there are six doubts that require attention. We shall begin with three that are based on ethical grounds and certainly require some discussion. Then we shall turn to three considerations of a more intellectual nature that make it difficult for modern men to believe in the life everlasting.

Doubt   First, there is the doubt growing out of the supposed selfishness of the Christian belief in life after death. Is it not really just a glorified version of man's self-love?

Response   This doubt arises from a misunderstanding of the Christian teaching. Whatever else it may include, that teaching cannot be narrowly self-centered. In fact, the Christian understanding of the life everlasting is one of its most unselfish features. The concern to share the gospel with men everywhere is partly motivated by the desire to encourage all men to share in the promise of the Kingdom of God both here and hereafter. The person who wants to go to heaven by himself is unworthy of it. The Christian understanding of heaven is ineradicably social. It is the new *society,* the *Kingdom* of Heaven.

Doubt   Another doubt arises from the supposed impracticality of the belief in the life everlasting. It leads men to look toward the life after death rather than toward responsible living in the here and now. Its theme is "pie in the sky by-and-by." This distracts men. It leads them to think that the present life is relatively unimportant. So the belief is impractical.

180

Response   This doubt has been expressed in many ways and it recurs again and again in the modern world. It has back of it an authentic moral concern. It grows out of the observation that many people have lost a healthy concern for this life because of their interest in the life to come. In short, those who think in this way are eager for men to get with it, "to get where the action is."

This doubt arises from two basic errors, one concerning the nature of Christianity, the other concerning the present temporal order. Regarding the first, it is supposed that Christians, who entertain the hope for life after death, will lose interest in the only life they now have. This is obviously impractical. The Christian teaching on the life everlasting, however, is that it begins now and the fruits of it are already evident in deeds of love, justice and mercy. Therefore, far from teaching the withdrawal from the arena of responsible living, Christianity, even in its affirmation of eternal life, calls for unselfish service to men in the world as we now know it. Jesus demonstrated this in His life. Many of the greatest Christians, though believing strongly in the life everlasting, have been men of action. They saw what Jesus clearly taught, that the way we live here has a direct bearing on the life to come. Strange as it may seem, God's promise of life after death is one of the main resources for creative Christian living now.

The second error that leads to this doubt is the assumption that this present life is adequate to satisfy the deepest needs of men. It is often supposed that men are realistic and relevant when they turn away from eternal life and concentrate on roast beef, rice, and potatoes. The truth seems to be, however, that when we fix our attention on the latter, only something basic is missing. Jesus said, "Man shall not live by bread alone." Men cannot help thinking of their finitude. They die. As someone has observed, *the statistics on death have not changed: there is still one for every man.* The plain fact is that nothing this present world has to offer can satisfy the needs growing out of the universal fact of death. Modern man, owing to his extensive technological achievements, too often accepts the illusion of the adequacy of this present realm. He supposes it is just a matter of time and technique. But this misses the chronic ineptness of this world to satisfy some of the deepest longings of the human spirit.

Doubt   A third doubt arising from ethical considerations concerns heaven and hell. It seems to many that the Christian teaching on heaven and hell goes against elemental justice and a proper sense of values. This is especially true regarding the idea of hell. Christians have said that the sinner goes to hell and suffers there forever. What value can there be in this? Where is the justice in it? No matter what sins and crimes a man might commit during a period of seventy years, how could this warrant being punished for the endless future? If God creates a situation involving unending punishment for finite souls, how can He be interested in the realization of values?

Response   These are important questions. It may well be that Christians need to rethink their ideas on hell in the light of the developing teaching of the Bible. Here is where we need to go beyond the Bible itself to what has emerged in the interpretation of the direction or import of the Bible. Three points are to be made.

First, it is unreasonable to believe that God would establish any society, be it hell or any other, in which no values can be realized. The God who revealed Himself in Jesus Christ is concerned to realize values through finite persons. Therefore, endless torture and a continuing society of moral degradation would seem to have no place in the total movement of the Biblical revelation. The doctrine of eternal damnation, though stated now and then, is not a part of the developing disclosure of God's aims for His children. Nothing is more needed at this point than to free the Christian religion from any and all grossly immoral conceptions of the nature of hell.

Second, this does not imply that there is no longer any meaning in the idea of hell. If God were to make no distinction between good and bad men, He would be no God at all. If God were to put Hitler and Schweitzer in the same category He would be repudiating His nature as good. The Biblical teaching, then, rightly urges that God makes a radical distinction between good and bad men, the faithful and the unfaithful. Their destinies are different. It makes all the difference between heaven and hell as to how we respond to God in this life.

Third, what is required then seems to be an understanding of a hell that retains its tragedy but does not make of it a realm totally devoid of value. There must always be the possibility of progressive realization of values in all dimensions of God's universe. This possibility is suggested in Jesus' story of the rich man and Lazarus in which the rich man, though in hell, still experiences concern for his brothers (Luke 16:19–31). There is also the recurring Biblical theme that in the end all men will respond to God or will come to see that Jesus Christ is Lord. Joel had a vision of this. Paul gave it Christian utterance when he wrote that God exalted Jesus Christ so that at His name "every knee should bow, in heaven and on earth and under the earth, and every tongue confess that Jesus Christ is Lord, to the glory of God the Father" (Philippians 2:10–11).

Doubt　　　A fourth doubt holds that the belief in immortality had crude beginnings and is really a projection of man's wishes. This view, though somewhat superficial, bears some serious notice.

Response　　　It may or may not be true that the idea of immortality was first suggested by the belief in ghosts or by fanciful interpretations of dreams. Whether true or not, many ideas with crude beginnings have turned out to be true. Chemistry began with alchemy and astronomy with astrology. *The origin of a belief has nothing to do with its validity.*

As to the main aspect of this doubt, namely, that the belief in life after death is a projection of man's wishes, two comments are in order. First, man's wishes often have their counterparts in reality. Man is thirsty and finds water. He is hungry and finds food. He needs companionship and finds other

183

persons. It is not a convincing argument to say that man's vision of life after death, being a projection of his wishes, is an illusion. He may desire it and it may take place. Second, there is a suggestion in this doubt that the desire for life after death is crude and therefore suspect. *But it is no more unreasonable to want to live after death than to want to live tomorrow.* This is simply an extension of the universal desire to live. What is suspect is the lack of any desire to move into the future.

Doubt   A fifth doubt about personal immortality is rather widely entertained by well-educated men. This is the doubt arising out of intellectual honesty. The belief cannot be proved. There is no convincing evidence for it.

Response   For those who believe that the only road to truth about reality is by way of science this is a strong argument. They would say that they do not rule out the *possibility* of personal immortality. If dead men would communicate or make their existence known, those who suspend judgment would accept the belief. But there is no such scientifically verifiable evidence.

Two suggestions are in order regarding this honest doubt. The first is that, as we have seen, science is not the only road to truth. Since the limitations of science have been discussed already, we need not comment on them in detail here. Some of man's most important truths arise from thought and reflection on the broad ranges of experience and value. These cannot be brought into a laboratory and tested. Besides this, where the belief in personal immortality is concerned, if the souls of men pass into a new dimension of existence when they die, it is unreasonable to insist that they must return and communicate with men in this present world. The brief period of communication by the risen Christ had a special purpose, namely, to reveal God's policy and to express His *promise* for the future. It was not to suggest that beyond death men will still live in this present world and deal with each other here.

The second comment on this particular doubt is that, though

there is no scientifically adequate proof, it is still reasonable to believe in the life everlasting. In the end everything depends on God and His policy regarding man's life on earth. The doubt here arises at last from the doubt about God. Once again we encounter the troublesome fact that men tend to doubt all other major religious teachings when they entertain serious doubts about God. If God is, and if He is concerned to realize moral and spiritual values in and through men, it makes sense to believe in the life everlasting. If not, there is not the slightest reason to believe in it.

The only real basis for believing in the victory over death is the power and promise of God. If this is a part of his over-all policy, then death will be conquered; if not, there is no reasonable hope for it. The resurrection of Jesus would have no sustained significance apart from the continuing policy of God which Christians claim is revealed by that special event. In the end, therefore, everything rests on what God does and will continue to do.

Doubt   There is a sixth doubt that requires attention also. This is the doubt arising from the universality and finality of death. It seems so obvious that death is the end. Involved in this doubt are the questions concerning the existence of the soul. Man is a physical being. Whatever soul is present is sustained in any case by the body. When the body dies, the soul, if there is one, dies with it.

Response   This too is an honest doubt. Many believers in the life everlasting return to it and experience it as a recurring possibility only to move on again to the belief in God's revealed policy.

Perhaps the best place to begin is with the problem of the relations between the soul and the body. This is also known as the mind-body problem. If a man is a living soul who has a body that is intimately related to the soul, then it would be at least possible for the soul to continue after the death of the body. I have already presented the reasons for believing that

185

the soul or mind cannot be reduced to the body (see chapter 7). The two are interrelated, they interact, and at the same time they are distinct.

Body affects mind, and mind affects body. If a man is knocked unconscious, his body collapses. His nervous system is still there. His body is there. But his mind is not there attending to the body. This shows that the two are distinct. In this present life the soul of a man is fragmentary and incomplete. Its states vary all the way from alertness to reverie to the dim edges of consciousness. Nevertheless, it is not the body, nor any part of the body, nor merely a function of the body. We see this when we converse with other persons. We are not addressing brains, nervous systems and the like. We are talking with conscious individuals. So is it when we know ourselves. I know myself as an abiding ego, or self, or soul. I recognize this only by introspection. Therefore, it does not necessarily follow that when my body dies my soul will perish too.

Some scientists may still believe that the mind or soul is a function of the body or an aspect of bodily processes. But science itself does not confirm this. What experiments can demonstrate that a thought is a nerve, or that love is analyzable into physical processes? Consider imagination. Who can show that it is nothing more than some bodily activity? Or consider man's freedom of will, his power of contrary choice. Is this merely some strange combination of biological or chemical factors? No scientific tests can establish such a view. Again, can purpose be reduced to bodily processes? When I am trying to understand the thought of Plato am I making a study of his brain or nervous system?

To ask these questions is to answer them. Even well-educated men are apt to err here because of the failure to think realistically and concretely. They fail to distinguish between what *affects* the soul and the soul itself. Beyond question the soul, or mind, or ego of a person is *dependent* upon the body for its present existence. In theological language this is to say that God convoys the human soul through this present life by means of the body. But since the soul is not the body (though dependent on it in this present setting) there is no inherent reason to draw the conclusion that when the body dies the soul dies.

Even if it were argued that man's soul must have its present body for any continued existence, this would not finally exclude the possibility of life beyond death. For God could, if He wanted to, raise up the elements of the body and form them into a new body for sustaining the soul.

The minimal Christian belief on this subject is that in the world to come God will furnish a body suited to that new setting, enabling the soul to do its work, to have satisfying experiences, and to have fellowship with others and with God. If this sounds fantastic, the necessary comment is that it is no more fantastic than our life in this present world. How the body, which is physical, can sustain the soul, which is spiritual, is an unfathomable mystery. Life itself is a mystery but we live it. Theologically speaking, God performs the miracle of sustaining the soul daily by means of the body for over three billion human beings. How God will supply the new body for the soul after death, we do not know. We only know that God is and that He has promised through the risen Lord that He will do so.

In summary of the chapter, we end up where we began. When the issues here are seen within the narrow circles of scientific perspectives, and not in relation to God's over-all purpose, it is easy to say that death gets the last word. But when God is taken with radical seriousness and when His promise for the future is fixed in our minds, then the scattered pieces begin to fit together. We begin to sense the direction in which God is determined to move.

With God endurance and value must go together. It is morally impossible for God to destroy what ought to have enduring value. He is not in the business of making men who feel, enjoy, think, work, create, love, and pray, only to abandon them at death. His policy is to conserve and to carry forward.

187

It should be noted again, as we consider next the Christian call to responsible living, that the teaching on an everlasting destiny with God moves the believer into the life of service in the here and now. Jesus made it forever impossible to separate the quality of life here from the promise of life in the Kingdom of Heaven. The judgment is as real as life and death. Therefore Christians look to God for help in carrying out the known demands of the love of Christ toward all men and particularly toward those in need. This is why Paul, after writing in the most sublime language on the conquest of death, moves swiftly back to this life. "Therefore, . . . be steadfast, immovable, always abounding in the work of the Lord, knowing that in the Lord your labor is not in vain" (1 Corinthians 15:58).

We shall begin the next part with a statement of general principles regarding passivity and activism. Then we shall select representative personal and social issues in which the Christian necessarily seeks to act redemptively and creatively for men.

Part V

On Responsible Living in Community

13

PASSIVITY VERSUS CHRISTIAN ACTION

Nearly all societies and cultures have been pervaded by the tradition of passivity. By this tradition I mean the belief, passed on from generation to generation, that we cannot, or need not, or should not do anything to redirect and manage the larger forces of nations and communities. This tradition makes men passive, submissive, or indifferent to the broader and more far-reaching forces of history. It belittles all efforts to improve the world by long-range planning.

What are the larger affairs of history? They are the political, economic, cultural, moral and religious forces that affect not only one individual or another but vast numbers of people in communities. The issue here is one of the most crucial in the modern world, both for Christians and non-Christians. From the standpoint of Christianity, the issue is whether or not the Bible and the church can be rightly used to foster the tradition of passivity, or to repudiate it in favor of Christian action in these larger affairs of man's life in community.

THE MAIN ALTERNATIVE VIEWS

Here we shall concern ourselves only with the views of various Christians toward their responsibilities in community affairs. Broadly speaking, there have been three main ways of looking at the larger affairs of men in this world. The first two will be discussed in this section; the third will be treated, as the main teaching of the Bible, in the section that follows.

189

First, some have said that the gospel is the good news to men as individuals. It is a refuge for the solitary soul and has nothing to say about the management of the larger affairs of community life. It addresses itself to the individual soul in his relationships with God both in this life and in the world to come. Along with this goes the thought that God alone governs in the larger affairs of the world and therefore we can and should do nothing about them. This, of course, is a form of the tradition of passivity within Christianity itself. This theme is so important for the church as it moves toward the twenty-first century that we must linger on it long enough to see it in historical perspective. Here it is necessary to go into more detail in presenting the major options regarding the involvement or noninvolvement of Christians in the control and management of national and international affairs. I have chosen to bring the issues into bold relief by reference to the tradition of passivity in two Christian leaders of the first magnitude, namely, Augustine and Luther.

Though Augustine was one of the ablest minds in Christian history his thought was pervaded by the tradition of passivity. It never occurred to him that Christians have a responsibility for reshaping and managing the larger structures of history or controlling its larger events. It might be said in defense of Augustine that his times did not permit it. Vico, who wrote, ". . . the world of civil society has certainly been made by men," came more than a thousand years later. Walter Rauschenbusch and the social gospel were 1500 years away. Our purpose here is not to stand in judgment on this man to whom all Christendom owes a debt. It is merely to state what is the case, namely, that Augustine's thought and influence moved heavily in the direction of passivity regarding the larger affairs of this world.

This is seen in at least five aspects of his thought in *The City of God*. (All the references to Augustine that follow are to *The City of God,* translated by Marcus Dods.) First, Augustine believed that God was in almost absolute charge of the rise and fall of nations. Rome was great and long-lasting only because of God's will (I, 36; V, 21, 26; XVIII, 22). Like the sun and rain, peace is given by God (III, 9; VII, 30). Both good and bad emperors were placed on the throne by God who acted in keeping with the times and seasons. That is, God saw when good and bad emperors were needed. So He gave the power alike to Augustus and Nero, to the Vespasians and Domitian, to Constantine and Julian (V, 19, 21).

Second, Augustine's explanation of the tragedies of history expresses this same passivity. For God sends these upon the people to correct, instruct and punish them (I, 8–9, 29; VII, 30). God distributes calamities among good and bad alike because both "love this present life" (I, 9). Sometimes Augustine explains these tragedies by saying that they provide the opposition and antitheses which, as in good literature, lend beauty to the whole. In this way, he said, the universe is even beautified by sinners, though considered in themselves "their deformity is a sad blemish." If God does these things, why should men try to change them?

Third, Augustine stressed the grace of God, but never for the purpose of showing how the divine resources could help men in the control of events and in the management of affairs. The most that can be hoped for is that God's grace will give courage and patience to see life through this present world (XXII, 22). It works to save men for the life to come. Augustine seems to be driven to this conclusion by his conception of the two cities. The overwhelming majority of men are already consigned to the doom that awaits the earthly city (XVIII, 48). So they are beyond the reach of God's grace. The rest, who belong to the city of God, are chosen by grace for their eternal reward (XIV, 1). These two societies move side by side through this world, but they are headed for two altogether different destinies. Neither can really affect the other.

Fourth, the tradition of passivity is implied in Augustine's view of man. Here the main point is that man is so sinful by his fallen nature that he has no real initiative for the good. He has the power only to do evil except when God intervenes. Augustine urges that the nature of men is vitiated by birth, corrupt, and under the sway of warring forces within. Men are now the slaves of vices and sins. As a result of man's first sin, writes Augustine, ". . . there originated the whole train of evil, which, with its concatenation of miseries, convoys the human race from its depraved origin . . ." (XIII, 14). What then can this fallen creature do about the management of the larger affairs of community life?

Once more, the tradition of passivity is found in Augustine's purpose for criticizing Roman civilization. He criticizes not to reform society here and now but to justify the Christian religion and to call people to seek God. His gaze is fixed not on this world with a view to its reconstruction but upon that eternal city whose builder and maker is God. For there alone is true happiness. Sometimes Augustine speaks like a modern Christian reformer in denouncing the evils of the Roman Empire. What are greatness and glory when they produce misery? he asks. He strikes against filthy plays (II, 4, 27), against the use of vital lies to deceive the people (III, 4), against constant warfare (III, 10, 13, 14, 18, 22, 24, 27, etc.), unjust laws (III, 21), and needless luxuries which turned out to be "more destructive than all hostile armies" (III, 21). Even the peace secured by Rome was an evil. Like a modern prophet he wrote, "Peace vied with war in cruelty, and surpassed it: for while war overthrew armed hosts, peace slew the defenceless" (III, 28). By any standard, Augustine was great in recognizing injustices, barbarities, and wickedness of all sorts. So much so that we would not be surprised to find him suggesting in the name of Christ a program for the reconstruction and management of society. Here, however, his moral insight was crushed by his theological perspective.

Augustine saw Rome as if it were a huge animal lying on its back afflicted by disease and racked with pain. But he saw without seeking to cure and diagnosed without offering a remedy. Why? Because the style of the Christian was to be a pilgrim through and not an active agent in the affairs of this present world. Christians were neither able nor expected to do anything about the large forces of history.

The second major figure to be considered briefly is Luther. He and Augustine confronted very different circumstances. Augustine fought for a Christianity threatened from without; Luther fought for a Christianity threatened from within. Both men, in their own ways, embody the tradition of passivity in their thought.

This is not to deny Luther's activism. Like Augustine, he was a man of immense vitality. His achievements along many lines have left their enduring marks upon the world. He fought against the political and religious domination of Rome. His treatise, "To the Christian Nobility of the German Nation," deserves a place among the notable essays on religious liberty. He was keenly interested in political affairs. His advice to princes in the third part of his treatise on "Temporal Authority" is a call to responsible and wise leadership in government. He championed the establishment of Christian schools. To this end he wrote, "We are living in a new world today and things are being done differently." He exalted the work of a teacher.

He concerned himself also with economic questions. He favored changes in the economic order. He denounced overcharging, he approved a "common chest" for the needy, and insisted as few men have done that all worthy work is a vocation and not merely a job. His special tribute to the vocation of the writer is among the finest in all literature on the subject. He believed strongly in good works even though they had no bearing on the forgiveness of sins. In the preface to his commentary on Romans he wrote, "O, it is a living, busy, active, mighty thing this faith; and so it is impossible for it not to do good works incessantly."

This suggests that of all men Luther would seem to have no place in his thought for the tradition of passivity. Nevertheless, it is an implication of many aspects of his thought. For the basic movement of his theological perspective is that men can do little or nothing to change and manage far-reaching events. It is even arrogant and out of place to think that he can or should. This is evident in at least four aspects of his theology.

First, it is seen in his absolute concern for the individual soul in relation to God. Because of his own spiritual struggles, and because of the external and artificial religion of Rome, he turned his eyes on the inner life and found the basic answer to his own problems in the doctrine of justification by faith alone. His exposition of this in his commentaries on Galatians shows the extent to which he took this principle. In the realm of the gospel everything had to do with the act of God in justifying the soul of a man. This is why Luther could write, "For if the doctrine of justification is lost, the whole of Christian doctrine is lost." He was so eager to guard this against any possible encroachment from other quarters (such as the law, works-righteousness, morality, government, and the like) that he called for a clear distinction between the two realms. On the one hand was the realm of the gospel; on the other, the sphere of law and political power. To be sure, the law functioned to warn of God's wrath and to show man his sinfulness. In a negative way, then, it prepared a man for the grace of God. But otherwise the two spheres were held apart by Luther. Beyond this it is clear that he found no organic interconnection between the salvation of the soul by faith and the desire to reshape society.

This brings us to the second aspect of Luther's thought involving passivity, namely, the almost absolute separation of law and gospel, secular and spiritual, good works and faith. Luther of course recognized the role of *human* righteousness in political, civil, legal and family affairs. He was aware that there were many good men even among pagans. But he urged that their kind of goodness was as nothing before God. Man's good works have no power to forgive, to deliver from death, to purchase life, nor to gain favor with God. Just as Augustine separated the earthly from the heavenly city, so Luther separated law and gospel, the secular and the spiritual. The dualism could not be absolute in either case. Nevertheless, it was as nearly so as was possible in both men.

Passivity is implied in this because it does not really matter what the Christian does about the affairs of this present world. He is not judged (as the Bible seems to teach) by his deeds but by whether or not he has faith. If he has faith, he may do good works but those deeds do not count one way or another with God. Luther urged that the Christian's good works please God only because of his faith and not because they produce the desired results. Here Luther, in the interest of preserving the important Biblical teaching on justification by faith alone, lost sight of God's aims for men on earth and of the authentic function of good deeds. At best the connection between grace and responsible involvement in the affairs of this world is very loose. Luther does not even want to say with the scholastics that faith does not continue to justify "except it be furnished by charity." The point is that as far as the gospel is concerned we need not bother about the larger issues of human societies. Curiously enough, then, in the realm of the deepest spiritual power, namely, the realm of grace, there is little or no clear and consistent connection with the management of affairs in this present world.

That this was the way his thought moved is seen clearly in his reaction to the twelve articles of the Swabian peasants. This may be taken as one instance out of many that might be cited. Luther wrote:

Not one of the articles teaches anything of the gospel. Rather, everything is aimed at obtaining freedom for your person and for your property. To sum it up, everything is concerned with worldly and temporal matters. You want power and wealth so that you will not suffer injustice. The gospel, however, does not become involved in the affairs of this world, but speaks of our life in the world in terms of suffering, injustice, the cross, patience, and contempt for this life and temporal wealth.

As long as the gospel remains the gospel it is necessarily separated from involvement in ethical responsibility for the larger structures and events in this world. Thus, in allowing man (even the man justified by faith) no merit before God for responsible living in community, Luther missed one of the finest springs of social action and, at the same time, misunderstood the revealed nature of God for men on earth.

Again, the tradition of passivity is present in a third aspect of Luther's thought, namely, that on the Christian in relation to the powers that be. This is a further specification of his general teaching on the two spheres of God's activity. Here the essential role of the Christian is that of acceptance and obedience. Those in authority are to be obeyed. For, whether good or bad, they are of God.

The theological basis for all this (in addition to Romans 13:1–7 and 1 Peter 2:13–17) is that God in His wrath controls fallen men by means of political authority. In this sphere God's love functions as law, coercion, punishment. ". . . the kingdom of the world is a kingdom of wrath and severity." For God established the political order to deal with man in his fallenness. That order is suited to that nature. It must not be defied, opposed, or disobeyed. Luther was thus a champion of the status quo and a political reactionary, because he believed that God had established the powers that be, and they were acceptable to God alone.

Therefore, Christians were not to do anything about them. It was not only that men were not to rebel against them, or rise in protest; it was also that, except for the rulers themselves, men were not to seek, in the name of Christ, ways and means of revising and improving the political structures.

The fourth aspect of Luther's theology that nurtures the tradition of passivity is his view of man as a fallen and helpless creature. This is expressed with surpassing force in his *De Servo Arbitrio* (*On the Bondage of the Will*), his only work other than his *Catechism* which he thought (according to his letter to Capito, dated July 9, 1537) should abide above all his other writings. Luther's view of human nature is that man, though able to do many things in the affairs of this world, is totally helpless in the spiritual realm. This is so stated as to imply that man seems to be incapable of doing anything good by his own free will. Left to himself, he is bound by the devil. Only when he is restored by grace can he begin to function on the good

196

side. Even here his nature is so polluted that there is no real righteousness in him. When a man has faith God graciously imputes a righteousness that is not present. These ideas are reiterated by Luther again and again.

This way of thinking about man tends to make him feel that all efforts at responsible involvement in the larger affairs of nations and communities is either futile or presumptuous.

There are other aspects of Luther's theology which, when brought together with those here considered, show even more explicitly how much he did to nurture the tradition of passivity in Christianity. These may be mentioned with very little elaboration. He believed that this present world was chronically evil and under the sway of the devil. The only real deliverance was not by changing it but by being released from it through a faith that enables men to rise above it. Beyond that, deliverance could come only by divine intervention. Luther believed also that in some mysterious ways God was at work in the larger forces of history to carry out His ends. The Turks were the instruments of His wrath and possibly the weapons whereby He would destroy the world.

Luther believed that the end of this world was imminent. The Lord would soon return. So there was no time-span in which man could do anything in any case. Hence, again, the tradition of passivity.

In contrast to all this, a second way of looking at the relationship between Christianity and the present world is marked by social activism. Here the Christian religion is understood almost wholly in terms of the moral responsibility for social change and betterment. This general approach came to clear focus during the first half of the twentieth century in the United States in the form of the social gospel movement. Many thinkers prepared the way for it. Immanuel Kant said that religion is regarding duties as divine commands. Matthew Arnold spoke of it as morality tinged with emotion. Countless others might be mentioned.

The social gospel grew out of complex developments in the modern world. There was the idea of progress. There emerged the idea that societies were made what they are by men, so they can be remade by men. Culture is the sum of all that man has invented and learned, namely, his tools, his machines, his ideas, his languages, his traditions, his religions, his standards and values, his institutions. Since man has created these, he can change them. Among the most important tools that have helped in this process are the behavioral sciences, especially psychological and societal studies. Therefore, the contemporary world has come within the range of a break-through in social improvement. We can now speak of the possibility of "social salvation."

Where does religion come in? Religion undergirds the moral responsibility to change and improve the human world. Just as some identify Christianity with correct belief and others with a certain type of feeling, here many identify it with moral concern. Religion is social action. The experiences of prayer, joy in the presence of God, worship, the awareness of the Lordship of Christ, communion with fellow Christians, and the sense of a meaningful future with God, these are viewed as relatively worthless unless they put men in a position to hear the one compelling call to act for community well-being. Social vision and community service are the sum of religion.

In this type of Christian activism the sermons preached and the classes taught are dominated by themes on community and world problems. War and peace, race relations, poverty, slums, overpopulation, family problems, and all major forms of injustice and inhumanity, these are the areas of concern.

The Christian activists, as we are considering them here, have little or no place for a living faith in God. Everything depends on man and is accomplished by man. Though these activists often express themselves with the aid of a vocabulary that is Biblical and Christian, they find all that is meaningful in Christianity in moral experience, duty, action. Religious faith is translated into moral concern, prayer is reduced to deeds of love and mercy, worship is turned into involvement in social action, and "the sense of the presence of God" is rendered "the sense of fellow feeling with men in need." They talk about the

United Nations, the ghetto, poverty, peace, job opportunities, education, the knowledge explosion, and social order as if God were nothing more nor less than man-in-his-humane-concerns-and-deeds. In many instances, if one were to ask what difference it would make if such activists were moralists only, with no interest in Christianity as a religion, the answer would be "none." That is, their total resource comes from the moral sphere with no assignable resource from faith in God.

The recent stress on secular Christianity is a kind of clarification of the thesis that God is totally present in man and in his interpersonal and cultural relationships. What man at his best strives for, God is doing; for God is nothing more nor less than man in his hopes and efforts for good. This is the real meaning of Jesus Christ. He is God acting for man because He is man acting for man. The unique importance of Jesus Christ, as understood in Christianity is almost totally obscured by confining His work to that of a moral example. The God Jesus talked about as Father is lost in the overwhelming concern "to get with it," "to get where the action is."

Sometimes this kind of humanistic and secularistic activism takes on extreme forms, as in the varieties of existentialism that stress radical discontinuity. Here Christian action may lead in any direction as long as it is toward change. The aim is not to secure human well-being (as the humanistic activist wants to do) but to find God in protest, in change, and even in the disruption of society. For after all, every situation has its own unique meaning. This type of activism recurs in every generation among at least a few. It shares in the kind of humanistic activism described in the foregoing paragraphs only in that God's action tends to be identified almost wholly with that of men.

THE BIBLICAL TEACHING

Two preliminary remarks are necessary before considering the Biblical teaching on the call to responsible participation in the affairs of this world.

First, that teaching is a part of a large pattern of developing ideas on the purpose of God for man's life. We cannot understand the Biblical perspective here merely by bringing together some widely scattered verses on one side or another. Here is where a principle of Biblical interpretation presented in chapter 2 becomes specially relevant. I refer to the principle of the organic unity of type. It will be recalled that, according to this principle, any major teaching of the Bible is to be understood in its development. It must be seen in its beginnings, its growth through succeeding prophets, teachers, and events, and its fulfillment in keeping with its essential nature. In the case of this teaching its full development moves beyond the Bible itself into the succeeding generations of Christians as they become involved in historical situations. There is first the seed, then the stalk, then the fruit.

The second preliminary remark is that there are passages in the Bible which, when taken by themselves, would appear to imply the idea of passivity. For example, God is said to have loved Jacob and hated Esau. There was nothing either man or his descendants could do about it. This is mentioned in several passages and even Paul makes use of the idea. Nations are used by God as instruments of His wrath. Romans 9 strongly suggests the idea that God is so much in charge of everything that little is left for man to do. Some men are "vessels of wrath" and others "vessels of mercy" and nothing they do can change this. The passages along this line are present in sufficient numbers for us to understand how Augustine, Luther, Calvin and others developed strong doctrines of predestination. The main point here is that while these passages are to be found throughout the Bible they do not represent the primary spirit and movement of the Biblical teaching, which required the centuries that followed to become more fully visible.

The Biblical teaching, in its main thrust, necessarily moves toward the belief that man has been called by God for responsible action in all the affairs his decisions can affect. Along with this there is the sustained idea that God will help him as he seeks to act responsibly in human affairs. Therefore, the social gospel movement of the first half of the twentieth century says something that is implicit in the Biblical teaching. Similarly, the contemporary call to Christian involvement in the secular world, with a view to learning from it and transforming it, is likewise implied in the Biblical teaching.

There are at least four major factors in the Biblical revelation that combine to express this activism.

1. There is the idea of God as acting to achieve His aims. This forward-moving, purposive nature of God is the primal source of Christian activism. This understanding of God has been discussed already so its bearing on the theme at hand may be stated without further development. The connection is obvious.

2. Implied in that understanding of God is the belief that man has a crucial role to play in this world. In contrast to all perspectives, East and West, which suggest that this present realm is either unreal or unimportant, the Bible teaches that man's life here and now is both real and decisive. God created the universe to realize His aims. He brought man into being for a meaningful career on earth. Consequently, man's response within the whole enterprise is of utmost concern to God. This divine concern is expressed on the one hand, in the "wrath" of God, and on the other, in the call of God. God's "wrath" expresses His disapproval of man and society as they are. The prophets were always warning men, showing them their folly, and calling them to fulfill their responsibilities in society. Consequently, there was the reminder of the judgment of God that was directly connected with man's management of his affairs in relation to the will of God.

3. The Bible repudiates passivity in the life and work of its most important characters. The outstanding leaders were men whose openness to God led them to be discontent with things as they are. The Bible is a book about moral and spiritual adventurers. The vision of God gave them a vision of the promised land, or of moral and spiritual renewal, or of the Kingdom of God. It was no accident that in the Old Testament the vision of the Kingdom of God was largely in terms of a new society on earth. After his encounter with God in Midian, Moses could

no longer be content to abandon his people who were enslaved in Egypt. When he was their leader in the wilderness he did not abandon them to social disorder. On the contrary, he organized them by means of law and covenant so they could continue to maintain their identity as a people. He was a master in the management of a disrupted people.

The prophets did not allow the masses, or kings and queens, or any others to forget their responsibilities for the present and future direction of human affairs. It was their mission, among other things, to show that God's thoughts and ways are not man's, and that man must expend his energies in trying to fashion into fact the demands of God for social change. Throughout the Old Testament there is the cumulative impression that men are called to participate in courageous and creative living with God's help for the improvement of society. Even in the midst of adversity there is the recurring appeal to hold fast to God in anticipation of the future community of Israel under Him.

In the New Testament there is the awareness of God's call to newness of life through faith in Jesus Christ. He came to deliver men from sin, mediocrity, disease and death. His mission was to men now. For God's energies were available to awaken those who put their trust in Him as their Father. The teaching on God as Father would seem to imply the ordering and management of community life for the well-being of all concerned. The New Testament teaching on Christian activism in relation to community affairs is largely undeveloped. It is there, implicit throughout, but it required later developments in Christianity for the implications to emerge. Certainly, Jesus and His followers demanded the kind of love that never could be confined to merely personal relations.

4. Closely related to this is the theme that implies the repudiation of passivity. This is the moral concern for the well-being of men in community that comes to fulfillment in the dynamics of Christian love. This love, of course, expresses itself in concrete acts. The cup of cold water for the thirsty, bread

for the hungry, clothes for the naked, and personal interest in the sick and the strangers, these are among the ways love expresses itself. Jesus, in His own example, demonstrated the direction in which love moves and must move.

Love is necessarily dynamic. The man who loves his fellow-men does things in their behalf. Christian love as exemplified in Jesus concerns itself with *results* that are beneficial to people. Paul too expressed this same concern for the physical and spiritual well-being of men, including the "outsiders" called the Gentiles. To be sure, in the New Testament love is understood primarily as it functions in the face-to-face situations of small groups. But in principle the Biblical teaching calls for the kind of love that reaches out as far and wide as it can to give men meaning and opportunity with God's help. Therefore, the Biblical teaching on moral concern and Christian love repudiates the idea of passivity. It requires responsible involvement in every area that significantly affects human well-being. In a developing world the simple individual expressions of Christian love necessarily take on far more extensive proportions. For example, the cup of cold water implies, in later developments, public water works with facilities for purification. So is it in relation to every other expression of the love that Jesus taught. This is another indication of how necessary it is in understanding the Bible *to move with the Biblical heritage into its authentic extensions in the contemporary world*. He who understands the Bible without reference to its developing implications for an ongoing world does not understand the Biblical teachings.

SOME MODERN DOUBTS AND RESPONSES TO THEM

The primary doubts about the Biblical teaching on passivism and activism concern the stances the church has actually taken on social issues. In particular, there are two criticisms of the church regarding her approaches to these larger issues. First, it is said the church does not really care. Second, when it does care, it gets on the wrong side. If the Biblical teaching on which the church claims to base its thought and life, leads to either of these ways of responding to the larger social issues, then is there not something radically wrong with that teaching? We shall consider these two criticisms in the order presented.

Doubt   The church does not care. That is, she is so pre-occupied with the inner life, comfort, the spiritual realm, and the world to come that her energies are used up without getting really involved in the issues having to do with the control and management of affairs in this world.

Response   Three comments are in order. First, there is painful truth in the criticism. Many Christians find in their religion a protective cathedral within whose walls they can shut out the world. There they worship, pray, meditate, sing, chant, and go through their familiar ceremonies oblivious to the vast sufferings and privations of their fellow human beings. They are quietists. They do not want to be disturbed. The charge that religion is the opiate of the people has enough truth in it to hurt.

Second, this undue stress on the inner life is not authentic Christianity; it is one-sided. It lacks balance. The basic Biblical teaching here is that the inner life must express itself in beneficial and responsible outer deeds, else it is not authentic even in its inner quality. Love must act to achieve the Father's ends, namely, the well-being of all His children. Jesus perfectly illustrated this combination of the inner and outer life. He prayed, He engaged in corporate worship; but He always moved into the world where men lived and worked and suffered. When He invited men to follow Him, He called them to inner rightness with God and to outer deeds in behalf of men. The Biblical teaching, then, requires both of these emphases, the inner life with God and outer results for men in community.

John Calvin and John Wesley, perhaps as much as any two men in Christian history, lifted up this essential combination of the Biblical heritage. John Calvin did it not by his stress on predestination but by his emphasis on the elect and their responsibility for leadership in this world.

John Wesley brought together the inner life of grace and the

outer life of responsible living by his distinctive ways of stress-
ing personal religion. He combined the truth of pietism with
the truth of Christian activism. He showed that while men are
justified by God's forgiving grace through faith, they cannot
continue in God's favor without constructive service to those
in need. He made it a special point to urge that the new life
born in men through forgiveness and grace is inherently connected with responsible living toward others here and now. For
him this meant involvement with men in need, such as prison-
ers, the ignorant, the sick, the poor, the enslaved, the drunkards,
and those who are considered the least among men. His war
against slavery is one of the finest achievements in Christian
statesmanship.

This combination is reflected also in Wesley's synergism,
that is, man's cooperation with God in the salvation process.
The leaders of the Reformation did not want to recognize any
human response as a factor in man's salvation. To be sure,
Wesley joined Luther in urging that men are justified by faith
alone. They bring no merit of their own. But he said also that
no man can be in a position to be justified by God's grace unless he responds to God. Every man has the built-in or God-
given power to respond to God, if he wants to. This teaching
has a direct bearing on Christian activism. For if man has the
power to respond to God in the salvation process, surely he
has the power to act toward his neighbor in ways that please
God.

In contrast to Luther at this point, Wesley taught that when
a man is justified he is regenerated. He is a new being and not
merely one who is called righteous because of Christ's righteousness. The idea that God imputes righteousness because of
Christ's righteousness is artificial and unreal. Wesley stressed
the realities here. If a man is not in fact just, it makes no sense
to call him just, even in the name of Christ. In Wesley all this
was given its highest interpretation in his teaching on goodness or holiness. He insisted that goodness is not limited to a
select few who separate themselves from the world but is available, with God's help, to every man who involves himself in

the world. In fact, God expects sanctity of everyone and consequently is eager to help him experience it and manifest it in his deeds of love. The point is that Wesley and his followers have something to offer the ecumenical movement and authentic Christian activism by this combination of grace and social concern that leads to responsible action.

More than this, the total direction of God's revelatory aims as made known in the Bible appears clearly to move toward this end.

There is a third response to the charge that the church does not care, namely, that Christians need to do some rethinking. In the light of this vast movement of the purpose of God, and in the light of recent insights from psychological and societal studies, a restatement of the Biblical and Christian stance is indicated. That restatement would necessarily bring together what have been too often separated: a strong re-emphasis on the dynamics of God's grace coupled with an equally forceful statement on the kinds of social involvement and action that necessarily flow out of the lives of those in the community of faith who are actually under the sway of Christ. The call in the name of Christ is for the responsible management of all human affairs.

Doubt   The second criticism of Christianity pertaining to social action is to the effect that when the church does care it is on the wrong side. Here the point is not that Christians are uninvolved or passive but that they absorb the standards and values of the world and consequently support the status quo. Consciously or unconsciously the church uses its power to maintain social evils and to stifle creative advance.

Response   Here again several responses are indicated. First, this too contains the kind of truth that hurts. The history of the church's reactions to nearly every effort toward cultural and social betterment is often disappointing. For example, its record in relation to war and peace, slavery, race relations, the advancements in science and technology, the developments in culture and civilization, is at best ambiguous and, at times, tragic in the extreme.

Second, there are two characteristics of the church just as there are of society in general. One is the deep-seated desire to conserve; the other is the dynamic prophetic urge toward change. Many observers have analyzed the workings of these two factors in human societies. When things are going reasonably well (at least for those who are in charge) the conserving tendency becomes predominant. The call is for law, order, stability as against disruption and anarchy. Generally speaking, men prefer tyranny to anarchy.

But there is also the tendency to be discontent with things as they are. Men require change and seek improvement. The modern mind has contributed especially to the techniques for improvement. The advances in science and technology, and especially in business and financial enterprise, have made men discontent with things as they are. Hence, in medicine, housing, urbanization, social welfare, business management, education, labor relations, and in many other aspects of society there are massive efforts to upgrade and improve the standards. Techniques for self-criticism and re-evaluation are extensively used. In all these efforts there is the natural drift toward mediocrity and toward an easy acceptance of things as they are. Nevertheless, the desire to improve is one of the major factors in the modern world. More than this, the techniques for improvement have been built into man's enterprises. It is this that makes the plight of the underprivileged nations all the more pathetic. Here the church must sit at the feet of the modern world and learn where she, in carrying out God's business, can do her part more effectively both in the management of her own life and of community life.

Third, within the Biblical heritage there has always been this prophetic and forward-moving tendency. The prophets were adventurers. They called for repentance and change in the moral and spiritual realm. Throughout Christian history they have risen to call for justice and love. Sometimes they have worked quietly and persistently to establish educational and other institutions for human well-being. At other times they have followed the path of protest. But in their ways the voice of God in judgment and concern has been heard.

It is not true that the church has merely championed the status quo and stifled the spirit of adventure. Her record is ambiguous partly because there is necessarily in all institutions that manage to survive a strong conserving tendency. But in nearly every situation of human need the church has raised up prophets and architects of a new day. Too often, perhaps, she has been heard in protest without helping in the call to responsible management. But whether in the prophetic voice of protest against injustice and inhumanity or in the more difficult prophetic work of reshaping society through institutions that give opportunity and meaning to life, the church has done its work for good in the larger affairs of mankind.

In the sphere of moral and spiritual renewal the church has no rivals. Sometimes her prophetic work has gone on for years without much notice until the time was ripe for massive social improvements. At other times her leadership has been more conspicuous in protest and in the cry for justice. But always she has sent into the world those who, under the sway of Christ, have called men to God and to the justice and love He requires.

Christianity is unalterably committed to the elevation and improvement of human beings and their conditions in this present life.

Fourth, the church has often been alone in urging that back of all human improvement there must be a moral and spiritual reformation. Without this basis the advances in science, technology, business, and even education become further instruments for man's selfishness, mediocrity, and inhumanity. Therefore, the church has a unique role to play in all the quests for improvement. That role is to call men to God and to the moral responsibility He demands. Without this, if we are to judge by the history of nations and civilizations, there is little basis for sustained hope for the future of mankind on this planet.

14

CHRISTIANITY AND THE
REVOLUTION IN SEX

As modern man looks toward the fantastic future just around the corner he wonders where he is headed in his sexual behavior. Old standards and values are giving way. The authority symbols are losing their grip. The revolution in sex is here. There is nothing new about abandoning Christian standards in sexual activities. Nearly every conceivable variety of sexual indulgence, from orgies, to perversions, to promiscuity, has taken place since ancient times. What is new is the more frank and widespread repudiation of those standards.

In no area of practical living is it more important to identity clearly the major alternative approaches, including the Biblical teaching, so that men may reflect wisely on this vital subject. Here, too, questions and doubts require credible responses. This is an age that has largely abandoned the idea of external authority. If there is to be any authority, it must come from persuasion. And persuasion begins with a clear understanding of the alternatives.

THE MAIN ALTERNATIVE VIEWS

There are no *new* options in sex. All of them have been thought of before and all have been practiced before. Nevertheless, there are several new factors that affect the attitudes and behavior of men in their sexual relations. These must be introduced into any discussion of the alternative approaches. There are at least four major approaches to sex that need to be considered within the context of the human situation on the eve of the twenty-first century.

According to one approach, man is primarily a physical being with strong sexual drives, and it does not make much difference how these drives are satisfied. The main thing is to get sexual gratification. Those who adopt this view do so not so much from thought as from instinct or passion. Theirs is an instinctive approach to sex. The theory, if stated, simply expresses the way some people want to live. In fact they feel compelled to express themselves in keeping with the sexual demands of their bodies. Just as men need food, water, and air, so they need sex. It is a corollary to this view that people should feel free to experience sex when and where and with whom they want. Neither society nor the church has any right to restrict its free expression. The possible ranges of sexual expression within this general perspective move all the way from promiscuity to abnormal forms of sexual behavior.

All this is given more plausibility in the modern situation by the recent methods of birth control. For example, the "pill," when used, has reduced the likelihood of pregnancy and prepared the way for a more free attitude toward sexual relations. Modern medical advances in the prevention and cure of venereal diseases have also tended to create more permissive attitudes. (As we shall see, however, during the 1960s venereal diseases in the United States showed a marked increase.) Other factors too make for a more easygoing involvement in sexual intimacies. These include the mode of dress, the easy access to privacy away from home and from the rest of society in automobiles (which are movable rooms), the readiness to talk about sex more freely, the "adult" movies in which intimate contacts between the sexes are so frequently portrayed, sex-saturated magazines and paperback books, and the general attitude toward external authority. As a result of this last there is in many minds the idea that both young people and adults have the right to experience the full satisfaction of sexual desires without stifling restrictions.

Second, somewhat related to this view is the theory of free love. Those who hold to this view insist that sexual intimacies should be entered into by young people not only for the sake of pleasure but also for experimental purposes. That is, they should feel free to discover for themselves, by direct experience, what sex is like. In this way they not only satisfy a basic need, they prepare themselves for a more informed sex life in the future. Few things are more important than the selection of a compatible companion for marriage. But how can people know what to look for without this period of experimentation? The idea here is that by entering rather freely into sexual intimacies either with one partner or with a variety of partners one is apt to discover what he is looking for in the choice of a mate. This approach too is found more plausible by the new factors in the modern situation mentioned above.

A third approach is that true love and sexual intimacies should go together whether the partners are married or not. This means, on the one hand, that when two people are not in love with each other, intimate sexual relations should not occur. It means, on the other hand, that two partners in love, whether married or not, rightly express themselves in these intimacies, including sexual intercourse. The body is an instrument for expressing this authentic love. Therefore, whenever such love is present (whether apart from any interest in marriage, or prior to marriage, or in marriage, or outside of marriage) such behavior is to be accepted. This view too is made more convincing by the modern improvements in birth control.

The fourth approach is the Biblical-Christian view to which we now turn for a more detailed elaboration.

THE BIBLICAL TEACHING

Many references to sex can be found in the Bible. Some passages express the crude ways of men. The story of Lot and his two daughters is an instance (Genesis 19:30–38). King David ordered his general Joab to send Uriah to the "forefront of the hardest fighting." He ordered him then to draw back from Uriah "that he may be struck down, and die." In carrying out this order despite its being a military blunder, Uriah and several of David's servants were killed. In his report to David explaining the costly mistake, Joab made sure that, at the end, there was the statement: "Your servant Uriah the Hittite is dead also" (2 Samuel 11:2–24). Why this murder of a devoted subject? Because David wanted Uriah's beautiful wife, Bathsheba, for himself. It would be difficult to find in all literature a story that more graphically illustrates how a man of influence and ability can stoop to the most reprehensible act in the interest of sex.

Jesus knew the problems of sex when He spoke of His contemporaries as belonging to "An evil and adulterous generation . . ." (Matthew 12:39). Paul was familiar with the sexual aberrations that have attended human existence in all eras (Romans 1:26–27). He dealt with incest (1 Corinthians 5:1), adultery (1 Corinthians 6:9), prostitution (1 Corinthians 6:15–16), and the power of man's sexual drives (1 Corinthians 7:5,9, 36). The Biblical writers did not live in a naïve dreamworld regarding sex. They knew the realities and they reflected on them in the light of God's will for men.

There is an essential unity in the Biblical teaching on sex. This is seen when we consider the major ideas bearing on this theme, which fit together, develop, and maintain their essential identity. There are at least six such ideas that go into the Biblical teaching.

First, that teaching begins with God who has a purpose for every major aspect of man's life. Like everything else, sex is understood not as an accidental human interest but as a factor in God's over-all plan for man's life on earth. In the Book of Genesis there are four thoughts about God and sex. 1. God made man male and female and ordered them to "Be fruitful and multiply, and fill the earth and subdue it . . ." (1:27–28). 2. He made man and woman for each other (2:18). 3. The relationship between the sexes comes to its proper expression in marriage. "Therefore a man leaves his father and his mother and cleaves to his wife, and they become one flesh" (2:24). 4. God was pleased with all this and saw that "it was very good" (1:31). These four teachings from Genesis emphasize the point that this deep-seated sexual drive was created by God when He made man, and its expression is a built-in feature of man's life on earth. He approved it as an authentic process in human dynamics.

There have been periods in Christian history when sex was looked on as a necessary evil. Some Christians today so regard it. But this is not characteristic of the developing teaching of the Bible. Sex is neither bad nor sinful. Rather, it is God's strategy of involving man in the continuation of the human race. In this regard Schopenhauer expressed in a secular way at least one aspect of the Biblical teaching. He observed that back of the love between the sexes is the mysterious urge to keep the race going (see his essay on "The Metaphysics of the Love of the Sexes" in *The World as Will and Idea,* translated by R. B. Holdane and J. Kemp).

Beyond this, God was interested in a suitable way of protecting and nurturing this race during its immature years. The words, "be fruitful and multiply," imply parental responsibility for the children. For this process involves a man and a woman, not just humanity in general. It is the policy of God, then, to use man's sexual drive to bind people together by intimate ties for the instruction, guidance, and economic support of human beings during their formative years.

The account in Genesis suggests also that God had another purpose for introducing sex into human relations, namely, to enhance the companionship of a man and woman for each other. This is at least a part of the meaning of the sentence: "It is not good that the man should be alone; I will make him a helper fit for him" (Genesis 2:18). It is a part of the thought too that husband and wife become "one flesh." Sex had to be a dynamic force in order to serve as a major factor in bringing a man and woman together in a deep and abiding relationship. The basic answer to loneliness at the human level was given by means of the two sexes. The helper suited to a man is a woman. The helper suited to a woman is a man. Therefore, in addition to the propagation and nurture of the race, sex is an important factor in meeting the need for an intimate companionship.

Second, the Biblical teaching on sex is a part of the larger understanding of man. Here, as we have seen in an earlier chapter, man is understood in his relationships to God. He is not viewed primarily as related to nature, nor as an animal among animals, nor as a creature in human society, nor as an object for psychological study. Without minimizing these other approaches, we may say that in the Bible man is understood as made by God, for God, to live and work with God in community.

The Bible teaches that man is a creature of body and spirit who is precious in God's sight. He has dignity because of his unique relationships to God. Without these he not only would have no dignity, he would not even exist. Man is a special kind of creature, made after the likeness of God. This means that, as in the case of no other known creature, man has special areas of kinship with God. Jesus put it this way: God is our Father and we are members of His family. By birth God has set His mark and seal on man and claimed him for Himself. God knows and loves His children.

All this implies responsibility to God as well as to other men in every aspect of life, including sex. Consequently, there are wrong ways of expressing sex, namely, in those sexual intimacies that disregard mutual respect and human dignity under God. This leads to wrong relationships with God and man, which in turn lead to emptiness and despair in this life and to tragedy in the next. Here the Bible teaches that it is not enough merely to say man turns away from God. We must say also that for some reason, not adequately explained in the Bible, there are in man built-in tendencies away from God. Sex is good, but like so many other vital impulses, it lends itself to evil. Man has a fight on his hands in every noble endeavor and in every effort to participate creatively with God and men. How a man treats another human being is organically connected with his relationships with God. If anyone has a cheap attitude toward another person in expressing his sexual impulses, or if he wishes to use other people for selfish gratification without regard to human dignity, then God is at war with him. The Biblical teaching at this point is as plain as that. God abhors the loss or corruption of human dignity and self-respect.

It is self-evident that anyone who takes seriously the Biblical view of man will reflect this in his attitudes and conduct. If a man thinks of himself as an accidental product of the blind, impersonal, chemical processes of nature, he will find it easier to take advantage of a partner in sex. For he will regard himself as an animal among animals who does not need to take seriously the questions pertaining to the soul, dignity, personality development, social well-being, and human destiny. Therefore, in the Bible man's sexual activity is understood as only one of the basic factors in the total process of living on earth. It is not to be expressed (any more than other major interest) apart from man's responsible relationships to others.

Third, the Biblical teaching comes to focus in a special way in Jesus Christ. What did Jesus say or imply regarding sex? He emphasized some things that were long familiar. He taught that by creation God made a man and a woman for each other. When married, the two become one flesh (Mark 10:7–9). The full force of His teaching is to bring love and loyalty together. He was radically opposed to those who move from one sexual partner to another. Jesus made it impossible for Christians to cheapen sex by disconnecting it from loyalty to and respect for the partner in sex. For this reason He took divorce seriously and regarded it as a major tragedy (Matthew 5:31–32). He repudiated promiscuity as a bad way of life. Jesus taught also that everyone should guard with care the inner quality of his desires and not let sexual lust run rampant (Matthew 5:27–28).

At the same time, Jesus urged that those who lapse into moral failure here should be treated redemptively and creatively. He knew that people made mistakes. Jesus condemned adultery. Nevertheless, He responded with redemptive love toward the woman caught in the act of adultery (John 8:1–11). He knew that she was ashamed of herself. He knew also that she was far more important as a person than any act she committed. He did not approach her with a sentimental attitude suggesting that "we are all human." He took both her misconduct and her value as a person seriously. He saw that He could not have helped her maintain her self-respect if He had approved her former acts. So He said to her, "Has no one condemned you?" She said, "No one, Lord." Then He looked at her and said, "Neither do I condemn you; go, and do not sin again." This scene, though somewhat questionable in its manuscript basis is one of the most spiritually authentic in the New Testament. There Jesus taught that no one is so free from sin as to condemn another person. He taught also that, where sex is concerned, any cheap involvement with a partner cuts a person off from God and from a high regard for oneself.

Similarly, when Jesus encountered the Samaritan woman at Jacob's well He knew that she had been living with five different men and that the one she was then living with was not her husband (John 4:16–18). But Jesus saw beneath the mistakes in her sexual behavior. He saw this woman as a person created by the Father for the new life of the Spirit.

A fourth part of the Biblical teaching bearing on sex is that self-giving love is the basic principle of action toward another person. Jesus said that there are two great commandments: Love God, and love your neighbor as yourself (Matthew 22:36–40). This love is not to be confused with sentimentality. It is not primarily a feeling. It is not the desire to let everyone have his own way. *Love is the sustained desire for God's best for everyone. Therefore it is purposive and dynamic.* It has a goal to attain. Just as God's love aims toward the enrichment and salvation of men, so Christian love seeks beneficial results for them. It seeks these in *every* aspect of life from the most elemental bodily needs to the deepest spiritual longings.

What is the bearing of this Biblical teaching on the sexual behavior of people? It bears directly on sex in three ways.

1. It fixes attention on the *whole* man. Sex is only one aspect of life. Christian love neither minimizes nor stifles the proper expression of sex. It places sex in the setting of life as a whole. The Bible never teaches that sexual values are the most important in the cosmos of values. They have their place within the total setting of higher values.

2. Christian love bears directly on sex in helping people to enjoy wholesome expressions of sex. For example, love seeks to free people from foolish attitudes and destructive habits that leave them emotionally empty, isolated, and guilty. Jesus came to bring the abundant life to all. Christian love, then, demands God's best for everyone in sexual relationships.

3. Christian love makes everyone think of the satisfaction he can bring others. Each person is precious in God's sight. Therefore, Christian love, both in the preparation for marriage and in marriage, calls for the sexual behavior that makes for the highest development of the persons involved. To mistreat a partner in sex by deception, or by regarding that person as merely a means to sexual gratification, or by disloyalty, repudiates the law of love. These things destroy personal values and separate men from God.

A fifth aspect of the Biblical teaching on sex is that its true meaning is realized in marriage. All other relationships involving sexual behavior are either preparatory to marriage or destructive of it. This is implied in the order of creation itself (Matthew 19:4–6).

This is not to say that men and women must necessarily marry. Jesus Himself never married. Whether married or not, life is far more than sex. The point should be made again and again that by Biblical standards it is no mark of failure to be unmarried. Some of God's finest workmen have chosen to be single rather than to be mismatched or to be matched at all. Nevertheless, the tendency to suppose that celibacy indicates a higher purity or a closer relationship to God is not in harmony with the essential teaching of the Bible.

When it comes to *sexual* relations, the Biblical teaching is that they come to their highest expression in marriage. Five major aspects of sex in marriage may be delineated within the Biblical teaching: (1) the responsible involvement in propagating the race; (2) the consequent economic support, nurture and education of children; (3) the control of irresponsible sexual behavior (". . . it is better to marry than to be aflame with passion"—1 Corinthians 7:9); (4) developing a lifelong companionship; and (5) mutual inspiration for courageous and creative living. Therefore, marriage is ordained of God as a further expression of His policy for man's moral and spiritual growth.

Sixth, there is another Biblical teaching that bears directly on sexual behavior. This is the idea that man's resources for

217

self-direction are inadequate until they are strengthened by God's resources. The Biblical writers are fully aware of the dynamics of sex. They know how difficult it is to live in harmony with God's purpose for man in his sexual behavior. So they emphasize the adequacy of God's grace.

God forgives for past failures. This is an incomparable gain. There is nothing that so perfectly prepares a man for a new beginning as the experience of being forgiven by God. He also helps him to overcome temptation. He empowers him for creative living. The struggling stream of duty is energized and amplified by the free-flowing rivers of God. Paul writes ". . . a thorn was given me in the flesh, a messenger of Satan, to harass me, to keep me from being too elated." We do not know what that thorn in the flesh was except that it was something in his life not easy to manage. He says further that he prayed for it to leave him. But God said, "My grace is sufficient for you, for my power is made perfect in weakness" (2 Corinthians 12: 7–9).

SOME MODERN DOUBTS AND RESPONSES TO THEM

Many doubts arise in the modern mind about the Christian approach to sex. These center largely upon the Christian teaching that sexual behavior comes to its proper and highest expression only in marriage. In particular, there are three major areas of doubt that call for careful consideration. First, there are doubts that concern the restrictive character of Christianity because of its stress on the spiritual to the neglect of the physical. Second, there are questions arising out of the new factors in modern life that bear directly on man's sexual behavior. Third, there are doubts about marriage and family life. We shall consider these in that order.

Doubt   There are honest doubts about Christianity because it seems to minimize the physical needs of men. Human beings are not merely animals. But they do have powerful sexual drives that require expression. Otherwise, they encounter frustrations that may lead to psychological as well as physical

218

damage. Does not the Christian approach to sex encourage the needless and harmful repression of a vital impulse?

Response   There have been Christian thinkers and groups who tended to ignore and beat down the legitimate claims of the human body. The physical world and the human body were regarded as beneath the special interest of the spiritually minded person. In ancient times, according to the Gnostics, the whole physical realm was said to be inferior. For them salvation consisted in some kind of deliverance from it. They even denied that Jesus had a physical body like that of other men. At times Augustine practically identified original sin with the sexual drive. The monastic ideal was prompted by the idea that a radical involvement in the life and affairs of this world (including its normal sexual activities) was inferior to the special cultivation of the spiritual disciplines. The celibacy of the clergy in Roman Catholicism is based partly on this idea.

As we have seen, the Biblical teaching is that man is a physical and spiritual being. Therefore, the legitimate claims of both body and soul have to be met. This is a structural feature of an authentic Christian perspective on sex. There is nothing in the Biblical teaching that requires us to regard the physical side of life as evil. God created the body. When He wanted to reveal Himself most clearly He did so through the man, Jesus Christ, who laughed and cried, ate and slept, bled and died. "The Word became flesh." Therefore, the modern doubts here arise more from a caricature of Christianity, or from one-sided views, than from a valid account of its teachings.

Nevertheless, it should be added that for all persons who make sustained ventures in the spiritual life there is the recurring danger of neglecting the legitimate claims of the body. This may be particularly true of those who do not have as strong sexual drives as others. It may be true also of those who cannot easily sublimate those impulses. Here there are differences in degree that amount to differences in kind. Paul recognized this when he wrote, "To the unmarried and the widows I say that it is well for them to remain single as I do. But if they cannot exercise self-control, they should marry" (1 Corinthians 7:8–9).

It is part of the Christian way of life to insist that vitality requires restraint. C. S. Lewis said that when he was growing up as a teen-ager the liberal writers on sex kept asking, "Why not treat sex as we do all other impulses?" But, says Lewis, he discovered that they really were asking people to treat sex *differently* from other vital impulses. For all dynamic impulses need to be controlled and often redirected.

For example, a football team is a study in miniature of what a whole community is like. Suppose a coach were to say to the players, "Do as you like; no curfew, no training rules; practice when you feel like it; develop no game plans and plays; do not bother about team spirit and teamwork; you have complete freedom." Everyone would know not to expect an effective football team from such a policy. In every civilized society two things are brought together, namely, vitality and order. This applies to sex as it does to all other basic desires. Rules and regulations are not oppressive but creative when men see their life-subserving purpose.

Another thought to bear in mind as we reflect on these modern doubts is that sex is both physical and spiritual. Only on the level of human beings do the spiritual aspects of sex become evident. *The idea that sex is merely physical and that in this sphere at least man is an animal among animals is a crude distortion of the facts.* Sex has its physical bases. The differences between the sexes clearly show this. There are the male and female bodies. But in sexual behavior at the distinctively human level there is always this fascinating interrelationship between the physical and the personal, the physical and the moral, the physical and the spiritual. Among human beings, therefore, all efforts to reduce sex to a particular sexual act is a mistake. Many psychological studies in recent years have shown the essential validity of this Christian insight.

It is to be observed further that Christianity rightly suggests that the exaggerated concentration on sex in the interest of catering to the physical urges can interfere with solid achievements. Beyond a certain point the returns from sexual behavior are minimal. When exaggerated beyond reason, sex becomes a distraction of such serious proportions as to disqualify some people from creative participation in the human enterprise. The Christian teaching contains a warning that sex, like all other vital impulses, readily admits of gross exaggeration and perversion. The consequences can be disastrous to an individual, to a family, and to some extent to a community.

Doubt　　　Second, there are honest doubts arising from the new factors and problems in the modern world that affect sexual behavior. For example, there are modern methods of birth control, including the pill. There are all the problems pertaining to the population explosion. How do these bear on sex? There are the new ranges of mobility. People get around more. Some speak of the architecture of modern homes, with their lack of privacy, as conducive to more freedom on the part of young people as they engage in sexual intimacies away from home. There are changed attitudes regarding transient physical intimacies. In the modern world there are so many occasions when such intimacies are easy and natural that the Christian approach seems out of date. Do not the magazines that concentrate on sex and offer alluring photographs have something relevant to say to the modern world? What about the nudists with their call to enjoy the natural state of the body? Have they something to say that supersedes or would modify the Christian approach to sex? Do not the claims of the "new morality" have point? Why have fixed rules and relationships? Why not let sexual behavior vary with the situations?

Response　　　Somewhere in here we come to grips with the major problems that modern man faces regarding all aspects of his life. These problems, insofar as they have to do with morality and sex, concern human personal and social management. How can men gain the advantages of self-expression and those of personal and social management at the same time? This is a crucial question.

More specifically, what about the new factors in the modern world? Here we shall consider three.

1. There are the improved contraceptives and there are medical advances that provide cures for venereal diseases. The pill has doubtless rendered important service to married couples by giving them freedom from the recurring fear of an unwanted pregnancy. Insofar as it has been used by women outside of marriage it has reduced illegitimate births. Nevertheless, it is important to note that while the pill may have reduced the fear of pregnancy, it has probably increased the incidence of venereal diseases. And, what is as important as anything, by reducing the fear of pregnancy it has multiplied the innumerable occasions of promiscuous, and therefore mediocre, sexual expressions.

Moreover, despite all the advances in modern medicine, we have entered the new decade of the 1970s with venereal diseases on the increase. During the 1950s it appeared that we were well on the way to maintaining a high degree of control over venereal diseases, but during the 1960s the number of cases in the United States increased markedly until, at the present time, they are among the most widespread communicables diseases in the nation. Their physical consequences—sometimes delayed for ten or more years—are often disastrous. Their effects in mental anguish to all involved are beyond description.

Have modern advances really changed anything substantive regarding the meaning of sexual behavior? They may have made people more permissive, more free and easy to engage in sexual intercourse prior to marriage and outside of marriage. But these new developments have not really changed anything basic concerning the meaning and responsible expression of sex. Long before the pill there were reliable methods of contraception. The pill is simply a further convenience. Sexual intimacies have to do essentially with *persons;* the various devices are secondary. The point is that the highest expression of sex requires the kind of mutual love and respect that can be present only within a total mutual commitment. Birth control devices have no substantive bearing on this because we are here concerned with the conditions under which human dignity can be maintained. At this point we may add that the official position of the Roman Catholic Church on contraceptives is neither required by the Biblical teaching nor in harmony with science and common sense.

2. There are the changed attitudes in the modern world. People have a more casual attitude toward sexual intimacies. They talk more freely about sex, and they are not as ready to condemn others for sexual looseness. This change has come from a combination of many factors. There are the doubts about anything that has come down from the past. There are the recurring contacts and social occasions when intimacy up to a point seems natural and proper. There are the vast quantities of books and magazines that perpetually keep the readers and viewers reminded of man's sexual interests. As we move toward the twenty-first century, the adult movies join the slick magazines in saturating the imagination with sex. Here man's technical advances in photography and mass media have enabled him to achieve a degree of boldness in experience and conversation which, in its range and freedom, is new. How far these changes have affected sexual behavior itself is not easy to determine. Does not this mood affect the relevance of the Christian approach to sex? Should it not bring about a rethinking of the Christian view?

The Christian religion can make adjustments at many points. It too can emphasize the necessity and importance of sex. At its best it has always done this. But Christianity has to do with the formation of authentic persons who have a destiny with God. Therefore it is impossible for Christians to regard sex as anything more than one aspect of life. It is equally impossible for them to view sexual behavior as disconnected from the whole network of responsible interpersonal relationships. Probably the vast majority of young people today who reflect on these matters would agree with this comprehensive approach. They might state their views differently. If there are some, however, who feel they must make a choice against Christianity in the interest of a free and easy sex-saturated mentality, they may do so. They will be at war with Christianity, and Christianity will be at war with them. This will not be a new experience for Christians because, at their best, they have always been at war with the one-sided and mediocre expression of life. The Christian religion can never accept a view on any subject that tends to destroy or weaken the sense of the dignity and value of persons.

The Christian view emphasizes the importance of sex and insists that it comes to its highest expression only in marriage. It emphasizes the dangers of permissiveness and of the obsession with sex which are characteristic of a considerable number of people in this modern era. Christians move toward the twenty-first century with the conviction that they will outthink and outlive their pagan contemporaries. For, among other things, they have an incomparably superior philosophy of sex to share with mankind.

3. What about the "new morality" in relation to sex? A critical evaluation of this general view has been given in an earlier chapter. What I wish to do now is to show both the weakness and untimeliness of this mood in relation to two of the most serious problems mankind has ever faced. These two problems are: first, the problem of the population explosion, and second, the problem of genetic standards.

The "new morality," which weakens the hold of men on rules and guidelines, tends to weaken the efforts toward controlling the population explosion. It does so primarily by suggesting more freedom, individuality and permissiveness than is desirable in this area of human behavior. The point is that it tends to create an attitude of mind in which the full seriousness of sexual behavior is not adequately communicated. This is not so much a part of the explicit statements of those who expound on the "new morality" as it is a consequence of their thought patterns, categories, and emphases.

As we move into the twenty-first century, we see increasingly the need for proper planning and management in all human affairs. This will be increasingly the case regarding man's sexual behavior. Man's sexual activity may not be the major factor causing the population explosion. There are several factors at work, including especially the triumphs of medicine over diseases that previously contributed heavily to a high mortality rate. Nevertheless, now that the earth's population is so largely made up of young people in whose lives the sexual activity is most intense, the need for the responsible expression of sex becomes all the more urgent.

The "new morality" is untimely also because it does not help with the problem of genetic standards. It tends to nurture permissiveness and freedom rather than the management of the reproductive processes in the interest of guaranteeing a high genetic standard. Here again it is not that in theory the "new morality" is against such management. Rather, it is that its mood and tendency suggest this in the minds of people. This is seen especially in the popular newspaper and conversational treatments of this theme.

Doubt   This brings us to a third type of doubt about the Christian understanding of sex. I refer to the questions raised about sex and marriage. According to the Christian view, sexual relations and marriage should go together. In the modern world this is subject to question. Some think marriage is out of date. If young people want to get married, well and good. But suppose they love each other and do not want to get married. Why should they be bound by an old custom? Or, suppose they are not sure and want to experience sexual intimacies with one or more partners to find out whether or not they should get married. Again, suppose people get married who are mismatched sexually and in other ways. What if a partner in marriage meets someone else afterwards and falls in love with him? Those who report on man's sexual behavior have mentioned some extremists who engage in temporary exchanges of married partners because they seek new forms of sexual excitement. Such persons too have their reasons for regarding the Christian view of marriage as outdated.

Response   Marriage does not seem to be losing in popularity. As we move toward the twenty-first century it does not appear that it will be superseded. The doubts to be considered here, then, have to do with the unyielding stance that sexual intimacies and loyalty in marriage must go together. There are doubts on this that require careful consideration.

Some are against the Christian view because they want to feel free to engage in sexual intimacies without regard to personal values. Promiscuity is a way of life. They believe that man's animal impulses should be expressed, and they feel free to go ahead without the stultifying reflection on the value of the persons involved. The only response to this is to insist that the Christian religion requires higher standards than this and is necessarily at war with any practice that ignores or minimizes personal values. The God revealed in Jesus Christ is at war with promiscuity and with any easygoing disregard of the value of persons. This cry for unrestrained freedom and self-expression is *just another way of yielding to the tyranny of the immediate present.* But God requires the management of human beings guided by a long-range vision of what life is all about.

As we have seen, one level of honest doubt is felt by those who believe that some experience of sexual intimacies is essential to the process of finding a life partner. Granting that marriage is the ideal, how do we know that two partners will be suited to each other for life? Is it not reasonable to allow for some preliminary experimentation with different partners or with the same partner? Several comments are in order.

This sounds more plausible than it is. To be sure, nearly all Christians agree that young people need to go through a period when they date different partners. They need to get acquainted with a variety of persons to have some basis for selecting a life partner. They may engage in moderate romantic activities. But the idea that they must experience the full expression of sex in order to identify a life partner is basically unsound for several reasons.

First, it cannot be an authentic experiment. People's emotions and values are involved. Besides this, the conditions are

226

so awkward and unreal as to make the experiment no test of what a person would be like in marriage. Unhappy experiments might cause partners to lose each other when they would be in fact very much suited to each other. On the other side, such experimental sex might deceive two people into thinking they would be suitable life partners when they are not.

Again, the idea is deceptive because it implies that the real test of suitability in marriage is sexual compatibility. The fact is that sex is a part of a whole network of interrelationships. The experimentation, if we wish to call it that, should involve the encounters of whole persons in whole life-situations.

Furthermore, this view fails to take into account the fact that some things cannot be experienced without irreversible tragic consequences. People may say, "Let's try everything." "Others are doing it, why shouldn't we?" Here it is easy to forget what happens to others. One choice excludes other choices. We cannot experience being a thief and a good citizen at the same time. A boy and a girl who have engaged in sexual relations with a variety of partners and with each other cannot know the experience of those who feel that marriage is worth waiting for. They cannot know the experience of those who reserve for their true love alone this unique relationship.

Again, there is good reason to believe that such experimentation is more apt to disqualify people for a happy and useful marriage than to prepare them for it. It would be interesting to know the facts about those who have found it difficult to build an authentic marriage because of their free and easy "experimentations" prior to marriage. The questionnaires circulated among high school and college students about their sexual behavior do not tell us much about how people *ought* to act. What would be of value here would be the answers of those who have been married for ten years or more. Some of them could report on whether or not premarital sexual experimentation was a sound method of preparation for marriage. They could report on what they would have done differently. *Premarital sexual experimentation may be preparation for postmarital promiscuity.*

Finally, the idea of sexual experimentation is nearly always a rationalization with unhappy consequences. Some of these consequences need to be noted. There is usually a good deal of deception, two people acting as though in love with each other when they are not.

There is still the fear of pregnancy and the danger of venereal diseases. Who knows who else an experimental partner has been with? These diseases are incurred almost exclusively through promiscuous sexual intercourse and sexual intimacies. The fear of pregnancy may be allayed by the use of the pill, but this does nothing to free people from the increasing menace of venereal diseases. Liberalized laws on abortion, while perhaps beneficial, will not reduce the incidence of these diseases.

Moreover, from sexual promiscuity there is the sense of shame or remorse, especially on the part of the girl. There is the haunting sense of emotional emptiness. There is at times the feeling of superiority and even contempt for the partner. There is the danger of so cheapening what ought to be beautiful as to make for a cynical abandonment of authentic sexual values. There is the feeling afterwards—which sometimes disturbs married couples because of their premarital promiscuity— that the full giving of oneself, which should have been reserved for the life partner, has been thrown away on inferior relationships.

Therefore, we come back to the Christian view that sexual relations and marriage go together because these relations require full mutual respect and full responsibility.

Perhaps the most understandable doubts about the Christian view of marriage arise in the minds of those who truly love each other, but who, for one reason or another, do not feel ready for marriage. Why not say, then, that true love and sex go together? Here the doubts are on a higher level than that of coarse self-indulgence. The love is felt as genuine. It is sustained. The two partners are committed to each other. In this type of situation, as in all others, a moral decision must be made on the basis of what happens to the persons involved, not merely in a moment, but in their continuing relationships. Several factors need to be kept in view.

First, there is a vast difference between being engaged and being married. Two partners can break up an engagement relatively easily. There is an even greater difference between an unengaged couple and a husband and wife. No blood tests or physical examinations are required for engagements. This, as well as many other factors, shows a lack of full seriousness in the relationships outside of marriage. Two people do not, in fact, assume the full measure of responsibility for each other apart from marriage. Society recognizes this by its laws which, by mutual agreement, bind the partners together in the eyes of the whole community; and these bonds are not only sexual, but also economic, legal, and cultural. They involve the whole range of life; therefore, society has much at stake in good marriages.

Second, there are the fears of pregnancy which linger in the mind despite all precautions. There are the anxieties concerning whether or not the love so strongly based on sex will be sustained. Do the partners love each other as persons or are they merely finding in each other a satisfaction of urgent needs? Besides this, there are the recurring questions about the sexual relations themselves, for they may be unsatisfactory owing to anxiety, feelings of guilt, and the fear that others would misunderstand. Married couples often require a considerable time to become sexually adjusted.

Third, those in love with each other who indulge in premarital sex often feel that something precious has been shared prematurely. There is much to be said for saving this most intimate and meaningful of all sexual experiences for the one to whom a person is committed in marriage for life. This adds a special quality to the relationship. There is a mysterious depth of experience and mutual appreciation when two partners agree to consummate their sexual relations only after marriage. Before God it gives sacredness to the bond between husband and wife.

Fourth, if it is morally right to have premarital sexual relations when two partners love each other, what can be said about extramarital relations when love is present? Does not the former tend to make for more openness to sexual promiscuity? The point is that it is not merely the love of two partners for each other that clears the way for sexual relations. Rather, it is their love and their total commitment in public and before God that rightly clears the way. *Both God and society have much at stake in good and bad marriages.*

Fifth, because the way is cleared through marriage, Christians can enter into the fullest and freest expressions of sex. They can share their bodies without restraint and with a sense of joy and mutual satisfaction. In and through it all, they can experience an ever-growing love, appreciation, respect and gratitude for each other. And as they have children together, grow older together, they continue to love and enjoy each other because of the innumerable ties that now constitute their marriage under God. Therefore, the Christian ideal, though not always achieved, calls for management and self-discipline out of respect for the sacredness of the life-subserving bonds of marriage. Christians believe that God brings something special into the relationship when two partners in love hold for each other the full consummation of their sexual relations. God also makes a covenant with them when they are bound to each other in this most sacred of all earthly ties.

In summary, the Biblical teaching on sex aims toward the formation within Christians and in the Christian community of built-in standards and values that can be recommended to all men. It has its intellectual and ethical content which makes it a constructive option among the theories competing for the minds of men. More than that, it calls for the development of fully responsible persons in the *management* of their dynamic sexual drives. Out of it there emerges a style of attitude and conduct that lends itself to a redemptive-creative approach to the personal and social problems having to do with the sexual behavior of mankind.

15

CHRISTIANITY AND RACE RELATIONS

During the past fifty years few developments in the intellectual world have been more important than those in the behavioral sciences. By means of these sciences modern man has discovered new instruments for understanding himself. There may be errors in the methods and theories, but there are also important truths and techniques. Here instead of accepting mere opinions and dogmatic statements concerning men in their associational relationships, the social scientists have looked for facts and credible theories. They have studied with care nearly every aspect of man's life in community. In the first half of the twentieth century they began to study racial and ethnic groups with some real seriousness. Since mid-century they have increased enormously their research activities in race relations. Consequently, we are living in a new world of facts and insights on the races of mankind and on the problems of living together in the same world.

Except among tyrants, the day is past when men can talk dogmatically about race. The day is past too, except among racists, when men can deal in ideologies and myths on this subject. On all important theories about race and race relations innumerable scholars and students are at work. They are like an intellectual army deployed in the effort to separate fact from fiction, truth from prejudice. The tempo of their activities has been increased during the past two decades by the racial crises of this period.

These two significant forces, the advances in the behavioral sciences and the racial crises, have converged to remind the modern world of one of its most critical social problems. There is no turning away from it. Nor can it be treated casually as if the best insights of the social scientists, the educators, and the political statesmen were of little account. The church too, in some segments of its life, has been aware for many years of the social problems that come to focus in race relations. The ur-

gency of facing the problems has been brought home to every-
body by the crises in the large cities of the United States within
the past two decades.

There are many theories on the origin and significance of the
races. We cannot discuss all of them. For the present purpose
we shall consider those views on race and race relations that
bear directly on the way men act in relation to each other. First,
there are the theories based on the supposed superiority and
inferiority of races. An excellent summary of these may be
found in *Contemporary Sociological Theories* (1928), by
Pitirim Sorokin. Second, there is the theory, with its consequent
practical applications, that the races are equal but made to be
separate. Third, there is the view that calls for mutual respect
and involvement with pragmatic and not absolute policies concerning the degrees of that involvement.

Since ancient times men have been aware of the inequalities
among people. Plato and Aristotle developed significant political theories based in part on the idea that some men are by
nature made to govern and others to be governed. These
ancient thinkers were not developing this as a racial theory. It
was inevitable for some men to come along who identified this
superiority-inferiority syndrome with races. They said that
some races are superior and others inferior. It was equally inevitable for them to suggest that the future of mankind depends
on the superior races. By the same token the degeneration of
mankind would follow upon the mixing of the races.

In 1855 Joseph Arthur, comte de Gobineau, completed a
four-volume work, published in Paris, on the inequality of the
races. He developed the theory that the rise and decline of
societies was based respectively on the purity and mixing of
the races. He urged that environmental factors, whether geo-
graphic or cultural, were entirely secondary to race in the
progress and decay of societies. He argued also that the races
were probably heterogeneous in origin. This accounted for the
relative superiority and inferiority of the races. Originally, said

Gobineau, there were three pure races: white, yellow, and black. All the others are mixtures of these. The white race, especially in its Aryan branch, created the major higher civilizations of mankind. But from conquest and other factors these races began to mix, and from that mixture there resulted the inevitable consequences of mediocrity and decline.

Others followed in the line of Gobineau. For example, Houston Stewart Chamberlain in his *Foundations of the Nineteenth Century* (1910) wrote:

In spite of the broad common foundation, the human races are, in reality, as different from one another in character, qualities, and above all, in the degree of their individual capacities, as greyhound, bulldog, poodle and Newfoundland dog. Has not every genuine race its glorious, incomparable physiognomy?

Chamberlain went on to state that the races are not only different, some of them are superior and others inferior to each other. These differences are not due to environment but to racial factors. Then he developed the thesis of the superiority of the white race. Unlike Gobineau, he did not regard the mixing of the races as bad. In fact, he said, all the nobles races came from fortunate racial mixtures. Like Gobineau and others, he stressed the outstanding influence of the Teutons and the pernicious influence of the Jews.

The theorists on the superiority and inferiority of the races have developed their ideas in all sorts of ways that need not be discussed here. According to some, the size and shape of the head was the key to the mental capacities of a race. For example, G. V. de Lapouge wrote in 1896 that because of the length of the cranium and brain the blond Aryan race had made nearly all of the major advances in Western culture. In fact, he argued that social progress or decay was dependent almost entirely upon the size and shape of the brain. Education can have only very little effect. If society is to improve, the most important need is, by a process of selection, to increase the number of people in the superior racial types and to diminish the number in the inferior racial types. Nevertheless, such a process has not been taking place and the future does not give any basis for hope. So the idea of progress is a utopian dream.

Others who emphasize race as the major factor in social progress and decay have made special studies of the hereditary differences among men. The differences between genius and mediocrity have been explored in detail with the usual inference that heredity is the primary factor at work on all levels of human success and failure. From this it is but a step to the theory of racial superiority and inferiority. The chief measure is the number of men of genius produced by a particular race. The assumption here, of course, is that race is the all-important factor in the production of men of outstanding ability.

During the twentieth century two major efforts to embody the idea of racial superiority and inferiority into social structures have forced their way onto the human scene. The first was in the form of the Nazi movement, which rose to prominence in the 1930s and was brought to a halt by the defeat of Germany in World War II. It is of course well known that Adolf Hitler came to power using the theme of the superiority of the Aryan race. The races, he said, may be divided into three groups, namely, the founders, the maintainers, and the destroyers of culture. The Aryans, being superior, were to fulfill their mission by overthrowing and subduing the inferior races. As we have seen, there were learned discourses on this theme that helped to prepare the way for Hitler and the Nazi movement. In addition to those mentioned and others like them, there was the influence of all those from Hegel to Nietzsche to Spengler, not to mention Richard Wagner, who championed modes of thought tending toward the illusion that Germany should dominate the world.

The Nazi movement represents the last racially oriented effort thus far to bring together large numbers of people in a national conspiracy toward world conquest. It used the myth of racial superiority to run interference for the ancient, audacious, and crude ambition of a nation to conquer the world. Here there was no pretense at scholarly justification. The notion of racial superiority was an ideology to be communicated not by teaching but by propaganda. Every thrust of Hitler in glorifying the Aryan race was deliberately aimed to gain national power. In the end this was a demonic myth used as a weapon to unite a nation for world conquest.

The second major effort in the twentieth century to embody the idea of racial superiority in community structures came in the form of conscious efforts to sustain policies of segregation which had long been practiced. Here the superiority of the whites and the inferiority of the blacks was assumed. In the course of the advancements of education and opportunity, increasing numbers of Negroes became conscious of the injustice of their plight in a segregated society. Many white leaders too, including especially innumerable churchmen, saw the injustice and called it to the attention of the world. They saw enforced segregation as a cancerous growth within the nation and within the church itself. This sense of injustice came to consciousness gradually throughout large elements of society in the United States. But it emerged as a mighty moral force in the person of Martin Luther King by virtue of the combination in him of the sense of justice and the policy of nonviolent resistance. Many others, including the black extremists, joined in the emerging revolution.

Against all these forces the segregationists struggled desperately to maintain the status quo. With the myth of racial superiority and inferiority still cruising about in their minds they fought against any and all efforts at social changes in race relations. Precinct by precinct, town by town, county by county, school by school, and church by church, this approach was for them a way of life to be maintained rigorously. This way of approaching race relations, so humiliating to many citizens and so offensive to the moral sense of mankind, has deep roots in nearly all individuals and societies throughout the world. The "consciousness of kind" runs deep and does not easily yield to essential sanity.

Segregationism as a policy differs from Nazi racialism in

several particulars. The latter, though latent for many years, emerged rather suddenly under the sway of an extraordinary dictator as a part of a larger strategy for world conquest. The idea of segregation as operative in the laws, attitudes and ways of men during the first half of the twentieth century, had deep historic roots. It did not involve the Nazi idea of extermination. It had to do wholly with keeping the black man "in his place." Segregationism formed the minds of men gradually and almost unconsciously until it was assumed, like the atmosphere and the earth, to be an essential part of the environment. Not until mid-century was this long-accepted way of thinking and living comprehended on a wide scale as unjust, inhuman, and humiliating to the blacks who were assumed to be inferior.

It came as a shock to innumerable sincere Christians (not to mention those who have no interest in God and human welfare other than their own) when prophetic leaders within and outside the church spoke out against segregationism as inhuman and un-Christian. These leaders, with assistance from the behavioral sciences, insisted that the complex network of ideas, attitudes, laws and practices that constitute segregationism is under the judgment of God. Political and legal minds showed that it was a repudiation of democracy.

A second approach to race relations that has emerged is expressed in the formula: equal but separate. Here segregation is not thought of as implying the superiority or inferiority of races. The emphasis is on recognizing the elemental fact of race and on acting in keeping with that inescapable reality. Some have gone so far as to argue on Biblical and theological grounds for this separation of the races. God made the races and intended to keep them pure. Here the arguments run all the way from those who speak of the tragedy of mongrelization to those who believe that the best interests of each race are served by a deliberate policy of keeping its identity. This view has come to expression in one way or another in nearly every century. The Jews, though not a race, have espoused it and in this way have maintained their identity without necessarily implying their superiority over others. Many members of the white race have insisted on mutual respect among the members of the several races while at the same time adhering to strict codes of separateness. This has emerged too as a characteristic approach among large segments of black men.

For example, the most vigorous exponents of this view are some of the advocates of Black Power. Here the focus of attention is on maintaining the identity of the black man, of awakening his sense of self-respect, and of using his resources cooperatively to gain opportunity and status in the world. Though deeply rooted in the fact of race, the Black Power movement also has historical and cultural roots. It seeks deliverance from social attitudes and structures that have conspired to hold down the black man. And it is based on the assumption that the black man must help himself toward that end. Consequently, Black Power is really a call to all blacks to unite in liberating the Negro people from humiliation and injustice. On the positive side, many Black Power advocates stress the separate identity of the Negro for the purpose of coordinating their efforts in providing opportunities for self-improvement. This means changed laws, new attitudes, political and social pressures for the purpose of securing higher levels of skills, better jobs, improved housing and cultural advancement generally.

In its extreme forms, the idea of Black Power is that the white man is the natural enemy of the black man. Therefore, the only hope of liberation and advancement is for the blacks to keep their identity, to take pride in their blackness, and to unite as a massive force for their own good. To this end, there is among the extremists the call to use any and every means, including violence, to achieve the desired ends. The idea is that any structure would be an improvement on the status quo. So it is better to destroy anything that exists, whether or not there are more promising structures to suggest.

In its more moderate forms the Black Power movement is a constructive effort to protect against injustice and humiliation and to call upon the black people to strive for increasing opportunities for themselves step by step.

A third theory on race relations is that along with mutual

respect among the races there must be mutual efforts at solving the problems of human society. Here the thesis is that it is a mistake of the first magnitude to base any policies on race as the primary factor in community life. The problems are primarily human and secondarily racial. Therefore, all questions concerning the degrees of involvement among the races, how they should act toward each other, how much they should associate with each other on all levels, whether or not and to what extent they should intermarry, these and all other interracial problems are to be worked out pragmatically. That is, with the well-being of all men in mind, decisions here should be made on the basis of what course of action makes the most sense. As here presented, this will be understood as the essential direction of the Biblical teaching as it bears on race relations.

THE BIBLICAL TEACHING

The Bible is not a book about race relations; it is a book about *human* relations. It concerns the purpose of God for *all* men in *all* major aspects of their lives. Therefore the Biblical revelation as a whole has a direct bearing on the major problems arising from racial tensions. In particular, there are at least six Biblical teachings that relate significantly to race and race relations.

1. God created and sustains all men. This means that He alone is the Ground of their being. Without Him they would not be. Why there should be different races of men is not disclosed in the Bible. Nor are we given to know how God formed the various races. Speculations on this, based on selected passages of Scripture, have been made by many, but they are all forced and futile. Whether the human race had a heterogeneous origin, or whether all races came from a single pair of human parents is an open question. If we hold that the story of Adam and Eve refers literally to the two original human beings from whom all men descended, the question is answered. But if that primordial pair is thought of as symbolizing original human parents, then the door is open to the possibility of a diverse origin of the several races.

238

In any event, the Biblical teaching is that God made them *all*. No race can claim for itself on Biblical grounds any priority in time or importance. God is the originator of all races, He alone authorized that they exist, and He made them kin to each other by virtue of their shared kinship with Himself.

To be sure, the Hebrew people wanted to claim God as theirs only; and at times He was thought of as interested only in Israel (Exodus 34:24). The descendants of Abraham were God's people, and He was their God. Even Jesus may be quoted as having limited His own ministry "to the lost sheep of the house of Israel" (Matthew 15:24; see also 10:6). This would shut out everyone except the Jews from God's providential concern; and it would run counter to the developing movement of the Biblical teaching.

That teaching necessarily moves toward the affirmation that the one true God rules over all peoples both as Creator and Sustainer. All the nations belong to Him (Psalms 82:8). They are His people (Zechariah 2:11). All races are encompassed in the thought that men live and move and have their being in God, for they are His offspring (Acts 17:28). The Lord is concerned about all "the children of men" (Psalms 11:4; 14:2; 33:13). This concern is seen in His call to Second Isaiah and to Jeremiah to report God's message "to the end of the earth" (Isaiah 49:6; Jeremiah 1:5). It may be noted also in the good news of the coming of Jesus which was for "all the people" (Luke 2:10).

2. A teaching of the Bible that bears directly on race relations is that of the "image of God." *All* men share in this image or in the essential kinship with God. If any creature is a man, he necessarily shares in this kinship. This becomes visible in the cosmos of values where goodness, love, beauty, truth, and worship cannot be confined to any race. It is seen also in the teaching of Jesus that authentic living before God and man cuts across racial lines. He took a hated Samaritan (of an alien ethnic group) and made him the hero of one of the greatest stories ever told. At this distance we are apt to miss the shock with which some men heard Jesus tell this story. For we do not

feel the heat of the ethnic prejudice that boiled in their hearts. *Not* the respected priest, *not* the honored Levite, *not* those who were supposed to be the spiritual leaders, but the *hated* Samaritan was the hero.

The Master's attitude toward the Samaritans perfectly illustrates how He felt toward people of other races. The Jews had no dealings with them, but He did. The plain fact is that Jesus responded to *all* who came to Him for help. He healed the centurion's servant (Matthew 8:5–13) and restored the Canaanite woman's daughter (Matthew 15:22–28). Jesus Himself made it impossible to exclude any race of men from the family of God.

If we follow the implications of the Sermon on the Mount as they began to develop in the early church, we see that Jesus' teaching on the Fatherhood of God and the sonship of men moves through struggle against prejudice toward the idea that *all* men belong in God's family regardless of race. In the teachings of Jesus there are no racial conditions for being kin to God, or responding to God, or belonging in the Kingdom of God. The developing teaching on this theme is that of the unity and kinship of all races because God has chosen them for creative participation with Him in His Kingdom both here and hereafter. This teaching is seen most clearly in the relevance of the salvation process to which we shall turn later.

3. Closely related to all this is a Biblical teaching that the human soul is distinct from the body that accompanies it. The body is important, but the soul is more important. The value and dignity of the human soul is not based on the body that sustains and convoys it through this life. For example, there are male and female bodies, but these physical differences are of no consequence in estimating the worth of souls. There are small bodies in babies and children and larger bodies in adults. This too is of no consequence in relation to the value of souls. Similarly, some men's bodies are black, others white, others yellow, and others mixtures of all sorts, but these have no special significance before the God who loves the souls of men. Similarly, the color of eyes, the shapes of noses, the varieties

240

of hair and the like, have no essential bearing on the soul and its relations to God.

This is the Biblical teaching on the solidarity of the race and its preciousness in the sight of God. Since the principles here involved have been elaborated upon in chapter 7, we need not go into further detail here. Some of the most important implications of all this will become visible in the paragraphs that immediately follow.

4. A teaching of the Bible bearing directly on race is that God's redemptive-creative process is available to men of all races. More than this, God seeks them all. The promise of salvation is for all. And they are all called to share in the dynamics of faith and grace in community.

If Abraham was chosen by God to be a pioneer in the spiritual life, *all* the nations and races were to benefit from his leadership. Again and again we hear the theme: "All the nations of the earth shall bless themselves by him" (Genesis 18:18, 22:18, 26:4; see also Acts 3:25; Romans 4:17–18, 15:8–12; Galatians 3:8).

There is also the persistent and developing teaching of the Bible that people everywhere, including all races, will turn to the Lord (Psalms 22:27–28, 86:9, 102:15; Isaiah 52:10, 66: 18–19; Philippians 2:10–11; Revelation 15:4). For some of the prophets Jerusalem became the symbol of true religion. With that in mind they said that "all nations" would gather in that city and come into the presence of God (Isaiah 56:7, Jeremiah 3:17, Micah 4:2, Zechariah 8:22; see also Mark 11:17).

Jesus spent most of His ministry working with the people of Israel. Time and again He taught in their synagogues and in the temple. Those whom He healed, with insignificant exceptions were the descendants of Abraham. He even said that "salvation is from the Jews" (John 4:22). Nevertheless, the good news He came to share was for the *whole* world, and His redemptive-creative work was done for everyone. In John's Gospel especially the good news about Jesus is addressed to all people. The most familiar verse there (3:16) summarizes the whole movement of the Biblical revelation on the divine love that reaches out for all mankind.

Jesus saw the failure of both Jerusalem and the temple. For this reason he could say to the Samaritan woman at Jacob's well near Mount Gerizim: "Woman, believe me, the hour is coming when neither on this mountain nor in Jerusalem will you worship the Father. . . . But the hour is coming, and now is, when the true worshipers will worship the Father in spirit and truth, for such the Father seeks to worship him" (John 4:21, 23). This broke down the walls separating Jews and Samaritans. In principle it destroyed all barriers, whether of race or nation or creed, that excluded any group from the sincere worship of God. One who was greater than Jerusalem and its temple (Matthew 12:6) had to come to inaugurate the new era of the faith that was open to *all* men. Jesus said that men do not enter the Kingdom by being of the seed of Abraham. Rather, they will come from the east and the west and share with Abraham in the Kingdom of Heaven (Matthew 8:11–12).

At first the apostles themselves failed to grasp this universal appeal of the gospel. In particular, they did not see that the gospel was for the Gentiles as well as the Jews. This is not easy to understand when we remember that they heard the risen Lord say that "repentance and forgiveness of sins should be preached in his name to all nations" (Luke 24:47). They knew also that He had called them to be His witnesses "in Jerusalem and in all Judea and Samaria and to the end of the earth" (Acts 1:8). They were aware of the great commission to "make disciples of all nations" (Matthew 28:19). Nevertheless, at first they did not grasp this teaching.

Deep-seated prejudices do not easily give way to the Holy Spirit. Even after that first Christian Pentecost, Peter and the other apostles at Jerusalem did not understand the gospel as God's good news for *all* men. The story of Philip and the Ethiopian shows that the dawn was beginning to break (Acts 8:26–38). But it required a special vision from God to open Peter's eyes to the Christian perspective regarding the Gentiles. This event was so important for the earliest Christian community that Luke devoted nearly two chapters to it (Acts 10–11). After that vision Peter entered the house of Cornelius, a Gentile, and said, "You yourselves know how unlawful it is for a Jew to associate with or to visit any one of another nation; but God has shown me that I should not call any man common or unclean" (Acts 10:28). After hearing of Cornelius' vision Peter said, "Truly I perceive that God shows no partiality, but in every nation any one who fears him and does what is right is acceptable to him" (Acts 10:34–35). Peter preached the love of God in Christ and many Gentiles received new life through the Holy Spirit. Then he declared, "Can any one forbid water for baptizing these people who have received the Holy Spirit just as we have" (Acts 10:47)?

After all this, however, it was not easy for Peter to justify his action in the eyes of the Christians in Jerusalem. The prejudices ran deep. They asked, "Why did you go to uncircumcised men and eat with them" (Acts 11:3)? Peter told them all that happened and concluded by saying, ". . . who was I that I could withstand God" (Acts 11:17)? Then the Christian leaders in Jerusalem glorified God, saying, "Then to the Gentiles also God has granted repentance unto life" (Acts 11:18). This was one of those momentous events that enabled Christians to break through the prejudices of a narrow provincialism and move into the whole world without regard to nation or race.

But it was Paul who, more than any other, saw that salvation has nothing to do with whether people were Jews or Gentiles. It is the free gift of God to all who have faith. Race has nothing to do with it. All are invited; all are wanted; all who respond are received in the name of Jesus Christ. Once Paul even had to rebuke Peter because, as he wrote, "he stood condemned" (Galatians 2:11). For Peter ate with the Gentiles until "certain men came from James," then he withdrew himself because he was afraid of the circumcision party (Acts 11: 2–16).

It has been said that Paul, for all his work among the Gentiles, still did not see the full reaches of the gospel because he approved of slavery (see Ephesians 6:5; Colossians 3:22). This is true. At the same time it needs to be remembered that Paul recognized slaves as chosen also for salvation through Jesus Christ. They were human beings who were to be treated "justly and fairly" (Colossians 4:1; see also Ephesians 6:9). Paul asked Philemon to accept his slave, Onesimus, "as a beloved brother" (Philemon 16). He gave instructions to slaves and encouraged them to gain their freedom (1 Corinthians 7:21–22). Moreover, one of the most powerful utterances in the long and brutal history of man's struggle for liberty came from Paul's pen. As much as any other statement along this line it summarizes the developing teaching of the New Testament. Paul wrote, "There is neither Jew nor Greek, there is neither slave nor free, there is neither male nor female; for you are all one in Christ Jesus" (Galatians 3:28). This profound utterance, repeated again and again (Romans 10:12, 1 Corinthians 12:13), cut across the standards, values, and traditions of a blinded and prejudiced humanity to give all mankind an enlarged vision of the purpose of God for all His children regardless of race.

The movement of the Biblical revelation comes to fulfillment in the vision that all men will respond to God's salvation in Jesus Christ. For God will redeem men from "every . . . nation" (Revelation 5:9, 7:9). And all shall benefit from the tree of life whose leaves are "for the healing of the nations" (Revelation 22:2).

5. Another teaching of the Bible that bears directly on race may be more briefly stated; but it is no less important. It is that the way we treat any man bears directly on whether or not we are acceptable to God. By implication, this encompasses the idea that the way we treat people of any race is organically connected with our rightness or wrongness with God. This is a complex idea. For it means also that the judgment of God functions against men when they are against any segment of their fellowmen. This can be so serious as to affect the destiny of the souls of men not only in this world but also in the world to come.

Here the standard of judgment will not be the traditions, customs and prejudices of men. Rather, it will be the love and justice of the God who has revealed Himself in Jesus Christ. For God's thoughts and ways are not our thoughts and ways (Isaiah 55:8–9). ". . . the tradition of men" (Mark 7:8) is not permitted to usurp the authority of God. In fact, unless the standards and values of men express His overarching purpose for the human race, they are at war with God.

This teaching came to climactic utterance in the scene of the last judgment found in Matthew 25. There Jesus pictures the separation of the good from the bad. At the left hand of the King are those who had no concern for their fellowmen. To them the King will say, "Depart from me, . . . for I was hungry and you gave me no food, I was thirsty and you gave me no drink, I was a stranger and you did not welcome me, naked and you did not clothe me, sick and in prison and you did not visit me." To their question, When did all this happen? the answer came back, "Truly, I say to you, as you did it not to one of the least of these, you did it not to me" (Matthew 25:41–45).

Those at the right hand of the King were chosen because of their sincere effort to help "the least of these my brethren." This, of course, has direct implications regarding race relations. For the assessment of who is important in God's sight is not to be based on the standards of men but on the concerns of God. And He is concerned for *all* men.

6. One more basic Biblical teaching that bears on race relations is this: All effective religion comes to fulfillment in community. We have already observed that the Biblical teaching emphasizes the realization of values in *community*. God speaks through the *people* of Israel. He speaks through the Christian community. Consequently, any force or forces that inherently separate those who seek salvation through Christ must of necessity be alien to the Biblical teaching. This is not to deny a place for the freedom of groups to worship and work in keeping with particular interests and areas of kinship. Nevertheless, whenever any such group is exclusive by nature and structure it represents a force alien to the Kingdom of God as inaugurated by Jesus Christ.

245

The Biblical teaching is that there is essential unity among those who are in Christ. This unity goes beyond any physical differences. The conditions of such unity are not in race, color, and bodily makeup but in faith, hope, and love. Therefore, the Biblical teaching moves toward this mysterious sense of unity in Christ which goes beyond all racial barriers to bring people together in the awareness of their common Lord, their common task, and their common destiny in the world to come.

SOME MODERN DOUBTS AND RESPONSES TO THEM

There are at least two major types of doubt regarding the Biblical and Christian approach to race relations as presented in the foregoing pages.

Doubt   First, there are doubts arising not so much from the Biblical teaching itself as from the obvious failure of Christians and the churches to live up to it. It has been remarked often that the most segregated groups in the United States are those meeting for worship on Sunday morning. It has been said also that the church will probably be the last institution to practice integration on a large scale. Athletic teams and events are integrated; theaters and schools are integrated. Business and labor are integrated. But the churches are lagging behind. Not only have they lagged behind, but in many instances they have lent sanction and support to segregation and, at times, even to racial prejudices of the most intrenched sort. So the question is asked: How can Christians say anything on race relations when the record of the churches has been so far below even the best achievement in the secular world? After 2,000 years why has not the spirit of Christ been able to awaken in Christians themselves a genuine acceptance of people of all races?

Response   Doubts of this kind frequently arise from the sense of having been betrayed by those who should represent the ideal. These doubts strike the mark and hurt because they are so often motivated by love and justice. The church is at

246

fault in many ways, and this is one of them. Among those who bought and sold slaves in the new world were many who called themselves Christians. And many who consider themselves Christians are moving toward the twenty-first century still cherishing the beliefs and values of hard-core segregationism. In even the best Christians there often remains the scar tissue of a once demonic racial prejudice. It is this that gives meaning to the truth that the church is not so much a community of saints as of sinners in need of God's mercy.

For this reason the prayers of repentance among Christians are always in order; and so are the prayers for illumination and for a right spirit. The effort to grow in knowledge and insight is necessarily characteristic of the authentic Christian community. And it is desperately needed here.

Having said these things, it should be remembered that among the most able leaders for improved race relations and civil rights have been men and women whose primary motivation came from the life and teachings of Jesus Christ.

Instances could be multiplied, but I shall illustrate this from the life and example of John Wesley and some of his followers. His basic principle for practical Christianity was that faith and good works must be joined. For him there was no Christian gospel separated from social responsibility. His Christian convictions led him to fight the slave traffic (on which England had gained a monopoly) with the full force of his mind and heart. In 1774 he wrote against it with devastating cogency in his "Thoughts upon Slavery." Wesley pictured the inhumanity of it. Against the idea that slavery was a legitimate business he asked,

But can law, human law, change the nature of things? Can it turn darkness into light, or evil into good? By no means. Notwithstanding ten thousand laws, right is right, and wrong is wrong still. There must still remain an essential difference between justice and injustice, cruelty and mercy. So that I still ask, Who can reconcile this treatment of the Negroes, first and last, with either mercy or justice?

Against the men involved in the slave traffic Wesley wrote: ". . . men-buyers are exactly on a level with men-stealers." He added, ". . . you know that they [slaves] are procured by means nothing near so innocent as picking of pockets, housebreaking or robbery upon the highway." He wrote all this to "respectable" people. He said to the slave-holders, "Now, it is your money that pays the merchant, and through him the captain and the African butchers. You therefore are guilty, yea, principally guilty, of all these frauds, robberies, and murders." He stated further, "Thy hands, thy bed, thy furniture, thy house, thy lands, are at present stained with blood." In all this Wesley was vigorously attacked, sometimes in peril of his life, by those who had invested so heavily in the slave trade.

He saw all of those involved in the traffic, from plantation owners to ship captains, as condemned before the tribunal of God and the moral order. He said that even some judges are on the wrong side of justice here. The desire for money and selfish gain is at the root of it all. Therefore, he called upon all Christians and others to unite in the suppression of slavery. He said, "Away with all whips, all chains, all compulsion! Be gentle toward all men; and see that you invariably do unto every one as you would he should do unto you." It was no accident, therefore, that the followers of Wesley were taught to regard the black man as their "brother in Christ." Nor was it any accident that as he lay on his deathbed unable to read, he asked his friends to do so for him from the autobiography of a black slave. It was owing chiefly to the work of Wesley, the Quakers, and other like-minded Christians that the slave trade was outlawed and slavery abolished by acts of Parliament in 1807 and 1833.

In America, when slavery became a formidable evil, many Christians gave their lives in opposition to it. For example, there was, among the followers of Wesley in America, Freeborn Garrettson. Upon his conversion in 1775 he announced at family prayers that God had revealed the wrongness of owning slaves. He then pronounced his own slaves free. Wherever he preached he urged that slavery was utterly contrary to the Christian religion.

It is significant that in 1778 Francis Asbury, the great leader of American Methodism, paid the following tribute to the Quakers for their effort to free the slaves: "This is a very laudable design; and what the Methodists must come to, or, I fear, the Lord will depart from them." In 1780 he led the way in getting a group of ministers to adopt a statement on slavery. He said of this occasion, "We all agreed in the spirit of African liberty." At the "Chrismas Conference" in Baltimore in 1784 the Methodist Church in America was created. Of special interest is the fact that, notwithstanding all the other concerns at that conference, time and care were devoted to approving a new anti-slavery statement. According to it, all Methodist laymen who had not drawn up within a year a plan for emancipating their slaves in specified stages were to be excluded. No one was to be admitted thereafter who retained slaves.

The later history of Methodism, as well as of all other Christian bodies, does not show the full measure of consistency and of persistence in the fight for justice for the black people. But always, like a mighty theme and force, there has been this continuing emphasis on the right to liberty and opportunity under God.

Within the church there have been in every generation black and white ministers and laymen working for racial justice and good will.

A study of the church school literature of most of the major Christian denominations would reveal how extensively the churches have been teaching their members Christian attitudes on race. The results of this are not easy to assess. But there can be little doubt that this kind of teaching has gone far to prepare the United States for the measure of mutual respect among the races that has been achieved. Many of the leaders of the church have been unsung heroes in the pioneer work toward improved race relations. They began with the fight against slavery. They continued in the struggle for justice and civil rights. Who can measure the influence of the various institutions of higher learning for black students in Atlanta and throughout the nation? Yet these were founded and supported largely because of the vision of Christian ministers and laymen. The first interracial committee in Georgia was founded in Atlanta by Plato Durham, a theological professor at Emory University.

What language can express the influence of Martin Luther King in his struggle for civil rights? Yet who could begin to understand him apart from his background in the home of Christian parents, his education up through the Ph.D. degree in Christian institutions, and his opportunity for leadership through Christian churches which he served as pastor and which he visited as spokesman. Whether or not men can approve of him in all points, all men of moral concern would have to agree in regarding him as perhaps the greatest single force for social advancement in behalf of the black people that the twentieth century has produced.

These brief illustrations, which merely serve to point to numberless others that are on record, show that Christianity, despite her many failures, has been and continues to be at work in the interest of civil rights and opportunity for black people and for men of all races. This work is not something tacked onto Christianity as an extra for these times. It is organically connected with the Christian teachings on God, man, Jesus Christ, the Holy Spirit, and the life everlasting. And, of course, it is implicit in the teachings and example of Jesus.

Doubt   The second kind of doubt arises from quite different motives from the first. It is that the Christian teachings are too naïve and unrealistic to come to grips with so formidable a force as racial tensions. Race is an elemental and inescapable fact of human existence. The racial differences are so marked and man's "consciousness of kind" goes so deep that the Christian religion seems ethereal and remote in its efforts to deal with racial problems. In this respect racial differences, like the differences between the sexes, cannot be adequately controlled and directed by Biblical teachings and religious faith. The very idea

250

that the Bible is not a book about *race* relations but about *human* relations serves only to lift up the problem. For, again, race is an elemental fact. Blackness and whiteness and yellowness and brownness and redness, these characteristics are ineradicable and paramount realities of human existence.

As a corollary to this there is the realistic stress on man's selfishness and even cruelty which leads him to look on the members of other races as his natural enemies. In this sphere it is a question of dog eat dog. The rest is mere talk. The black people must look after themselves. They must rise up and work for their own good. For in addition to the racial differences that lead whites and blacks to dislike and misunderstand each other there is the demonic factor of man's ineradicable selfishness and pride.

Response   In response to this, six comments are in order.

First, it is true that Christians, on the basis of the teachings of Jesus, may too easily overlook the obvious facts of racial differences. These are certainly among the elemental facts of life. And it is beyond reasonable doubt that they complicate the problems of community life in many ways. This is why patterns of segregation are so persistent. Christians have a built-in way of recognizing the dangers of man's pride, whether racial or otherwise, in the teaching on original sin and on man's constant tendency to turn away from God. Therefore, Christians can ignore these factors only by naïvely repudiating the implications of their own religion. Christians must avoid simple and sentimental solutions.

For example, it is so easy to suppose that integration is the answer when it is only a part of it. One of the most pressing needs of black people and nearly everyone else is for a better quality of education. Among the urgent needs also are those for better housing and improved opportunities for the development of skills so minority groups can share increasingly in the advantages of living in the modern world. These problems have to do only partly with integration. The hard facts here concern not only race but political, cultural, and economic factors as

251

well. The question of integration will always be relevant. But it does not always go to the root of things. It cannot be too often said that neither segregation nor integration is a moral principle. The sense of dignity has far deeper sources than can be tapped by any one formula. Basically it comes from faith in God and from a sense of achievement that arises from actual accomplishment.

Second, while recognizing the importance of racial differences as factors in social tensions, Christians can never yield to the cynical attitude that men are doomed to mutual hostility because of them. Nor are they willing to be satisfied with any philosophy of mutual indifference regarding the races. The Christian philosophy is that, with God's help and with proper opportunity and training, all men can learn to respect those of other races and work together toward worthy goals for all. This is not easy, but it has been accomplished already in the lives of many Christians and others.

Third, it has been supposed that the combination of racial differences and human pride require a deliberate strategy of separatist action on the part of the underprivileged races. This is the call to separatism. That is, the black man must take pride in his blackness, in his physical characteristics, in his heritage, and unite with other black men in liberating himself. So Black Power becomes a major theme and a basic strategy.

The Christian response to this would seem to lead in three directions.

1. First, it is good for any man to have some degree of pride in his body, in his race, and in his heritage. Moreover, there may be some truth in the idea that the black man is in a unique position to understand the black man. Only he knows by direct experience the humiliation, the privation, and the injustice of his plight. This leads to the inference that in a special way the black man is called upon to concentrate on helping himself and his race. Both black and white Christians may recognize a limited function in these times for temporary forms of black separatism to seek and nurture the identity and claims of black people. If an oppressed minority—toward whom the oppressor

does not respond with full acceptance—wishes to unite in its own behalf on a separated basis, there may be a great deal of value in that as a limited option. But as a long range philosophy and method it is inadequate. Exclusivism, whether white or black or yellow or brown, is at war with God and his new era of love.

2. Second, it needs to be observed that the quest for black identity, like that of white or yellow or brown identity, is always in danger of becoming another instrument of man's universal egoism. The Christian doctrine of original sin has relevance to men of all races. And all alike are called of God to avoid those delusions about race which feed the pride of men without giving substantive nurture to their authentic existence. It is one of the saddest aspects of the history of mankind that men have used race to run interference for their pride and meanness. It would be a moral blunder and a breakdown of intelligence of the first order for the black man to imitate the sins of the white man in allowing race to become a basis for egoistic illusions of identity.

Moreover, because of man's pride and egoism, there are large elements of illusion in the notion that blacks, or whites, or any others are going to unite solidly for their own self-advancement as races. There are inevitable and extensive polarizations among all peoples, including the black people. In some measure each person has his own idea, makes his own way, and is concerned with his own immediate needs and those of the people closest to him.

3. A third response to Black Power as a strategy is now indicated. The Christian philosophy implies that in a world like this there can be no morally acceptable long range solutions to the problems of race relations on the basis of black, white, yellow, or brown separatism. Whether we like it or not, we live together in one world. Whether we like it or not, we share in the same government and economy. We breathe the same air and are nurtured by the same soil. We are in fact interdependent. Most important is the fact that God calls us all to the life of love, which means mutual respect and helpfulness. Persistent thought will reveal that in the United States, and in the long run,

throughout the world, the greatest good for men of all races can be gained neither in the ghetto nor in the white suburb but in the larger communities where mutual respect, solid achievement, and cooperative involvement occur.

There is some real danger that, in concentrating on black identity and Black Power, we may lapse into the kind of provincialism which runs counter to the Christian concern for men of all races everywhere. The Bible proclaims a world religion. It offers help and God's good news in Christ to *all* mankind. While Christians necessarily seek to aid those nearby minority groups with their special needs, they can never allow their vision of the needs of the whole world—which are often more desperate than those close at hand—to become obscured. Therefore, as we seek to create a better society immediately around us we require also to let our world outreach be extended rather than diverted.

This brings us to a fourth comment on the doubts arising from a hard-core realism on race. The different races can contribute significantly to each other. There may not be any fixed ways of reacting that are distinctively racial. Nevertheless, the members of the black race in the United States have undoubtedly rendered innumerable services to the building of this nation. These have not often been recognized. Besides their many other contributions, they have helped to put "soul" into life. They have brought qualities of feeling and value from which all men can learn. They have added immeasurably to our economic life. They have demonstrated the highest qualities of patriotism. They have shown skills in communicating humor, they have developed athletic prowess, they have excelled in the ability to entertain in music and the theater, they have contributed significantly to our literature as well as to our religious faith and insight. I am assuming here the ever enlarging contributions of black people in all areas of human work and enterprise. But these are not so much illustrations of racial factors as of our common humanity. Life in the United States and in every nation, however complicated by racial differences, is nevertheless incalculably enriched by the presence of these different racial groups who are called of God to live together in full mutual respect and appreciation.

Fifth, the problems of living together in the contemporary world carry us far beyond the narrow bounds of race. All races are alike in having to face together their common enemies: war, overpopulation, pollution, crime, poverty, ignorance, and de-humanization in urban and technological societies. In an era of the proliferation of nuclear and other destructive weapons men of good will of all races are called to join in the common enterprise of overcoming war. As we look toward the twenty-first century we face the mounting problems of overpopulation, famine and poverty. The awesome dangers of the pollution of air and water and of the depletion of land and natural resources —these force us together. They force us to unite across racial lines in a compact of concerted efforts to survive with dignity and opportunity on this precious little planet. Everyone, regardless of race, is affected not only by the common problems of ecology but also by the problems of ignorance, illiteracy, prejudice, cultural privation, and the radical secularization and consequent trivialization of life.

Sixth, the Biblical-Christian teaching rightly urges that, after full recognition has been given to the realities of race, the deeper realities have to do with the common elements of humanity in men of all races. Therefore, the effort to find either final identity or long-range solutions of human problems on the basis of blackness or whiteness or yellowness or brownness is, from the standpoint of Christianity, an error of the first magnitude. As we have seen, the quest for black identity may have a temporary function. But no man can really find his identity on the basis of bodily characteristics. He is a living mind or soul. The body is secondary to the spirit or soul or personality. In the mind-body syndrome the mind or spirit has priority in value and in function. One man may have a small body, another a large one, another a medium-sized one. These differences are obviously there but they are entirely secondary in the sphere of religious values. One man may be black, another white, another yellow, another brown, another red. But these are alike incidental to the realities in the cosmos of moral and spiritual values.

Nobility is what it is regardless of race, nation or creed. Faith, hope, and love are beautiful in whomever they abound. The Biblical revelation, and consequently the church, rightly affirms the *unity and solidarity of the human race.* In the qualities that make for this unity, racial characteristics have no more significance than factors of size, sex, fingernails and toenails.

The first hints of this unity and value of all human beings appear in the universal capacity to participate in goodness, beauty, truth and worship. Kant said that man is a creature of supreme worth because he is a unique bearer of the moral law. This, like the other ideal values just mentioned, knows no boundaries of race, nation, or culture. If the Indian can build a Taj Mahal, the Chinese a Temple of Heaven, the Turk a Suleiman Mosque, the European a St. Peter's Basilica, and the American a Lincoln Memorial, then in the realm of Beauty they are all brothers. If the Indians can produce a Gandhi, the Japanese a Kagawa, the Italians a St. Francis, the Russians a Tolstoi, the Germans a Schweitzer, and the black Americans a George Washington Carver, then in the realm of the good they are all brothers.

We probe deeper still into this solidarity of the human race when we put it into its religious dimensions. Man was made for God. His capacity for participating in these ideal values is to be understood as one aspect of God's call to all men to join Him in the affairs of His Kingdom. No man and no race has any privileged status here. All alike stand on the same level before God, equally needy, equally chosen. The yellow man has no seat of honor that is not also reserved for the brown man. The white man has no privileges in the Kingdom that are not available to the black man. Race is entirely secondary and trivial. The value of all men rests alike ultimately upon the relationship with the God who created them, accepts and chooses them in Christ for participation in the Kingdom, and calls them to an everlasting life of creative adventure.

According to the Biblical and Christian teaching this is the only solid ground on which to stand and work in a world of racial tensions. Consequently, Christians are at war with racism in any form. Their standards and values strike against those who select their own race for special privileges and look down on others. They seek God's best for men of all races under the leadership of Jesus Christ in and through the community of faith and through all other constructive agencies of reconciliation.

16

CHRISTIANITY AND SOME NEW PROBLEMS

The purpose of this chapter is to consider the relevance of the Biblical teaching to some of the *new* problems facing mankind in the immediate future. No effort will be made to treat any of these in detail. For the aim here is primarily to suggest the direction in which the Biblical revelation tends to lead men as they come to grips with some of the commonly recognized *new* problems. Here again it will be assumed that we cannot make a direct move from the Bible to the issues arising out of contemporary experience. It will be necessary to follow the more troublesome way of considering the live options, facing the honest doubts of many people, and striving to show the plausibility and indispensable contribution of the Biblical heritage to modern man as he looks toward the twenty-first century.

It is often supposed that there is nothing new under the sun. The so-called "new theology" of each decade is known, by all who are historically informed, to be little more than ancient ideas in modern dress. The "new philosophies" have in them little that is really new. There are swings of the pendulum, changes of emphasis, unusual and sometimes even odd combinations of ideas, but very little is really new in theological and philosophical reflection. So the temptation is to deceive ourselves into believing that nothing is really new at all. Human nature is the same. The basic problems remain unchanged. The strong conservative tendency in men leads them to cleave to the old and familiar and, wherever possible, to settle down for a more or less routine approach to life.

Whether fortunately or unfortunately, this is no longer possible. It is true that there is very little novelty in the sphere of basic ideas. But in the realm of the human situation and human *problems* this is not the case. We are beginning to live in a new age. A new environment is being formed around us. And that includes the environment of the new problems facing mankind. These are primary factors in the cultural atmosphere surrounding nearly everyone in the more privileged nations. They constitute increasingly the atmospheric pressures of the contemporary world. What are some of these distinctively new problems? I suggest, out of larger possible lists, seven such problems.

First, there is the possibility of destruction by nuclear and other modern weapons which places mankind under a new threat. This is the threat of the destruction not merely of a Carthage, or of Naziism, or of some part of the earth, but of civilized existence on this planet. Some scientists, who know the capability of nuclear and other weapons, are very pessimistic about the future of mankind. For, they say, more and more nations are bound to learn how to make these weapons. Human nature being what it is, sooner or later, the availability of such weapons on a large scale across the world, will inevitably lead to war. And from here on out war will mean the destruction of civilized community life. The earth itself may be rendered uninhabitable. Others give the human race a fifty-fifty chance of survival. Still others suggest, hopefully and wistfully, that these new capabilities for destruction may deter men from taking the desperate plunge into oblivion.

In any event, all mankind is faced with the problem of survival because men have created the new possibility of planetary death. This risk has never been faced before by any generation.

Second, for the first time in history man is confronted by the threat of overpopulation, with the inevitable consequence of mass starvation. Over a hundred years ago Charles Darwin wrote, "Even slow-breeding man has doubled in twenty-five years, and at this rate, in less than a thousand years, there would literally not be standing-room for his progeny." That timetable has been speeded up fantastically since Darwin's day because of the advances in science, technology and medicine. It is no accident that K. Sax has written on this theme under the grim title, *Standing Room Only: The World's Exploding Population.* The present population of over three billion will jump to six billion by A.D. 2000. Teilhard de Chardin, in *The Future of Man,* summarized the situation when he said, "But now we see the saturation point ahead of us, and approaching at a dizzy speed."

William and Paul Paddock in their book *Famine—1975* (1967) remind us that the time is fast approaching when famines will begin on a mass scale in various parts of the world. These famines, they say, are inevitable. They cannot be averted by scientific and technological achievements. This is partly because the earth's resources are limited. It is due also to the continuing rapid increase in the number of people, particularly in those parts of the earth where there is neither sufficient land nor ability to meet the problem. They say that the methods of birth control are either too slow or unacceptable to people. For people want children. They love them. They are going to have them. Besides this, medical advances have enabled men to live longer. This is a major factor in the population explosion. The only choice, according to the Paddocks, is for the nations that can avoid mass starvation for the time being to deploy their food resources wisely both in their national and international interests. This too is a new problem.

Again, there are the new problems pertaining to the extensive pollution of the air, water and land. These are closely related to the problems of overpopulation. We are now in a position to foresee that unless men act with wisdom regarding the use they make of their environment, they will be in serious trouble as they look toward the twenty-first century. Land and topsoil are limited. Water resources are limited. Even the air can absorb only a limited amount of pollution. The natural resources which have been taken for granted can no longer be so regarded. The new problems of ecology require new systemic studies and solutions.

A fourth new problem is that of the polarization and depersonalization of human existence. These are big words that refer to experiences long familiar. But they are a part of man's contemporary experience in more extensive ways than ever before. Consider first polarization. The earth has its North and South poles. We speak of men as being poles apart. They are separated by race, geography, culture, work, interests, specialization. Every man inhabits the ghettos of his own world separated from others. He may live in the same apartment complex and never know his neighbor. Worse still, he may never care to know him. Men move in different orbits. What used to be called the primary or face-to-face social groups, though still present, have lost much of their quiet power to affect life. The secondary groups, where the more intimate personal ties are lacking, tend to predominate.

This leads to the depersonalization of human existence. Men are identified by numbers. They are judged by the measurable quantity of their work. They can cut or sew so many gloves an hour. They can prepare or put together so many pieces of wood in making chairs and tables. They can attach so many parts of a car or plane during a day and thus measure up to a standard set by the efficiency experts. The sense of artistic achievement from creating a whole product is confined to very few men. There is no way to avoid this. The man who cannot keep the pace becomes a liability to the company. The wages have to be paid, the products have to be put on the market. The salesmen, often under instruction to make a show of personal interest, keep in mind their one aim, selling their quotas. That is their role. It too is inevitable. For the products manufactured must be distributed. Otherwise, the collapse of the company and the loss of a livelihood for thousands are inevitable.

When he wrote "Technology and Human Values" (see *Human Values and Advancing Technology*) Huston Smith was addressing himself to this theme.

. . . society has become an impersonal mechanism and with its increasing complexity is growing more impersonal daily. More and more our lives are consumed by role behavior, that is, behavior in which *what* is done, not *who* is doing it, is the important factor. Since within roles persons are interchangeable—any number of persons could fill the roles of bus driver or bank teller without affecting the character of the roles themselves—the more our lives are lived in terms of roles, the more our individuality idles, or rather never comes into being.

Colleges and universities often get caught up in this same process. The large numbers of students, who are herded into classes and who never really get to know their teachers, reflect other aspects of this same process of depersonalization. Though some men tell us differently, Ortega y Gasset seems to have a point when he speaks of the dehumanization of art in the contemporary world. For, he says, the artists no longer seem interested in painting the everyday things and people. Instead they portray things that seem to come from another world, whether ultramicroscopic, or from outer space, or from the sphere of impersonal design. They have done some fascinating things. But it would be difficult to see how they could more effectively express man's contemporary experience of depersonalization than by what many of them are creating. Men in the various professions live in their own ghettos, isolated, oblivious to the work of their fellowmen in the other professions and even in their own.

In the intellectual sphere the polarization and depersonalization of life are evident everywhere. The "knowledge explosion" illustrates this. In 1960 UNESCO estimated that throughout the world there were 332,000 new volumes published annually. But a more recent study for the National Science Foundation reports that in the sciences alone there is an increase in published materials at the rate of 1,000,000 book equivalents each year. And there is no end to it. As E. A. Reitan wrote in the *Journal of Education* (July, 1966), ". . . beyond the fitful flickers of learning's torch lies an ever deeper and darker void luring the investigator into impenetrable realms of mystery."

The knowledge explosion (or, more accurately, explosions) becomes far more bewildering when we realize that there is no unifying culture in which the new knowledge can be given some semblance of order. C. P. Snow has spoken of the two cultures, represented by the scientists and the literary intellectuals. In *The Two Cultures: And a Second Look* he writes, "Between these two groups . . . there is little communication and, instead of fellow feeling, something like hostility." Snow has been severely criticized for confining his observation to two cultures when in fact it would be far more accurate to speak of a plurality of cultural orientations which are as far removed from each other as the North and South poles. They cannot now intercommunicate. The extent of the difficulty is suggested further by Carleton S. Coon when he writes that ". . . specializations within specializations have proliferated to such an extent that many mathematicians and physicists cannot even talk to each other intelligibly." And those interested in God, faith, and the church move in still other worlds.

Add to all this the new worlds of technology, including automation and cybernetics and the picture is still more complicated. We are moving rapidly into the era of the computer and all that implies. Instances from all areas of modern culture could be multiplied. These will suffice.

A fifth kind of new problem arises from the amazing advances in the biological sciences with their bearing on medicine and the future of man. I have in mind several kinds of new developments. For one thing, there is the new world opened up by discoveries concerning life formation and the genetic code. These have fantastic implications for the future. For the first time in history man is on the threshold of having to decide whether or not and how extensively he should be permitted to experiment at will with the genetic code in the formation of selected types of genetic inheritance. This could certainly be of untold value if it could help to eliminate mental retardation, other abnormalities, and improve the chances of normal births.

No reasonable man wants to stifle scientific advances. But every man can see here implications that go far beyond the ranges of science. Both good and evil possibilities loom on the horizon here.

Closely related to this is the relatively new world of experimental studies of specific physical and chemical events located in the brain.

Then there are the new developments in medicine having to do with transplants. As long as these are confined to hearts, lungs, livers, hands and the like, few significant new problems are involved. Granting that the donors are available by death, no good reason can be given for holding back in order to extend the lives of the recipients. But serious moral problems would arise from the efforts to transplant the brain or possibly parts of the brain. For here the question of selfhood and self-identity would seem to be at stake. The brain would seem to be the one organ of the body that provides the basis of personal identity and continuity. As we have seen, the brain is not the person, or mind, or ego, or soul of a man. But in this world it seems to provide the primary physical basis for personal identity. After a brain transplant, what would happen to the husband and wife relationships, the friend and friend relationships. What would happen to one's work? Would the same arms, legs, face, lungs and digestive system mean that a man was in fact the one whom his wife would want to live with? Innumerable personal, legal and other social problems emerge here. They have never before had to be faced in quite the same way.

Another new range of problems is emerging from the new discoveries in space exploration. These developments are too much in their infancy to know where they will lead. Are there habitable planets near enough to the earth for men to reach them and colonize them? Will there be other intelligent beings on them? Or, are there possibly innumerable other planets throughout the universe where intelligent creatures have developed extensive civilizations? If so, would they be friends or enemies? These and many other questions arise, in ways only dreamed of before, as bona fide practical issues now. So here too we are moving into new possibilities and problems.

A seventh new problem has to do with the major negative theme of this book. It is that for the first time on such an extensive scale men are expected, as sensible folk, to handle the problems of life and death and destiny with a world-view that assumes God to be irrelevant. One of the most interesting recent statements along this line comes from Huston Smith of the Massachusetts Institute of Technology. He writes

> We have described the new world in which man lives as one which, left to its own devices, depersonalizes. This world derives from technology. But while creating a new *world* with its right hand, with its left hand technology (and its progenitor science) has created a new *world view*. With great assurance this world view depicts a nature that is majestic beyond belief. But its import for man is obscure. This is unfortunate, for an essential condition of human well-being is possession of a self-image (together with the sense of orientation a self-image can confer) that is passably clear, convincing and efficacious.

This need not be elaborated on further because of previous observations. But it may become, in the long run, the most critical of all the problems facing men in the modern world.

THE MAIN ALTERNATIVE VIEWS

The various approaches to be mentioned here will concern how the Biblical teaching and Christianity bear on these new problems. Broadly speaking, there are four major options which, in the light of all that has been said in the foregoing chapters, may be stated very briefly.

First, there are those who hold that the Biblical teaching has nothing of consequence to say about these new problems. The Bible belongs in a different dimension of reality. The believer in the Bible as God's Word may hold that it has little relevance to these unique problems of modern man. It concerns man's personal relationship to God in this life and in the life to come. Therefore, it should not be used as a guide to men in coming to grips with these new problems, which pertain to this present life only. The Bible simply does not speak to such issues.

Second, there are those who suggest that man has created this new world with its problems, so he must work his way through them without reference to God or any teachings about God such as those found in the Bible. These are the skeptics who suggest that at its best the Bible is poetry and mythology with some ethical insights. At its worst it is a collection of books of superstitious utterances without any real bearing on man's contemporary experience. In fact, the sooner men get away from it the better.

A third approach is made by those who identify God almost wholly with man's higher aspirations and efforts. They see God as almost identical with the human historical processes. God is in the secular world. In fact, religion, pure and undefiled, is secular. In one generation this idea may be called nontheistic humanism, in another, secular Christianity, and in the generations yet to come it will doubtless be given other names. The reality is substantively the same. The basic ideas are essentially similar. The chief emphasis is on the divine immanence to the neglect or repudiation of the transcendence of God. So, we are told, if we are to retain any viable or assignable meaning in the word "God" it must express something of contemporary man's struggles, processes, fears, disillusionments and hopes. The Bible illuminates these, expresses them, and shares in them. Consequently, it has relevance as an interpreter of contemporary experience. Moreover, the Bible is relevant to the new problems because, when rightly interpreted, it helps us to identify (as the prophets and Jesus did) the divine action within the setting of the problems arising where men live. As the prophets and Jesus spoke to the distinctive problems of their day, so we are to identify and speak to the distinctive divine-human involvements of our day.

A fourth view is that in the Biblical revelation God has revealed certain things about Himself and His dealings with men that can render immeasurable service to mankind as it encounters new problems. This will be elaborated upon in the exposition of the Biblical teaching.

THE BIBLICAL TEACHING

I shall deal here with those major Biblical teachings that seem to bear most significantly on man's new situation. Here there are at least seven such teachings which will be discussed at varying lengths depending upon how extensively they have already been treated and on their relative importance.

First, there is the Biblical teaching that no matter what the problem is that men have to face, they are not to forget the primary importance of its religious and moral dimensions. The Bible, whatever else it contains, expresses a total world-view. This means, among other things, that its teachings bear on every major aspect of man's life. War and peace, poverty and affluence, sex, marriage and family life, business and labor, recreation and work, man and community, these are within the sphere of its teaching. In other words, everything that affects life, whether new or old, comes within the range of its interests.

But men are always trying to solve their basic problems without God. This becomes an impossible approach in the light of the Biblical teaching. The God of the prophets and Jesus, who spoke through them about peace, is all the more concerned with the issues of war and peace in this nuclear age. Therefore the Biblical writers can speak to modern men by calling them, amid all their deliberations and gropings, to recognize *the religious and moral dimensions of the new problem arising from man's capacity to destroy human life on this planet.*

Similarly, the God of the Bible, particularly as revealed in Jesus of Nazareth, is concerned over the population explosion whenever it affects such elementals as food, clothing, housing, and opportunity to realize the values that go with a creature of dignity. This problem too has its religious and moral dimensions, which the prophets and Jesus call upon men to remember. So is it with all other new problems mentioned. The Biblical teaching, then, is that a part of the proper management of life in these times is to see and interpret both the new problems and the answers to them in their religious and moral dimensions.

Closely related to this is a second Biblical teaching that bears on man's new problems. The Bible teaches that the only values worth striving for in the end are personal and interpersonal. We have already heard the theme, which runs through the preceding chapters, that God created and sustains man for the purpose of realizing moral and spiritual values in community. The Bible teaches that there are no other values worth seeking or worth the pain of existence. Money and property exist for people. Social status and acceptance have their meaning only for people. Scientific advances that threaten human existence must be turned into life-subserving instruments. So is it with all the new discoveries and activities of men in community. Do the Biblical writers have anything to say about the modern processes of polarization and depersonalization? The God of the Bible is at war with all societies in which these processes are not counterbalanced by ample opportunities for the realization of moral and spiritual values in community. Further still, God is at war with all human activities that cannot in some way bear on or contribute to the actualization of these personal values. Chief among these values are those of faith and worship and the experience of the presence of God. But they include also the privileges of friendship and love, of humor and co-operation, of beauty and hope.

Therefore, the Biblical writers speak to men today by saying that no matter what new problems they may face the answers must be sought in terms of their tendency to increase or enlarge the personal and interpersonal values which alone are worth seeking above all else. For man alone, among the creatures of this world, is supremely precious in God's sight.

A third relevant Biblical teaching is that love and the wisdom it implies is the law of life. We have already considered the nature and centrality of Christian love as expounded in the New Testament. The Greeks did not know it. Even among the writers of the Old Testament it was not really grasped in any comprehensive way. Jesus taught it by precept and example.

What we are apt to overlook is that the Bible teaches or implies the wisdom that love requires. What love *implies* is as much a part of the Biblical revelation as love itself. *Love implies the wisdom and management of human affairs in order to accomplish its aims.* This is the inner movement of the Biblical teaching in its inherent implications. This is why, for example, all Christians who have sought to do the work of love by establishing and supporting life-subserving institutions have felt themselves to be expressing the will of God.

This has a direct bearing on man's new problems because the Bible, when rightly understood, involves the call to minister to man's needs. Love aims to accomplish goals for mankind. In its implied call to wisdom and the management of life, the Bible speaks to the modern world as it faces its desperate new problems. All this includes the command of God to be resourceful, to use all the insights and techniques available in working on these problems.

A fourth teaching of the Bible that bears on these new issues is that the leaders of men must be transformed by the grace of God so that their inner desires are purified increasingly by love. Otherwise, the necessary self-giving love will be either too fitful or too weak to do the job.

Here the Biblical teaching takes with utmost seriousness the obstacles in human nature itself to a passionate, sustained, and courageous concern for human well-being. There are the strong pulls toward pride and selfishness. No casual efforts can deal with these dynamic forces in human nature. There is the weakening force of distraction, so often unnoticed and so universally debilitating. There are the innumerable factors in the environment and culture that put a damper on the manly creative concern for human well-being. Therefore, the Biblical teaching is that the leaders of men will not rise above these without God's help. The prophets and apostles, are concrete demonstrations in history of the power of God to change men's lives and strengthen them, despite all obstacles, for service to others. Transformed leaders are as necessary as any other single factor in dealing with these perilous new problems.

Fifth, the Biblical writers insisted that God's aims are attained not merely through individuals but through like-minded men in community. The *people* of Israel are important. The church or the *community* of faith is essential. Jesus worked with and through His disciples and others. Out of such beginnings came the vast movement of the Christian church, which is an extension of the Biblical idea that God does His work with men in and through community. Here the Biblical heritage, rightly interpreted, calls for the cooperation of all men of good will, regardless of race, culture, nation, or religion, in dealing with the ominous problems of these times.

Sixth, the Biblical teaching on the destiny of mankind beyond this present life on earth, when kept in proper focus, has the effect of aiding in the efforts to work with the desperate issues of the contemporary world. This seems like a contradiction. But, curious though it may seem, some of the most vigorous and creative efforts in the service of men have come from men who entertained the lively hope for everlasting life beyond death. The plain fact is that all men will die. They were not made for a life on earth that goes beyond a limited time. Their days are numbered, their capabilities are radically limited, and their hopes are easily frustrated. Because of this situation men easily despair of all human efforts to solve the problems of history. There is nothing more demoralizing with respect to the desperate and difficult larger problems of history than the silent, sustained, peripheral awareness that death will get the last word.

In contrast to all this, the New Testament assures men of continuing opportunities for creative advance with God. But a primary condition of this is the sincere and resourceful effort to serve men as long as we live on this earth. It is no part of the teaching of the New Testament that this present earth and universe were intended by God to be a permanent setting for His Kingdom. This temporal order, while unbelievably wonderful in so many respects, is strikingly inept at satisfying the deepest longings of the human spirit. Therefore, the Biblical teaching on the life everlasting is a dynamic source of morale in the fight to overcome the perils of this present world.

One more feature of the Biblical revelation that bears directly on the new problems threatening mankind need not be elaborated upon, but it is of utmost importance. I refer to its presentation of a total world-view with a personal God as the only ultimate Ground of reality, meaning and value. Without some such total perspective, and without an accompanying faith in such a God, despair is inevitable; and there is no sustained basis for morale. Morale, as here conceived, is the will to continue heroically and resourcefully in working to improve life for all men. Without God every thoughtful man will see himself as just another fish caught in ever-shallowing waters. And that provides no basis for hope. Therefore, the Biblical world-view, in contrast to the assumed materialisms or naturalisms of the modern world, offers man an adequate basis for the morale so urgently needed in the struggle to make his way through the mounting dangers of life on this planet.

SOME MODERN DOUBTS AND RESPONSES TO THEM

The most searching doubts about the relevance of the Biblical teaching and its continuation in Christianity may be reduced to four.

Doubt   First, there are the doubts that Christian communities with their Bible can overcome their chronic bondage to the past sufficiently to approach the new problems of mankind with scientifically informed openness. The Biblical teaching is simply too archaic. For example, consider the strong pronouncement by Pope Paul VI on birth control. At a time when men are struggling desperately with the problems of overpopulation, hunger, and war, the largest segment of Christianity is ordering its members to refuse to use certain available means of contraception. The times call for the *management* of activities pertaining to population. Because of the Pope's stand on this issue, however, intelligent decision-making for millions of people is precluded. The issue is made even more complicated by the problem of defective or low quality births. If it is said that this is a theological problem relating to souls, possible souls, and their right to be born, then why should such theology be taken seriously? Nothing in the Bible requires this. Nor does experience confirm it. There is a confusion between what can become a soul and what is a soul; that is, between potentiality and actuality.

Similarly, it is urged that the decision-making processes and modes of operation of the Christian churches are archaic and out of date. The basic point of the doubts along this line is that the Bible was written in ancient times to meet ancient needs. Its writers were speaking to men in nomadic rural societies. They lived in a different world from men today. Therefore, it is utterly unreasonable to expect the Biblical teaching and the church which is based on it to have significant bearings on the new problems of men who will be living not merely in metropolitan centers but in what has been called "a megalopolitan environment."

Response   By its very nature Christianity is an historic community. Its roots are in the past. It builds on the foundation of the prophets, apostles, and Jesus Christ. Nevertheless, it has recognized over nearly twenty centuries, often against the severest of persecutions, that its existence is in this present world. For this reason, in each succeeding generation Christians have sought to show the relevance of the Biblical revelation to life. The question is: Has this possibility been exhausted by the new achievements and problems created by the revolution in science and technology?

The doubts here seem to arise from three basic errors.

1. There is the error of supposing that the Bible cannot speak to men today because it is scientifically and technologically archaic. As we have seen, the Bible is not and was never intended to be a textbook in science. If it speaks at all, it speaks to other dimensions of human existence than those to which science and technology address themselves. If there is one thing that clearly emerges out of this modern era with its new setting and problems, it is precisely that *the basic issues of human societies cannot be handled merely or essentially by*

science and technology. It is interesting in this context to note that one of the most technologically advanced nations of the twentieth century, Germany, sold itself to Hitler, probably the most ruthless dictator that the world has ever seen.

What men need, *precisely in technologically advanced societies,* are those personalizing and balancing factors that can enable them to retain and enjoy their freedom and humanity. Here is where the Biblical teaching, with its stress on faith and personal values, has a unique contribution to make to the modern world. If the Bible is viewed as a textbook in science, it is archaic, pointless. But if it is seen as God's living Word of love and hope in a technologically conditioned age, then it takes on a new significance. For man cannot live by technology alone any more than he can live by bread alone.

2. There is the error, arising from the doubts under consideration, based on the assumption that the Bible is to be interpreted literally rather than dynamically. One of the tragedies of so many modern sophisticated people is that they have never really understood what the Bible is all about. Sometimes they have come from very restricted religious backgrounds where the Bible was interpreted with a method of rigor and vigor. Then after a brief exposure to science in high school and college they simply closed their minds to the possibility that the Bible has anything to say to the advancing modern era. Others, without much background in the study of the Bible, have abandoned it as superstitious and mythological. They have accepted, without searching analysis, the theory that God is nothing more than a man-made idea. So the whole Biblical perspective is swept aside as so much rubbish. Neither of these two groups who misunderstand the Bible is likely to have any encounter in depth with the main currents of the scholarly and broad-gauge Biblical studies of the present century.

It is unfortunate that, on all sides, we have to do elemental work regarding the Bible. Everything here depends on the way we understand the Bible as God's living Word. I have already presented the basic principles that, in my judgment, are necessary. This much needs to be said here: the Bible is a book about the God who loves men, who seeks their well-being, who desires the realization of moral and spiritual values in community in every era. He does not operate whimsically but in and through the laws, both physical and spiritual, of His own making. He calls men to live and work hopefully toward an increasingly meaningful future. Consequently, the Bible is a book about the *dynamics of interpersonal relationships* between God and man and between man and man as they move together into the future. This is precisely what modern men need if they are to be delivered from the illusion that their basic problems, whether new or old, can be solved by technology alone.

3. There is the error, leading to doubts about the relevance of the Bible to these new problems, arising from the inadequately challenged assumption that ideal personal values can change. On the human side the most basic of all principles is that human life is important; man has dignity and meaning. He is an end-in-himself and not merely a means. Without this principle, or primordial value-judgment, all other moral values collapse. Yet, in this era of polarization, depersonalization, and alienation, this is precisely the value that is being stifled by the developments and problems of a technological civilization. Technology would structure everything. The computer is based partly on the principle that everything it handles is structured. But *human beings cannot be squeezed into these structured molds without losing their identity and dignity*. The values of freedom, friendship, humor, beauty, love, joy, faith, prayer and worship belong in a unique realm beyond the sphere of technology. They do not basically change.

Doubt   Second, there are the doubts about the relevance of the Biblical teaching that are based upon its built-in impotence. It is not only archaic. It is too weak to make any real differences in solving the problems of the modern world. The church, which is based on the Biblical revelation, exhibits this very weakness. What can it do about the issues of war and peace? How can it lift a little finger to solve the problems involved in the population explosion? What can it do about the

273

awesome implications of an increasingly technological and computerized society? What can it do about pollution? Stalin is said to have asked how many divisions the pope had. Men live in a world of power politics. The new problems will have to be solved by men who are tough enough to deal with power struggles. How can those who come under the influence of the Bible, with Jesus as the supreme teacher, make any real difference in a world of hard facts and desperate needs?

Response   It is true, of course, that the church, with its foundations in the Biblical revelation, does not exert much power in terms of military force, or political prestige, or economic pressure. And if these are the only or the most important kinds of human energy used to work on the new problems facing mankind, the church has little to offer.

But, may it not be that moral and spiritual force is even more necessary in the modern world than ever before? Regarding the twenty-first century Donald M. Michael of the Center for Research on the Utilization of Scientific Knowledge of the University of Michigan, writes,

> I am assuming, then (recognizing that the assumption may be dead wrong), that to a large degree men's motives will still be corrupted by power, that the iron law of oligarchy will still prevail—that is, that organizations become ends rather than means and, as such, institutions will be needed to contain power, to change power and, very importantly, to alter institutions.

He goes on to say,

> The point is that, as far as I can make out, the church and the theater are the only two existing institutions in this society that are not immediately perceived by everybody as totally corruptible by the large system. Certainly you can't expect the sciences to play this role, or American philosophy, at least as we have known it in recent years.

This role, this kind of external criticism, is absolutely crucial for responsible society. In filling this role one vitally important function for the church and theater is to be the device for discouraging what I call "petit Eichmanism." That is, as we move into larger institutions, larger bureaucracies, more highly rationalized operations, dealing with larger social aggregates, in more complex information processing systems, it becomes harder and harder for individuals within the system to take a stand, even if they want to. By the same token it also becomes easier and easier to avoid taking a stand about the ethicalness of what they are doing.

In regard to the above comment on philosophy in the United States, it is one of the tragedies of this era that when men have been striving for human values the philosophers have had so little to say to give guidance on basic intellectual and moral principles. One reason for this may be that large segments of the departments of philosophy have been so preoccupied with the meaning and function of language that they have not bothered to reflect creatively on the meaning and purpose of life.

The church is in a particularly strategic position for calling the attention of men in the modern world to the life-subserving purpose of all institutions, including herself. For she ever seeks to see the world, its actions and its needs, in the light of *God's purpose* for all men. This provides the religious and ethical basis for critically evaluating the institutions and ways of men in society. In this way too the church can affect the direction of man's life even within the centers of worldly power.

One reason for believing that the church is not so ineffectual as men often suppose is that at least it has managed to survive through the most severe tests of history. The Roman Empire, though lasting a thousand years, could not show such staying power. What are the chances of survival of the Democratic party, or of the Republican party, or of the United States as a world power? We may hope that, much improved, these will long endure. But the church has already demonstrated that it can survive through the passing of the nations. This is in part due to its built-in demands for self-criticism. By continuing to exist as a thriving community, the church affects the larger affairs of history. Men often belittle institutions, and especially the church as an institution. But a sufficient response to such critics is this: Unorganized good will is no more effective than any other kind of unorganized power. *The future will be shaped by those institutions that have a future.*

The church has not only survived. It has shown the way many times by starting group efforts to overcome war, poverty, disease and ignorance. But its personnel has been limited and its financial resources woefully inadequate. Nevertheless, at the fountainhead of nearly every wide-reaching social agency today was the work of Christians who built institutions to improve the lot of those in need. The church began what was later taken over by governments and other agencies.

The church cannot now compete with these agencies in feeding and clothing men. It cannot compete with governments in teaching their citizens to read and write and to learn trades and skills. It cannot compete even in the healing and welfare agencies in the world. It cannot compete in working out the problems of pollution and ecology. But it can do its part. More than this, it can do what governments and other agencies cannot do. It can furnish men with those inner moral and spiritual resources that take them into business and labor, government, education, medicine, the arts, and family life with the determination to live responsibly in all human relations. It can equip men with compassion and mercy without weakness. It can awaken the sense of justice. It can call men to build on those moral foundations without which no society will have the opportunity to move toward the higher attainments of civilization.

Moreover, the time may have come when men begin to see that the new problems cannot be solved or even properly faced by raw power. As the world now is, nations require military prowess, but it seems increasingly evident that the most desperate issues now call for moral and spiritual power. The words of the ancient prophet are not less relevant, but more so:

". . . Not by might, nor by power, but by my Spirit, says the Lord of hosts" (Zechariah 4:6).

Doubt   Closely related to all this is a third kind of doubt. It arises from the apparent fact that the Biblical teaching seems to have a built-in call to withdrawal from this world. Much of it seems aimed to condition men to get away from the seething struggles of history. The emphasis is on prayer, worship, singing God's praises, and meditating on His law and gospel. Jesus Himself illustrates this tendency. He was not much concerned with practical affairs. According to the Biblical writers, this present world is inept at satisfying man's deepest needs. The Kingdom can never come here. How then can the church, based as it is on the Bible, have any real interest in becoming an effective agent for meeting the new problems faced by mankind? Does it not counteract its very nature whenever it attempts to enter this arena?

Response   There is a strange paradox here. One of the reasons why the church can be specially relevant to the issues of men in this world is precisely because of its ability to see dimensions of reality beyond it.

William Ernest Hocking has written of the "principle of alternation" in religion. It is that there is a necessary movement in the life of faith from withdrawal to involvement, involvement to withdrawal; here the self moves from a vision of the whole to practical action with the partial. This practical activity is always limited and is never altogether consonant with the vision of the whole. There is something self-defeating about attention to the whole. It is equally self-defeating to concentrate wholly on the task at hand. Therefore the movement of man's life in this present situation must swing between these two. As Hocking writes in *The Meaning of God in Human Experience,*

With the idea of God, one loves the world; and then with the idea of the world, one loves God again;—and the two loves, or ambitions, are of one substance, though they involve alternations in the history of the empirical will.

No one really understands the Biblical heritage and Christianity without grasping this principle. The church calls for withdrawal in meditation, prayer, worship, sharing. But this is only one side of a total process. At the same time, therefore, the church calls for involvement in the struggles and needs of men. This is the meaning of the cross.

The relevance of the Biblical teaching here, then, is that unless as a matter of policy men turn to God for occasions of meditation, aspiration, prayer and worship, they will not have the inner resources for the level of creative leadership and management needed in the twenty-first century. For in such occasions men get a vision of God and His aims, of man and his needs, of the task and its glory.

Doubt   A fourth kind of doubt about the relevance of the Bible to these new problems arises from its failure to bring people together in unity. The new problems require a *united* moral and spiritual effort. But the Biblical teaching, on which the churches are based, has not brought them together. How can it bring the world together? There are some two hundred and fifty denominational bodies in the United States alone. These are often at odds with each other and teach conflicting approaches to the social problems of the modern world. Is not the church too divided to lead?

Response   This doubt is like the voice of God, speaking both from outside and from within the church, reminding all Christians to work together in Christ. The doubt is inevitable in the face of the extensive fragmentation of the church. Moreover, it is beyond reasonable question that the church's ability to help mankind through the new problems of this era is crippled by its own lack of unity. Christians themselves are under the judgment of God.

Several further comments are in order. First, in the providence of God, the ecumenical movement has begun in earnest. It is on its way. Protestants, Evangelicals, Greek Orthodox Christians and Roman Catholics are beginning to communicate and share as never before. Second, there are significant co-operative efforts among Christian churches even though they are not seeking organic union with each other. These are seen in the many united efforts in the world mission of Christianity. They are evident also in the various Christian councils in the metropolitan areas and in the nation. These joint efforts are seen further in the intercommunication and cooperation among the boards, commissions, theological schools, and other agencies of the several denominations. Third, there is far more essential unity within Christendom than we see when we look at the number and variety of Christian denominations. All of them are based on the Bible. All look to Jesus Christ as Lord. All emphasize the moral and spiritual values that can come only from God. Their interpretations often vary (and these differences are not to be passed over lightly) but, in contrast to secular and nontheistic world-views, they present a united front.

The ecumenical task of bringing this essential unity of the churches to bear upon the new and desperate problems of the modern world is a priority item on the agenda of the church as it moves toward the twenty-first century.

Bibliography

Anderson, Bernhard W., ed., *The Old Testament and Christian Faith*. New York: Harper & Row, 1963.

Barr, James, *Old and New in Interpretation: A Study of the Two Testaments*. New York: Harper & Row, 1966.

Barrett, C. K., ed., *The New Testament Background: Selected Documents*. New York: Harper & Brothers, 1961.

Cauthen, Kenneth, *Science, Secularization and God*. New York: Abingdon Press, 1969.

Gardner, E. Clinton, *Biblical Faith and Social Ethics*. New York: Harper & Brothers, 1960.

Gustafson, James M., and Laney, James T., eds., *On Being Responsible: Issues in Personal Ethics*. New York: Harper & Row, 1968.

Heiler, Friedrich, *Prayer: A Study in the History and Psychology of Religion*. Translated by Samuel McComb. New York: Oxford University Press, 1958.

Hendry, George S., *The Holy Spirit in Christian Theology*. Philadelphia: Westminster Press, 1965.

Hocking, William Ernest, *Science and the Idea of God*. Chapel Hill: University of North Carolina Press, 1944.

Hough, Joseph C., Jr., *Black Power and White Protestants: A Christian Response to the New Negro Pluralism*. New York: Oxford University Press, 1968.

Huxley, Julian, *Religion without Revelation*. New York: Harper & Brothers, 1957.

Jeremias, Joachim, *The Parables of Jesus*. Translated by S. H. Hooke. New York: Charles Scribner's Sons, 1963.

King, Martin Luther, *Where Do We Go From Here: Chaos or Community?* New York: Harper & Row, 1967.

Lonergan, Bernard J. F., *Insight: A Study in Human Understanding*. London: Longmans, Green & Co., 1958.

Miller, Samuel H., *Religion in a Technical Age*. Cambridge: Harvard University Press, 1968.

Niebuhr, Reinhold, *The Nature and Destiny of Man*. One-volume edition. New York: Charles Scribner's Sons, 1947.

Outler, Albert C., *Who Trusts in God?* New York: Oxford University Press, 1968.

Schilling, Paul, *God in an Age of Atheism*. New York: Abingdon Press, 1969.

Simpson, Robert L., *The Interpretation of Prayer in the Early Church*. Philadelphia: Westminster Press, 1965.

Stace, W. T., *Religion and the Modern Mind*. Philadelphia: J. B. Lippincott Company, 1960.

Tillich, Paul, *Biblical Theology and the Search for Ultimate Reality*. Chicago: University of Chicago Press, 1955.

Trueblood, D. Elton, *A Place to Stand*. New York: Harper & Row, 1969.

Vidler, A. R., ed., *Soundings: Essays Concerning Christian Understanding*. Cambridge: University Press, 1966.

Vos, Geerhardus, *The Pauline Eschatology*. Grand Rapids, Michigan: Eerdmans Publishing Company, 1966.

Whitehead, A. N., *Science and the Modern World*. New York: The Macmillan Company, 1935.

Index